Help, Comfort and Hope

after

Losing Your Baby in Pregnancy or the First Year

Hannah Lothrop

FISHER
er
BOOKS™

Publishers: Bill Fisher
    Helen Fisher
    Howard Fisher

Editor: Sarah Trotta

Indexer: Michelle B. Graye

Book Design: Deanie Wood

Production: Deanie Wood
    Randy Schultz

Cover Design: FifthStreet*design*
    Berkeley, Calif.

Published by Fisher Books
4239 W. Ina Road, Suite 101
Tucson, Arizona 85741
(520) 744-6110

**Library of Congress
Cataloging-in-Publication Data**

Lothrop, Hannah, 1945-
    [Gute Hoffnung jähes Ende.
      English]
    Help, Comfort & Hope after
Losing Your Baby in Pregnancy or
the First Year / Hannah Lothrop.
    p. cm.
    Includes bibliographical
    references and index.
    ISBN 1-55561-120-6
    1. Grief. 2. Bereavement--
Psychological aspects. 3. Children-
-Death--Psychological aspects. 4.
Miscarrage--Psychological aspects.
5. Fetal death--Psychological
aspects. 6. Stillbirth--Psyshological
aspects. 7. Loss (Psychology)
I. Title.
    BF575.G7L68 1997
    155. 9'37'085--DC21   96-48501
                     CIP

Printed in the U.S.A.
10 9 8 7 6 5 4 3 2

Dedication

In love and gratitude

for Rob
who has shared my life for more than 30 years
and without whom my contribution to serving humanity
would not have been possible

and

for Cara
who has left her impression on our hearts
and on this earth
even though some may say
she never lived

Contents

Foreword

As a maternal/child health nurse, I often worked with families experiencing the death of a child. My first in-depth exposure to grief came in 1974 as I worked with Pam and Bob Sampson in Decatur, Illinois. Pam became eclamptic, and during a convulsion their unborn baby girl died. Pam was rushed to the hospital, where Anna Marie was delivered by Cesarean. Pam was in a coma for three days. When she woke up, she missed her daughter's birth, death and burial. She had no pictures, no memories, no mementos or rituals to help her through the grief process.

Because of complications, Pam was hospitalized for a month. The families, grateful for her survival, avoided speaking of the death of the baby, adding to Pam's pain. But she needed to talk. During Pam's hospitalization, both she and Bob asked me to spend time with them. I learned a great deal about the pain parents feel after the death of a baby. In the following months, Pam and Bob returned to the hospital because they needed to be with others having a similar experience. They asked me to start a support group for parents like them. I had no models for doing so. I began to search for ideas, and they continued their search as well. In 1976, Bob learned of AMEND, a St. Louis-based support program for parents. This was the first nonhospital-based support network in the United States for newly bereaved parents. Bob and Pam asked for my support as they explored beginning an AMEND chapter in Decatur. Through my participation, my awareness and sensitivity to their needs was enhanced. For the next 16 years, I dedicated myself to the support of bereaved parents whose baby had died.

Following a move to Springfield, Illinois, and at the urging of psychologist Dr. Glen Davidson and bereaved parents, I began to build a hospital-based support network. I saw the value of integrating the philosophy of support so that every person who comes in contact with these families is aware of and sensitive to their emotional needs—from admitting clerks, housekeepers, physicians and nurses, to social services, pastoral care and the billing departments. There was need for periodic in-services, to change policies and establish protocol or guidelines for those who responded to the families. It was clear a team approach was necessary to meet all the needs: from the time of anticipation of loss, during the initial period of grief and for follow-up support. In the fall of 1977, St. John's Hospital gave birth to SHARE (Source of Help in Airing and Resolving Experiences). Today there are more than 150 groups in the United States and other countries.

At the invitation of Hannah Lothrop, whom I had met when she lived in Florida and who then moved to Germany, I gave a presentation in Holzhausen, Germany, in 1987. That event was followed by 13 more presentations here and abroad. The universality of the grief experience became evident to me. Over the years, parents, our best teachers, have continued to educate others on bereavement following perinatal loss. Hannah has enriched joint workshops in the United States with her special knowledge of Middendorf Breathwork, a holistic body work that can be healing to the bereaved and of which we learn in her book, and through what she has learned in being there for parents during labor and delivery during a stillbirth and afterwards.

Hannah Lothrop's book is long overdue, but is well worth the wait. She reaches out empathetically to the bereaved and to their caregivers. Her writings come from the heart and her own experiences, as well as from those of many others with whom she has shared the journey. Hannah has helped others to experience a "good death" that Avery Weisman speaks of in his article, "Death and Responsibility: A Psychiatrist's View" (Weisman 1996): ". . . doctors, midwives, nurses, pastoral care associates can help to see that death under certain existing conditions will be experienced as a 'good death'—in overall agreement with certain values. . . . With a 'good death,' survivors can live in peace, not without pain . . . but knowing the peace flowing directly from the lifestyle of the parents . . . their wishes and aspirations. When we speak of a 'good death,' we imply that it is appropriate, not only for the deceased, but also for their principal survivors."

The death of a baby does not seem "right." All their potential for life and fulfillment is snatched away. The parents cannot love and nurture their baby as they hoped. The "good death" in this case comes when parents have the opportunity to parent their baby, even though the baby is dead, and to say good-bye. This happens if parents are involved at the beginning, have control over decisions and are informed of their options—those many details that Hannah illuminates in this book. To experience a "good death" will likely come only when there have been knowledgeable, sensitive caregivers and family who have "been there" for the parents during the time of anticipation, at the time of death and burial, and also in the weeks and months that follow.

The bereaved do not expect us to take away their pain. They do ask us to listen and to allow them to explore as they process their grief. As you stay with them, remember that you have two eyes, two ears and one mouth. It seems to me that we are to listen and observe four times as much as we speak. Listening is our greatest gift to the sorrowing.

We must give families "permission" to feel what they feel and to request those things they want for themselves and their baby. We have taken a long time to grasp this concept. It was made clear to us the first time when a couple who experienced a miscarriage at home brought their baby to the hospital. When it was time for the mother's discharge, the parents asked to take the baby home with them. This was not our protocol, and initially we refused their request, as if it were our baby. Then we asked ourselves, "Whose baby is this—ours or theirs? Whose right is it to decide about this baby? The parents brought this baby here. They could have left it at home. They were not required to bring the baby to the hospital. They took care of it." And the light began to dawn on us—the baby was theirs, and they should be able to decide what happened with it as long as their decisions conformed to state regulations. With this realization the solution was fairly simple. We established guidelines to provide this option for others in the future. Note that it was by listening to the parents that we learned, and their heart's desire was fulfilled. I encourage caregivers to listen to those wishes and to give them careful consideration. Depending on the significance of the request, the parents' future grief course may be significantly altered by our support in responding to it.

And, parents, you need to know that Pam and Bob's request resulted in the beginning of SHARE and affected perinatal-loss issues internationally. And when the other parents took their baby home, it not only satisfied their wishes, but also changed a hospital's policy—which affected policies in other hospitals. Parents, my message to you is, *listen to your heart* and follow the impulses that flow from the love you wish to express for your baby. This is one of the ways your baby makes a difference in our world. Some may not respond as you hoped, but others will pick up your message and pass it along.

We will never have a perfect formula for responding to the bereaved or for our own grieving. My experience has been that more than 90% of parents do not need anything special from us, only our presence and support. Each person will work through grief from a personal perspective. Guidelines help, but aren't the complete answer. Each of us—parents and support persons—respond based on our own personalities, coping styles, personal history and experiences. Intuition, along with listening, is a great gift. As we take the journey together, light begins to shine at the end of the tunnel. Hannah's book helps us walk through that tunnel with awareness that the light is there, and the darkness can never put it out.

SISTER JANE MARIE LAMB
Founder, SHARE
Springfield, Illinois
January, 1997

Acknowledgments

Innumerable persons have in their way contributed to this book, and I am grateful to all of them. My thanks go above all to the many bereaved women and men who allowed me to share in what were probably the most anguishing and difficult times of their lives. They told me their stories and bared their emotions and thoughts, or let me be with them at the stillbirth of their precious baby and during the weeks and months to follow. I am certain their stories will touch the hearts of many people.

This book could not have come about without the help of my dear friend Sister Jane Marie Lamb, founder of SHARE support groups. My thanks and love go to her for her friendship, kindness, readiness to help and her generosity in sharing her experience and materials with me. I enjoyed tremendously doing workshops with her, and I learned so much from her. She and Cathi Lammert, the new director of SHARE, took a lot of their time to go over the manuscript and make helpful suggestions. Thanks, Cathi, for the information you and your staff supplied! Deep thanks to Sister Marianna Kosior, who initiated the American version of this book by beginning (and finishing) to translate an earlier German version.

My special gratitude and love go to my husband, Rob, who assisted me with the research for this book, elaborated on the American version over and over and became a pathfinder for me in the world of the Internet.

I feel deeply grateful to my friend of many years, Mechthild Fuchs, who by simply being there helped me over the many hurdles of the often not-so-easy "labor" and who read the book with great care and counseled me with her wisdom.

Thanks to the women in Florida who freely passed on their professional experiences to me: Pat Stauber and Ann Coon from North Shore Hospital in Miami, Chris Pfeffer from Baptist Hospital in South Miami (also for helping me make the first contact with Sister Jane Marie), Edie Kaplan and Barbara Woodward of the Compassionate Friends in Plantation, and Edie Stark, who enlisted me as an ADEC member, as well as Dorothea Luytjes, who encouraged me at the beginning of this project. Thanks also to the women in other parts of the country: Cathy Romeo, Marilyn Unger, Sandy Gould and especially Dr. Susan Hodge for the many ways in which she supported me.

Thanks to Dr. J. William Worden for permission to use concepts from his book, *Grief Counseling and Grief Therapy*, in this one. Thanks also to Dr. Glen Davidson for the information from his book, *Understanding Mourning*, about the phases of mourning and Dr. John Bowlby and Dr. Collin Murray Parkes, from whose work these stages are derived. Thanks to Thomas Attig, Susan Scrimshaw and Daniel March, and Richard Boerstler, Barbara Kehrer-Kremer, Judy Tatelbaum, Howard Cupp, Pam Burden and others from the Compassionate Friends, whose work inspired me in some way. I want to express my appreciation to Dr. Gerd Eldering and the OB/GYN team at Vinzenz-Pallotti Hospital in Bensberg for integrating me into their team as a doula for bereaved parents in such a harmonious and uncomplicated way, and also to Dr. Eldering and to M.S. for allowing me to publish the letter at the beginning of chapter 7.

Thanks to Howard Fisher, Sarah Trotta and J. McCrary of Fisher Books for their interest and belief in my book. Thanks to the many others across the country who give so freely of their time and love to be there for parents in their darkest hours.

Thank you, Anya and Kerry, my beloved children, for your understanding and patience when the development of this book took much longer than any of us had anticipated. Last but not least I am forever touched by and grateful to my daughter Cara, who taught me many lessons and brought a much greater depth to my life than I could have ever fathomed.

HANNAH LOTHROP
March 1997

Introduction

"Who would buy it?" was the first comment many people made who knew I wanted to write a book on perinatal bereavement. "Expectant parents want to look forward to the birth of their child, not feel scared about it." Yet many parents who lost a baby and couldn't find support from the people around them really appreciated getting some help at least from a book.

> *When our baby was stillborn, I felt extremely isolated. No one could put herself in my shoes, no one could fathom my emotions. My husband didn't take my crying very well. I'd have loved to hear from other parents who had the same thing happen to them. I needed to know I wasn't alone. But there was no one. . . . At least I could read in a book that I hadn't gone crazy, that I was just a normal mother in grief—with the same kind of behaviors, feelings and the same thoughts as other mothers in a similar situation. I needed assurance that one day I would laugh again, and this lead weight would be lifted from my body.*

In 1984, my husband's and my life changed in a moment when we learned that our baby, growing inside of me and with whom I had already formed a strong bond, wasn't healthy. I got to know the excruciating pain of loss from first-hand experience. But I also learned the night would eventually end and that life would blossom anew.

I don't know how I would have coped if I hadn't happened to attend a workshop on perinatal bereavement two years earlier at the Annual Convention of the International Childbirth Education Association. What I learned there gave me a certain orientation. It was clear I couldn't run away from my pain. I held our daughter in my hands and absorbed her looks and her features, her image imprinting itself forever in my heart, while I cried. I shared with my child everything that was on my mind and in my heart, and great peace came over me. I think that made it easier to let Cara go. I had faced up earlier to the fact that pregnancies don't always end happily, and that helped me overcome this blow.

In earlier times, death was a normal part of our lives. People died at home and were attended there. Today, 90% of all people die in hospitals or nursing homes, away from loved ones. Many people have never seen the body of a dead person. Death has become foreign to us. Separated from our lives, it feeds our fears.

It is estimated that every fourth to sixth pregnancy ends in a miscarriage (some professionals guess that 50% of women go through the experience at least once). According to figures from the National Center for Health Statistics (1992), about every 80th baby is stillborn or does not survive the first weeks of life. But we just don't think it could happen to us.

So, most parents are totally unprepared for death. It comes out of the blue. We are overwhelmed by having to make decisions we never thought about before. We are in completely unfamiliar territory, without guiding principles to show us what to do. Often we live through it alone. Rituals are often experienced as superficial, without personal meaning. Church ceremonies may be denied when our baby has "not lived."

Too often physicians and nurses are themselves stunned when a baby is stillborn or dies after birth. Many of them haven't been taught how to deal with situations like this. It is a terrible feeling for anyone to be unable to help. Perinatal bereavement support teams can help here. With regular meetings, obstetricians, pediatricians, midwives, nurses, social workers and clergy (cooperating with and supporting each other) can develop constructive plans that can help resolve this situation.

Where obstetric and nursing personnel aren't aware of the stages of grief and concepts of attachment and separation, they have tended to "spare parents the sight of their dead child" or to prescribe tranquilizers. They don't realize that in doing so they prolong and complicate the grief process.

Relatives and friends also feel helpless, insecure and often paralyzed.

No one treated me in a way that was helpful. Everyone felt sorry, but no one thought of just holding me. I could have used some comfort, but everything seemed so cold.

The people around us may try to relieve our pain by making soothing comments. But that may only increase it. On the other hand, caring support from others can do a lot of good. The guidance and support parents receive from their caretakers at this time decisively influences how they will cope with their loss.

In a follow-up conversation at the hospital three weeks after the stillbirth of her daughter in the 33rd week of pregnancy, Barbara (32) described it this way:

I'm glad we delivered in this hospital. The staff was with us totally. The loss of our baby is certainly the worst experience I ever had in my life—

far worse than anything else that has happened to me—and yet there was also a beauty to Naomi's birth. I experienced such peace and harmony.

To those who haven't had a similar experience, this statement may sound strange. But a baby, though dead, can be born with caring and dignity, and a sick baby can be allowed to die in peace and dignity. When that is allowed, a positive feeling can emerge from within the terrible event to comfort the parents and support them for a long time to come.

Part 1 of this book is primarily written for bereaved parents. My understanding is that mourning is an individual experience and a more or less orderly process. I guide parents through the four phases of grief, offering concrete suggestions for living through these phases. I have based myself, with some adaptation, on the work of Dr. Glen Davidson, author of the insightful book, Understanding Mourning, who, after a 10-year study of 1200 adult mourners, confirmed research conducted earlier by the British psychiatrists John Bowlby and Colin Murray Parkes. Part 1 of my book is also valuable reading for professional caregivers, friends and relatives of the bereaved, offering them insight into the depth and nature of the parents' experience.

I incorporate quotes from my talks with bereaved parents (shown in italics). You may find many of these comments echo your own feelings, even if time has passed. They may help you feel less alone. At the end of many sections, I include a list of questions the reader may ask her- or himself. These questions are meant to help you sort out feelings and decide if you would like to take any action at this time.

Part 2 is directed to those caring for and those wanting to support bereaved parents—hospital staff, gynecologists in private practice, clergy, psychologists and counselors, leaders of bereavement-support groups, childbirth educators and funeral directors as well as relatives, friends and neighbors.

Help, Comfort and Hope after Losing Your Baby in Pregnancy or the First Year is based on many interviews with grieving mothers and fathers in the United States and Germany, my attendance at group meetings of SHARE, The Compassionate Friends and other bereaved parents' support groups, my personal contact with hospital personnel in Florida, and above all my ongoing exchange with Sister Jane Marie, the founder of SHARE. It reflects my five years as a *doula*, a labor companion for parents whose babies had been stillborn at Vinzenz Pallotti Hospital in Bensberg, Germany, including first-year aftercare, and the founding and leading of a hospital-based SHARE support group—all of this against the background of my own painful experience over my daughter Cara. As a therapist in private practice, I have walked with many bereaved parents through their grief, in individual sessions and in group settings. I continue to gain insights through encounters and personal exchanges with many of the thousands of people who have taken part in my workshops in the United States and Germany over the past seven years and from letters I receive from many of them after the seminars.

The interest and willingness, especially within the ranks of hospital caregivers, to feel their way into the lives and the situation of bereaved parents in order to be better able to lend them a supporting hand has been great and is commendable. Just as a stone thrown into a pond creates ever-widening circles, so sensitivity in hospitals towards parents and their dead or dying children is ever-expanding—to the benefit of the parents who are so very dependent on the immediate support they receive.

Part 1

Working through Grief

*You can't prevent the birds of sorrow
from circling over your head, but you can prevent
them from building nests in your hair.*

(Chinese proverb)

1

Losing a Baby

Death has many faces. Some time ago, my grandmother died at 91. We had become close in the last years of her life. And yet I could let her go, perhaps because of that. She had run her life's course and in a lot of ways had come back to the beginning—a well-rounded life! What remained were memories of intense moments of closeness, understanding and affection. In the last year of her life we took leave of one another in little steps—at times with tears in our eyes, at other times calmly facing the inevitable reality. That was OK—it was as it should be.

The death of a baby is entirely different. Nothing is OK about it.

> *I thought any minute now I would be a mother. And then within a heartbeat I was told, "Stop! You can't go that way any more!"*

With the death of a baby, there are no common memories of a life lived together, no memories to share with friends and relatives.

> *It felt like the burden of what happened rested on me alone. The trouble is, I'm the only person who knew the baby. People don't grieve over someone they didn't know. I was completely alone in my grief. Everyone said, "You can have another baby. It's not the end of the world." But it was the end of my world.*

Death nearly always finds us unprepared. It seems so unfair that this child of ours will never see the sky, the sun and the budding of nature in the spring, that we cannot cradle him in our arms, that we will not be able to see our baby grow and develop and make his contribution to the world. The death doesn't seem in keeping with our sense of order. We expect children to outlive their parents, not the other way around. Our dreams, hopes and plans for the future die with our children. With them, a part of us dies.

The death of a baby can occur at various stages of development. I will go over losses through miscarriage, stillbirth, newborn death and sudden infant death syndrome, first covering legal and medical aspects, then describing them through the eyes and hearts of stricken parents. The issue of the birth of a special-needs child, which in itself can be considered a great loss, is touched briefly, as is the intrauterine death of one twin. And finally, I will cover complicated losses considered taboo by parts of society, such as losing a baby through the termination of pregnancy based on prenatal diagnostic findings, losses of single mothers or giving up a baby for adoption. Each situation is somewhat special.

Miscarriage: Loss during Pregnancy

Legally speaking, in the United States and Canada, babies who die under 20 weeks' gestation are designated as a *miscarriage* in most states. This applies to an *embryo* (a doctor's term for a child during the time of organic development) as well as to a *fetus* (as it is called after the twelfth week of pregnancy). A death certificate is issued only if a burial is desired, in order to obtain a burial permit. However, the death is not registered.

A miscarriage in the early weeks of pregnancy may surprise you in the midst of your normal routine with strong cramps and heavy bleeding. Or your gynecologist may discover at a routine examination that your baby is no longer alive or, to use medical terminology, that your pregnancy is "no longer intact." What procedure is used depends on the stage of pregnancy and the situation. It may mean a *curettage* (a D&C or scraping the uterus—see page 38), by which the dead embryo or fetus is removed along with the placenta at your doctor's office or the hospital. But it can also mean, between the fourth and sixth months of pregnancy, regular vaginal birth, accompanied by strong contractions, of a fully developed baby. (In this case, labor may be induced.) After a spontaneous miscarriage, a curettage procedure is usually necessary. Frequently at such an early stage of pregnancy the placenta isn't expelled completely, making curettage necessary. It can be performed under spinal or general anesthesia. Approximately 75% of all miscarriages occur in the first trimester of pregnancy.

Causes of Miscarriage

When I picture what happens at the conception of a baby and in the weeks that follow, I'm in awe. What a miracle, that through the union of a tiny little ovum and an even smaller sperm cell, a person is created who can see, hear, speak, feel, think, sense, run, laugh and love! It's amazing that this succeeds with such precision in most cases. Yet it doesn't always work.

When nature fails and development doesn't follow the master plan, nature generally helps herself by interrupting the pregnancy with a miscarriage. A flaw in development can originate, for example, from a defective ovum of the mother or a defective sperm cell of the father. Or something can go wrong during the multiplication and division of the millions and millions of cells that make up the growing baby. It can be harmful to the baby if the mother is exposed to radiation, certain medications, chemicals or other injurious environmental factors. Certain infections may negatively affect the baby's healthy growth. Alcohol and nicotine abuse may play a role. A study conducted in England has shown that the father's genes can be mutated by radiation, and have the potential to adversely affect a baby at conception. Miscarriages for these reasons occur mainly before the twelfth week and represent the majority of cases.

Some miscarriages can also be due to problems of the uterus, such as a *myoma* (a benign tumor on the uterus), inflammations, scars from operations or an intrauterine device (IUD). In each of these cases it is difficult for the embryo to implant itself in the womb. Every now and then a pregnancy has to be surgically terminated, often as late as the eighth to twelfth week of pregnancy, when an *ectopic* or *abdominal pregnancy* (a pregnancy that develops outside the uterus and is a grave danger to the mother) is diagnosed. Hormonal imbalance can likewise cause miscarriage. A miscarriage can be induced by trauma, such as a shock, an accident or a prenatal diagnostic intervention—for example, amniocentesis or chorion villus sampling (prenatal diagnostic methods for recognizing certain defects in the baby; see page 12). Another reason for miscarriage can be an incompetent cervix.

Sometimes no obvious medical explanation for a miscarriage is found. Sarah (24) had her first son when she was very young. She reflected on her subsequent four miscarriages this way:

> *Maybe I was too set on having a second child and on handling things better this time. I moved directly from my family of 12 children into my marriage, and soon after Gabriel was born. I never had time for myself. Maybe this is why my body kept rejecting each new pregnancy. Deep inside I wasn't ready to immerse myself into childrearing again.*

The probability of a miscarriage increases with the mother's increasing age. A 40-year-old woman has three times the risk of miscarriage as a 20-year-old. Often miscarriages are a one-time thing. But there are cases in which women who had five or more miscarriages in a row then had a perfectly healthy child.

Experiencing a Miscarriage

People without personal experience of it may have difficulty imagining that a miscarriage, especially at a very early stage, could be experienced as a great loss. Many bereaved women hear, "That wasn't a child yet." But, as we know, bonding to a child begins long before his existence is detectable. The Chinese say that a baby is a year old at birth.

How parents experience a miscarriage depends upon many factors. Most of the time the reaction to a loss is more intense than is generally assumed and more intense than parents often permit themselves to acknowledge.

> *It's as if nothing happened. I went to the hospital but I don't know why . . . Something was there, and now it's gone. I can't tell anyone why I am so sad . . . (crying) the baby wasn't real to other people . . . no one would understand. . . .*

> *At first it wasn't so bad. But when I got home, it hit me just how crushed I felt by it. I haven't become pregnant to this day. Three years have passed, but it still hurts when I talk about this miscarriage. For me, there was a child even though I had only known about the pregnancy for a week.*

With habitual miscarriage, especially with advancing age, a fear often develops of maybe never being able to have more children. But we differ in our power to meet our fate—some people are even strengthened by an experience of loss (see page 149). If more dramatic losses have preceded the present loss, this experience, by contrast, may be perceived as not as serious.

> *This time it was as if a nail had been removed. With the other pregnancy I felt as if my heart had been ripped out.*

You may not be asked if you want to see your miscarried baby. Depending on the situation, it may not be possible. That makes it more difficult, as a rule, to grasp the reality of what has happened. If the miscarriage occurs before the pregnancy becomes outwardly obvious, few people may have known you were pregnant. That situation can leave little room for grief. It often gets repressed or must be expressed in private.

One's depth of grief may vary, but it's always there. Our society doesn't make it easy to live through the grief of a miscarriage in a healthy way.

I was so relieved recently to find a magazine article about miscarriages and to have my own experience validated. Before, I had thought to myself, "You must be crazy. You aren't quite normal. That wasn't really a child. But I cried myself to sleep over it every night.

Stillbirth: Loss before or during Pregnancy

In most states, when a baby over 350 grams or over 20 weeks of gestation, showing no vital signs at birth, dies before or during delivery and was expected to live, it is considered a stillbirth. But some states have a different definition. In Canada, a baby who weighs at least 500 grams or has a gestational age of 20 weeks and shows no sign of life at birth is considered a stillbirth. (Definitions vary slightly from province to province.) At the time of the birth and death, you fill out paperwork that goes on file with the state. Many states don't issue a birth/death certificate. You may only receive an acknowledgment letter. You may give a name, but naming is not required. You may give a name later if you wish.

Causes of Stillbirth

Babies can die during pregnancy or delivery due to strangulation, a knotted umbilical cord or because the placenta has detached. In each case the baby's oxygen supply is cut off. The death can occur because of anomalies or developments that make it impossible for the baby to survive. Certain infections can also take the life of the baby. Sometimes an autopsy can't determine the cause of death.

Experiencing a Stillbirth

Some women become alarmed when they don't feel their baby moving for a period of time. An ultrasound scan may confirm that their child is dead. Other women "know" suddenly, with absolute, shocking certainty, that their baby is no longer alive.

I had a sudden, strange sensation that I can't describe to anyone. I felt I was going completely numb inside . . . I started to cry and told my husband, "My child just died." I drove to the hospital and was connected to the fetal-monitoring machine. There were no heartbeats.

Often women or someone close to them have dreams or even premonitions that in some way prepare them.

I had a dream six weeks before my due date: I feel the baby in my abdomen. I am in labor, I push . . . the baby comes out and is dead. When Tim was actually stillborn, I wasn't completely unprepared. He was five or six weeks behind in his development. It seemed to me that in my dream, Tim had said good-bye to me. He even turned to a transverse position at the last minute . . . there was no reason to face downward [since] he didn't have to come out.

Some women go for a routine checkup not suspecting anything is wrong. One moment they feel fine, and the next they learn that their baby is dead.

I had an appointment with my doctor. The baby hadn't dropped, and the doctor seemed a little concerned. He tried very cautiously to prepare me for the fact that, under these circumstances, I might need a Cesarean. I thought, "Well, OK, if we have to." We talked a little about the results of the last ultrasound scan. Then he said, "OK, now let's take a look to see how things are today." He searched but he couldn't find a heartbeat. I felt like I had been knocked over. I knew immediately: It's all over—my baby is dead.

When parents learn that their unborn child has died, it is as if, within a heartbeat, they "close up the book called *Baby*." They no longer want anything to do with it. Many assume that the baby will be removed by a Cesarean section. That isn't the case. A baby who has died is usually born in the same way as a child who is alive (the birth is discussed more in chapter 2). The staff is just as shocked. There may be a heavy silence. Often news of death is communicated in a seemingly heartless, blunt manner.

If your baby dies during the birth, you have little chance to prepare yourself. You may be more overwhelmed than parents who have had a few hours or days to process the terrible news.

I came to the clinic with contractions. My membranes were ruptured, and an electrode was connected to my baby's head for fetal monitoring. There was a good heartbeat audible. The amniotic fluid was somewhat stained by meconium. The atmosphere was relaxed. I was a little nervous but the doctor calmed me down. I received a spinal to ease my pain. The baby came into the world, and the doctor said, "It's a boy." I said to my husband, "Can you believe it—we have a boy!"

The next 45 minutes were the worst of my life. Daniel wasn't breathing at all, and they started to suction him immediately. An alarm went off, and 12 people tried everything they could to resuscitate our little boy. I heard the doctor say, "He's breathing. I hear his breath." I was relieved. But after a little while, it became very quiet again. Then the neonatologist came to me and he said, "Something terrible has happened. We were unable to get your baby to breathe."

Neonatal Death:
Our Child is Born Alive but Can't Survive

If a child is born alive but dies within the first 28 days, we call it a *neonatal death*. If the baby took only one breath, its umbilical cord pulsated, or its little heart only beat once, its legal status changes to that of a person who is officially entered into the birth and death registries.

Causes of Neonatal Death

In 1992, 21,849 U.S. babies did not live beyond their first month of life, most within the first hours of life. The majority are born prematurely and, in spite of intensive neonatal care, their vital functions cannot be sustained. (Today, 90% of all babies with a birth weight between 1000 and 1500 grams and 30% to 50% of babies with a birth weight of 500 to 700 grams survive.) Other babies die from congenital problems with the circulatory system, the nervous system, the digestive organs or from severe chromosomal problems or problems with the respiratory system. A few die from complications of the placenta, the umbilical cord or the amniotic sac or due to infectious diseases.

Experiencing the Death of a Newborn

Rita (27) describes the loss of her second child, Anne, whose faulty heart development hadn't been detected during pregnancy and delivery:

"A girl!" my husband exclaimed, "She looks perfect!" As the umbilical cord was being clamped, Anne turned blue . . . She gasped for air and whimpered softly just once. She was immediately wrapped and taken into the next room, before I could even take a look at her. The doctor came over and said the baby didn't look as rosy as he'd have liked, but not to worry. They assumed she had gotten amniotic fluid into her lungs and were in the process of suctioning her.

Then the pediatrician came over and said, "Mrs. K., your baby isn't completely well. We don't want to take any risks and are sending her to the

Children's Hospital for further observation." It was as if I died inside right then. Imagine waiting so long to finally be able to cradle your child in your arms and being full of joy and anticipation, and then abruptly everything switches! We waited two endless hours. Tears kept welling up, but inside I felt as if I were in a thick cloud—completely out of it. I just couldn't comprehend what had happened. It seemed like a terrible nightmare. Then the heart specialist called saying our child had such a severe heart defect they couldn't save her, and she would die.

At first I thought I wouldn't be able to look at our baby, knowing I couldn't keep her. My brother-in-law drove us to the Children's Hospital for a talk with the doctor. When the doctor asked whether we wanted to see Anne, my husband said "yes," so I went along. I stood in front of her crib and could see that Anne was breathing irregularly. She was attached to a lot of tubes. She had been sedated so she wouldn't suffer too much. I stood there in tears and thought my heart was going to break.

Rita's husband, Peter (29), shares his reactions. Right after the delivery, he had been called into the adjacent room where their child was being supported with oxygen.

I thought, this can't be normal. There must be something really wrong. But the doctor reassured me that the baby probably had aspirated amniotic fluid into her lungs and would be OK in two weeks. I wanted to believe him so much. I told Rita what he said. "Two weeks . . . !" But we thought if that's the way it is, well, OK. We hung on to each other while we waited for the call from the Children's Hospital. Then the news came that she was incurably ill.

Even though great fears may prevail, in retrospect most parents feel comforted if they have had a chance to see their child, touch her, and care for her in their own way, even if only for a little while.

In the Children's Hospital, we stood at Anne's side next to the incubator and touched and caressed her, and she grasped my little finger. I will never forget that. I am sure it meant "hello" and "good-bye" at the same time.

The priest we had called came to administer an emergency baptism. Then he drove us home. I finally started crying then. Later, I went back to the hospital with a camera and took pictures of Anne. When I called my father-in-law at home, he wanted us to try to get a heart transplant, however possible. He would have offered everything he had. We called the centralized organ databank but there was no heart available.

Sudden Infant Death Syndrome (SIDS)

In spite of much ongoing research, sudden infant death syndrome remains a mystery. There are many theories, but as yet, no conclusive explanation. In 1994, SIDS took the lives of 4,073 babies in the United States and 269 in Canada. Most who fall victim to this syndrome die between the second and the fourth month of life. The babies are happy and healthy when tucked into their cribs in the evening. But when the parents look in on them the next morning, they find them dead. Thank goodness their number is shrinking—we're learning more about monitoring babies who may be at risk.

What makes the situation even more difficult for parents after a sudden infant death is that the police are frequently called to investigate whether the baby had been neglected or abused. A coroner's examination may be ordered. The majority of officials behave with tact and respect, but not all of them. The overzealous policeman who came to Karen and Bruno's house when their second child died of SIDS at 11 weeks added to their agony. Bruno remembers:

> *The young doctor was stunned himself and could only confirm that our baby had died of sudden infant death syndrome. Because he hadn't filled out the appropriate form before, he checked with the police, emphasizing that there were no signs of abuse or neglect. But the police decided to investigate the case anyway. Our child was confiscated, put in a plastic bag and taken away. We were already in complete shock. Added to this, we weren't allowed to see her again, not allowed to say good-bye.*

Karen, who attended one of my grief seminars with her husband, had an extremely hard time overcoming the harm done to her body, mind and spirit. It was only softened a bit after she gave birth to another baby. The policeman had misinterpreted the red marks normally appearing on the skin of a dead baby as a sign of maltreatment. But no one from the police force called to apologize to the parents.

Parents question themselves mercilessly for possible causes of their child's death, for what they might have done wrong.

> *If only I had taken him into bed with me. Maybe I would have noticed he wasn't breathing, and I could have resuscitated him right away.*

Even an outside confirmation that parents aren't at fault doesn't prevent these feelings. You may need support to deal with your guilt feelings rationally—perhaps through discussion with others who have had the same experience, by attending a support group or by seeking counseling.

Children who die of SIDS are torn out of life in the midst of the baby's and parents' "honeymoon" together. An exciting, joyful time has just begun, when the baby starts to make contact with her surroundings, imitates her parents and smiles at them. Love and bonding have grown deeply. On the other hand, memories of the baby's short life span remain—memories that no one can ever take away, and this can help the grief process.

Special Circumstances

We Don't Know If Our Baby Will Survive

Thanks to today's new technologies and medical advancements, tiny babies weighing less than a pound and just big enough to fit into the palm of a hand can sometimes survive. They spend weeks or even months in incubators. Their parents don't know whether their baby will live or what disabilities it may have in that case. In others, children are born sick and their fate is unknown.

Many parents, unless guided by caring and knowledgeable staff, are reluctant to form an attachment to their baby in this situation. They are afraid of possibly increasing their pain and grief later. Yet direct skin contact between mother and child, which some healthcare providers encourage, is very beneficial to the baby. For parents, it also facilitates the acceptance even of a baby with severe disabilities.

The birth of a sick child or one with disabilities *is* a shock. Even if the child survives, parents have a loss to grieve—the loss of the healthy child they anticipated. If the baby dies, this short time of bonding will ease their farewell (see page 41). If you have problems handling the situation on your own, do seek counseling.

A Twin Baby Doesn't Survive Pregnancy

"Oh, there's a second placenta!" our midwife exclaimed after the birth of our son Kerry in 1975. This was before ultrasound scanning was done routinely during pregnancy. I hadn't a clue that I was carrying a second child. There was no sign of it except for this second placenta. I had had a happy, uncomplicated pregnancy.

I was amazed to learn of research (Levi 1976) showing that about 70% of the pregnancies diagnosed as twin pregnancies before the tenth week of gestation ended in the birth of only one baby. Placental problems were the dominant probable causes for the death of one of the babies. Another cause was a blood transfusion from one baby to the other. In the case of one woman I cared for, who had originally been diagnosed as carrying triplets, one baby died early on in pregnancy, one died during the 20th week, and the third was born healthy right around the expected due date. Babies who die early in the uterus can "vanish" through bleeding during pregnancy. The bleeding stops on its own or is reabsorbed in the fetal tissue. When a twin is too large for that when it dies, it is carried, to be born together with the healthy baby. If many weeks have elapsed between death and birth, the dead baby is born as a dehydrated, very small fetus.

It is desirable to give the live twin as much time as possible in the womb to avoid prematurity, which is the major risk factor to babies' health. Therefore, a pregnancy is usually continued as long as possible—possibly until the 38th to 40th week of pregnancy—under close medical observation and possibly even hospitalization towards the term. A mother can simultaneously carry a dead baby and a live baby for several weeks without danger to the surviving baby pre- or postnatally, or to herself (Riehn 1982).

Emotional processing in this case is very difficult, of course. Parents are faced with having to mourn one child while at the same time looking forward to their other child, whose safety they worry about—which means doing emotional "splits." In the womb as well as after birth, the live baby needs attention and bonding from her parents. At the same time, parents need to be able to mourn their dead child so that grief doesn't manifest itself in an unhealthy way. They may find themselves in an environment that tries to tell them that they should be happy that they have one healthy baby.

The parents' relationship to the surviving twin can be overshadowed by the loss of the other. The baby may become a living reminder of the twin who did not survive. Feelings of anger and disappointment over that may continue rather than resolve. Kristen Swanson-Kauffman, a nursing professor at the University of Washington, writes, "Parents who have lost a twin should be encouraged to express these feelings and should be forewarned that such feelings may occur." (Swanson and Hoffman 1988) Because the loss of a twin is an extremely challenging and intricate situation, parents may wish to validate their feelings and find support. Appendix 4 lists a number of organizations that can help.

Losses Surrounded by a Taboo

When you lose a baby through miscarriage or stillbirth, you usually sense others' bewilderment and sympathy despite their possibly unhelpful reactions. A loss shrouded by taboo, depending on the circumstances, complicates the situation. Perhaps you are the only person to know about the loss, so you can't receive support from others. In this situation, you are left without an important safety valve for your emotions—another person's empathy. Or, if other people do know, some may withhold "social permission" for you to grieve; others may reproach or condemn. It's common for parents in such a situation to repress all their emotions and feelings.

When we sense that our loss is surrounded by taboos, that we have done something that might not be "sanctioned" in some people's eyes, it may be especially difficult to obtain support. But we very much need people we can trust to help us through such a complex, emotional situation. We need friends with whom we can share openly, who won't judge or point a finger and who will help us process the guilt we may carry, so we won't suppress it in an unhealthy way.

Termination of a Wanted Pregnancy

The loss of a baby, inflicted by forces beyond our control, is difficult enough. In the case of a spontaneous miscarriage, for example, the decision is out of our hands. There's nothing we can do about it. But to be confronted with the fact that something is terribly wrong, then asked to decide about our baby's life or death and assume responsibility for that decision makes our distress that much greater and the grieving process even more complicated.

Prenatal Diagnosis—Curse or Blessing?

Prenatal diagnosis has become increasingly common in the past decade. Through maternal serum tests (determination of alpha-fetoprotein level and other factors during the 14th and 16th week of pregnancy), amniocentesis (amniotic fluid analysis between the twelfth and 16th weeks), chorionic villus sampling (examining a test sample from the placenta from the seventh week on), and by routine ultrasound examination, severe anomalies in a fetus can be determined during pregnancy instead of discovered after delivery. One recognizable defect is Down syndrome. Its probability ranges from 0.9% to 2.3% for women between the ages of 35 and 40, and up to 7.7% for those between the ages of 41 and 46. But having access to certain information means "the loss of innocence." At first glance, it seems wonderful to be able to recognize certain abnormalities beforehand. But knowledge has its price: One out of 100 women undergoing diagnostic amniocentesis will miscarry as a result, and the risk of a premature birth is also increased. What's more, we can't anticipate the emotional and ethical dilemma that results when we know certain facts.

I was asked to play God. I was in the position of having to make a decision I felt I could not rightfully make, that was too great for any human being to make.

The decision of whether or not to submit to diagnostic testing isn't easy. Women who decide *for* the tests, according to research, are often plagued with guilt, doubt and ambivalence. (Golbus, 1974) Some women I talked to would have decided *against* undergoing amniocentesis or chorion villus sampling, but went ahead because of pressure from their husbands, other family or friends.

Julia lost her child after an amniocentesis test in the 19th week of pregnancy:

In a dream in my 13th week of pregnancy I heard a voice say, "Whoever sins against the sea will be swallowed up by it." Immediately the amniocentesis came to mind because I saw it as a transgression. But I didn't dare go against my husband's wishes because I was afraid that he would reject a child with disabilities if it came to that, so I had the test done anyway.

Some families decide in favor of a diagnostic test fully aware of the emotional trauma it can unleash. They do so without self-reproach because they know from first-hand experience what life with a child with disabilities is like.

After seeing what the first baby went through, we didn't think twice in deciding to abort. It is hard to feel guilty after seeing that baby suffer.
(Blumberg 1975)

Another woman wanted to protect her oldest child from life with yet another brother or sister with disabilities who would need their mother's constant attention.

But sometimes we agree to a prenatal diagnostic test naively and conceal from ourselves what it actually means. That's how it was for me in my third pregnancy at 39:

It was supposed to be a routine exam, because the doctor said you usually have it done at my age. I only acknowledged to myself what the test really meant during the preparatory talk at the hospital, when I was told that there was a 97% chance that the baby was healthy. "And what if the results aren't normal?" I asked, with tears already forming in my eyes.

Susan Hodge, a geneticist on the medical faculty of a large university, had an experience like this during her third pregnancy. Susan published this letter in *The New England Journal of Medicine* (1989):

> *I drafted the following letter to the editor one week before I received the results of my amniocentesis:*
>
> *I am 40 years old and 19 weeks pregnant with what will presumably be my third child. I am on the basic-science faculty of a medical school. When I teach medical students about amniocentesis, I occasionally mention the difficulty for the woman of having to wait well into the second trimester to receive her results.* (Cell-culture results from the examination weren't available for three to four weeks. —author's note) *. . . I am in that situation myself now, awaiting my results. And before experiencing it, I was unprepared for two phenomena. One was just how difficult this wait is. Pregnancy is always a time of waiting, but now time has slowed down to an extent I did not anticipate. The other, more disturbing phenomenon is how the waiting has affected my attitude toward the pregnancy. At many levels I deny that I really am pregnant "until after we get the results." I ignore the flutterings and kicks I feel. I talk of "if" rather than "when" the baby comes; I am reluctant to admit to others that I am pregnant. I dream frequently and grimly about second-trimester abortions. In some sense I am holding back on "bonding" with this child-to-be. This represents an unanticipated negative side effect of diagnostic amniocentesis. And all this, even though my risk of carrying a chromosomal abnormality is less than 2% . . . I presume I am not alone in these reactions, yet I have not seen this problem mentioned in the literature, nor did my physician or genetic counselor discuss this with me . . .*

Susan, as had most of the women with whom I have spoken, made an effort not to develop attachment—a process that is so important, even during pregnancy, for the development of a child's basic sense of trust in others and the world. Yet 93% to 99% of women undergoing diagnostic amniocentesis do receive the desired results. Susan wasn't one of them.

> *The next day, before I mailed this letter, I received the results, and unfortunately they were the dreaded ones: trisomy 21 [Down syndrome —author's note]. I have since then had the grim second-trimester abortion. From my current perspective of grief and shock, I encourage clinicians to help their patients avoid the denial described in my letter. My husband and*

I spared ourselves no pain by holding back emotionally. It has become a cultural expectation that one will keep one's pregnancy a secret until one has the "all clear" from the amnio. One reasons, "If we get a bad result, we won't have to tell anyone." But I now believe that reasoning is wrong. After our bad result, my husband and I did tell everyone. Sympathy and support from our friends, family, and colleagues have helped us to survive the ordeal of aborting a wanted pregnancy. By keeping the loss a secret, we would have cut ourselves off from such support when the feared outcome did happen. (Copyright 1989 Massachusetts Medical Society. All rights reserved. Adapted with permission.)

Her statement speaks for itself.

An Agonizing Decision

Susan Hodge, who has also written under the pseudonym Rose Green, and her husband had decided 95% to terminate the pregnancy, should they receive a bad result.

But when it did happen to us, when we were faced with the reality of trisomy 21, the decision was simply 100–0. . . . I had anticipated that it would be "really sad" to have this happen, but I had no idea of how emotionally devastating it would be. (Green 1992)

After four long weeks of waiting we, too, were told that our child had a genetic abnormality—one that occurs in one out of 10,000 children. Our decision process was not easy.

"We'll manage!" I thought at first, when our gynecologist friend described the genetic malformation . . . the second female gene missing . . . dwarfism . . . no ovaries . . . not possible to develop into a woman. The real shock came when I saw in a medical dictionary the photo of a girl with a webbed neck growing directly out of her shoulders, her shortened arms turned inward, and read what other severe symptoms our child might have. "My God, I can't handle that; we can't handle that!" . . . I had felt my child's movements from the 13th week . . . she was already very real to me and my entire family . . .

Parents' adrenaline levels rise as a natural reaction to such news. That clouds their thinking abilities and makes even the smallest decisions hard to make. At the same time, parents are asked to make probably the toughest decision of their lives.

I went through the hardest and most torturous time of my life. These thoughts popped up over and over again: "I really cannot make this decision . . . no human being can. That damned test . . . !" "What is better for my child—life, even with a genetic abnormality, or to spare her this suffering?" One way or the other—reproach . . . one way or the other—I am accountable . . . ! We can no longer not decide. Even if we do not make a decision, we have made a decision. My husband and I have never been closely confronted by anyone with disabilities. In our despair, we consult dear friends. A minister arranges a talk with a woman who describes life plainly with her disabled daughter. The fact that the spectrum of possible symptoms is so great—ranging from mild to very severe disorders—makes everything even more difficult. No one can predict the degree of disability. No one can take the decision from us, make it for us. I can only make such a decision from within myself—by going deep inside myself . . . I am pleading, but the answer doesn't come . . . Time is running out . . . we're urged to make a decision—but I feel blank.

We have a second test done, not daring to hope, yet hoping for a miracle. But we are already grieving. No matter how we decide, our life will never be the way it was. Our children suffer terribly. They were so excited about having a little baby brother or sister. Our son has tremendous difficulty in school. Then the previous test results are reconfirmed by a second laboratory . . .

After four long weeks of agonizing struggle to find an answer, we can no longer postpone the decision. Time is running out. We drive to the hospital, still not sure of a definite answer. . . . Through a profound experience in the hospital chapel, a deep peace overcomes me. I can agree to having the birth induced. I don't want anesthetic—I do not want to leave my child alone at the last minute. I feel it is part of my moral responsibility to be with my child in full consciousness. The anesthesiologist tells me not to look at my daughter, that it will be unbearable for me, that I will never forget that sight, that it will haunt me. After two long days of labor, I hold Cara (this name came to me during labor and means "the loved one" and "grief" in two languages, as I learned later), my daughter, in my hands for what seemed like eternity and say good-bye to her. It's true—I will never forget that sight, but in a much different way than the doctor supposed. Her face was so peaceful. The deep, painful grief, the emptiness, the aggressions, came later. . . .

Talking to your baby, telling it about the situation, listening for answers rather than avoiding inner contact, will help bring peace and forgiveness even at this very difficult moment.

Another couple learned by ultrasound shortly before birth that their child had hydrocephalus, the condition sometimes called *water on the brain*. The husband, who worked among people with disabilities, knew well what kind of life their baby could expect if he survived. They decided against a Cesarean section, which would have been the only way to bring their son into the world alive, and so they assumed responsibility that he would die at birth.

One family, after learning their child had Down syndrome, decided *against* terminating the pregnancy. They were understandably concerned and anxious over the potential extent of the disability. During the time remaining until the delivery, they gathered information and prepared themselves (including their other children) for the task ahead. Some people are challenged to grow by living with a child with disabilities, others through separation and loss.

Despite different expectations, studies have shown there is no difference in the grief reactions of women after a termination in early pregnancy based on a chorionic villus sampling and those who lost their child very late based on an amniocentesis test. However, to give birth to the child following labor induction, to be able to say hello and good-bye, despite the increased physical discomfort involved, seems to be more beneficial for processing the experience in the long run than to remove the child through medical intervention.

Special Circumstances

Society and the medical profession urge us to use the "wonderful" resource of prenatal diagnostics "to be on the safe side." Not having the test is perceived as irresponsible. Some physicians won't accept older pregnant women as patients if they don't agree to prenatal diagnostic testing. Those who decide against it may have to sign a release form.

Many people automatically advise us to terminate the pregnancy if we have taken tests and gotten adverse results. If, after painstaking soul-searching and inner struggle, we decide to terminate the pregnancy, we may find no understanding for our grief. On the contrary, we may be ostracized for it. People who may have advised us before to end the pregnancy may now say that they *would have also* accepted a child with disabilities. Perhaps that is just their way of clearing their consciences retroactively. Many others can't understand why we still grieve when we have "opted" for the death.

"Are you sad?" my gynecologist asked me with a surprised look. I had just walked into his office for a checkup two weeks after the loss, with traces of tears on my face. On the way to the office, I recalled how happy my

husband and I had been during our last visit, when we saw our baby for the first time on ultrasound. The tears helped. But my doctor was taxed by my sadness, and to this day he hasn't understood that I wanted nothing more from him than not having to feel obliged to act cheerful when I was sad.

Grief after such a loss is more complicated and takes longer to resolve. (Korenromp et al. 1992) A study showed that extended, strongly depressive periods after a termination of pregnancy for this indication were much more frequent than they were after the termination of an unwanted pregnancy. (Lloyd 1985) We need people around us, professionals or friends, who are aware of our decision and our loss and with whom we can share many feelings over the loss of a loved child—including guilt, doubts, inadequacy and naturally deep pain—so that we don't repress them.

It's important to find people who are supportive and who won't pressure us one way or the other. Supportive friends and professionals will help us find our own answers: Tests, yes or no? Termination, yes or no? The more we talk, the clearer we become on the many "voices" in us, and the better we can make a choice with full consciousness of and responsibility for it.

Many people are afraid of sharing their decision because they are afraid they will be judged for it. Contact with others who have been in a similar situation is invaluable. A hospital social worker or a genetic counselor might arrange that for you. Individual counseling may be necessary.

Addresses of organizations and groups providing support for parents facing such difficult decisions, literature and addresses of societies who have information and resources regarding your child's specific problem can be found in Appendix 4. Talking to parents who live with a baby that has the same problem as yours, or spending time with him or her, may help you make a decision, because your mind won't be working well enough to make such big decisions just by thinking about the situation intellectually. There are self-help groups for parents who decide for a pregnancy termination and for those who decide against it. How I wish I had had access to all the support that is available now!

Termination of an Unwanted Pregnancy

A patient came to a therapeutic-massage therapist complaining about severe pains in her hip. Over the course of treatment, as the therapist worked with her, the woman suddenly began talking about a past abortion. At the time she hadn't regretted the abortion. There was no room in her life for a child then. While she spoke about that experience, all the feelings she had repressed for so long resurfaced. At once her hip pains disappeared.

Even when an abortion may seem to be a relief from a currently unmanageable situation, consciously or not, it also means separating from a part of ourselves. It's common for women in this situation to hold back and deny their feelings. But it's important to allow the emotions of grief and guilt, and maybe even anger, to surface. They need to be expressed so they won't crop up later in a camouflaged way. You need people who will listen to you, who will not judge, minimize or rationalize your feelings, and who are not afraid of your tears. Talking with a counselor is helpful for some women.

Giving Up Your Baby for Adoption

Some women who become pregnant are unable to raise a child, financially or emotionally. Instead of having an abortion, they opt to give up the baby for adoption. Having given their baby the gift of life, these women give away their baby because they don't feel they can provide what it needs for healthy growth. This is usually done out of love. Many times teenage mothers are forced to take this step by their parents. In one case, a young girl was sent away so the baby would be born far from home. This was so the family would be spared disgrace and so the event wouldn't "ruin" the girl's life. Who can conceive of what it means to a woman or a young girl to give birth to her child, not to be able to get to know it, what it looks like, not to be able to say goodbye, not to know where and how the child lives—not even to know whether it is still alive?

These women do not receive support or sympathy from society. They can't let go gradually and free themselves for new commitments. For a while they may be able to repress their grief, but sooner or later they will come to the phase of searching and yearning for what they lost. Instead of passing through it as a natural part of the grief process, they will endure it as a life-long condition—unless they start a successful search for their child. Only then can the process continue, though perhaps not as they might have wished. This was 56-year-old Sally's experience. She "found" her child after 31 agonizing years of yearning and wondering.

Thirty-one years ago I gave birth to my daughter out of wedlock, which was a catastrophe at that time. The baby's father was married and denied paternity. I didn't want to marry him anyway. I hadn't finished school. I was studying to be a pharmacist and financing it myself. My father was against the idea of my child being raised in his home, which would have been feasible. . . . In my sixth month, I decided to go to another state to have the baby and give it up for adoption. The last few months of my pregnancy were beautiful and at the same time difficult. I had doubts about whether adoption was a good idea. I'd rather have kept my child. But in the end I couldn't find another acceptable solution. I didn't want my daughter to grow up in an institution or with foster parents. Consultation with the adoption agency didn't happen in those days.

My daughter and I had a long, hard birth. I didn't cooperate much because I didn't want to give away my baby, and I knew I'd lose her as soon as she was born. At least I got to see her for a moment—my only memory of her. After the birth I was more lonely than before. I was totally paralyzed and began to build a wall around me so no one would learn my secret. And nobody who did know asked me how I was able to live with it.

I didn't feel entitled to mourn because I considered myself such a terrible mother. I developed tremendous guilt feelings. My self-confidence took a nosedive. I didn't let anyone get too close.

All my repressed feelings broke out in full force with my father's death. I fell into total despair and finally started therapy. I've learned to say out loud, "my daughter," "my child." I've learned to talk openly to other people about the adoption. I have "come out" as they say these days. I met resistance, rejection and being silenced, but also received understanding, human closeness and warmth (unfortunately not from my elderly mother) or simply ignorance. Since I've opened up, I've made new contacts. I've read a lot about adoption. I've had many talks with others—those who were adopted as well as mothers who gave up their child for adoption, with adoptive parents as well as professionals.

My grief was compounded when I lost my daughter a second time. In the spring of 199-, I finally had the courage to search for her. I found her and wrote to her last November. She answered, refusing to see me . . . I became sadder still. She apparently didn't feel any connection to her biological parents, or any interest. That was hard.

But it's good that I can express how I feel about all this. It has been a huge relief to know that my daughter still lives, what her name is and that she is doing well outwardly at least. She has taken shape for me and has enough character to have answered me and not ignored me. She also learned that

I'm not indifferent toward her. I hope one of these days she'll be ready to get to know her roots. This hope keeps me strong, although I know that my giving her up and 31 years of life in different worlds lie between us.

Bereaved Single Mothers

While reading books on bereavement, I notice that on almost every page there is reference made to "the parents." I agree it is important to include the father in mourning. But there are women who carry their baby alone, who bring their dead baby into the world alone and after the loss are much more isolated than "parents." I'm one of them. My boyfriend deserted me when he heard I was pregnant.

Single bereaved mothers feel even more alone than couples who can grieve their baby's loss together. Barbara, who works in a hospital, describes this situation:

These women usually don't have anyone with whom to share their troubles and grief. Because they are often very young and not yet financially established, most people think that the baby's death is the best thing that could have happened. Often this opinion is voiced to the woman with little consideration. It's dramatic when a young girl keeps her pregnancy secret from her parents, friends and others, who only learn of the baby's death when contractions begin. The parents may be called to the hospital thinking their daughter is in the surgical unit with appendicitis and find her in the maternity ward. Often the young woman or girl is lectured and reproached. . . . The parents decide how to hush up the "story," and frequently the baby's death is not entirely unwelcome. Parents don't take into consideration that their daughter developed motherly feelings during the pregnancy, that she anticipated childbirth with a mixture of fear and joy, and that she is now under enormous emotional pressure. For the young woman, many problems will never be voiced, many tears will never be shed, and many emotions will never be expressed . . .

Some relationships end because they aren't strong enough to bear the loss (see pages 87 to 90). Women deserted by the father of the baby who has died and women who are alone need a lot of attention and support from other sources. A special support network for grieving single mothers is needed.

2

When It Happens to Us

Grief is real, and it is human. . . . It is important for us to accept our passage through the levels of grief. . . . It is fighting our feelings that causes our suffering, not our feelings. (Anne Wilson Schaef)

The Nature of Grieving

Grief is an entirely natural response to the loss of something or someone we loved and valued. We can work through grief in the context of our families or other social networks. We were "given" the mourning process so we could say good-bye and integrate the loss into our lives. Through the grieving process, we reach a new order and eventually find new meaning in our lives.

Grief is a powerful energy. It can heal or destroy. Even if we try to block it with all our might, sooner or later it finds a way of expressing itself. The high price we pay for unexpressed grief can be depression, chronic pain, overweight or underweight—even life-threatening illness. Or it can prevent us from experiencing life's joy. A lot of energy can be tied up in unlived grief. Entire families can become depressed and sick through repressed grief, unable to truly give and take love.

There is no simple way to process grief, though it must be done. **To become whole again, to be able to live and love again, is only possible if we dare to live through the experience consciously. We must**

feel those emotions and be shaken by them.

It takes courage to face painful emotions. If we don't work up the courage needed for this task, however, we automatically replace it with its opposite—fear. We may shy away from forming new attachments. Grief must be given its place. When we allow ourselves to feel grief, we learn it has the power not only to heal but also to help us grow.

At first you will probably feel worse than if you had blocked your feelings. But in the end, the wounds will heal better.

> *[Grief] is like a deep wound. It has to drain to prevent infection—you have to take care of the wound so it can heal.*

As unlikely as it may seem at first, when you really allow yourself to grieve, this painful experience can contribute to your own spiritual growth and lead you to a new understanding of your place in the world.

> *It takes courage and love for ourselves to believe that living through all these emotions will, in the end, help us to dissipate the pain.* (Tatelbaum 1980)

> *I felt a terrible sadness that I've never felt before in my life. But at the same time, I've also experienced joy—the joy of being alive, the joy of each moment, that I had never known before. And I don't want to lose that again.*

The Journey through Grief

> *It's been seven weeks and I am slowly coming to accept the fact that it will not be over in two weeks or a month or two. It will be over when it is over. I'm beginning to think it's something about which we'll never stop being sad.*

Most parents who have lost a child are surprised at how much time they need for the recovery process. The acute grief lasts as long as the pregnancy and often longer, depending on possible previous losses (not only death), individual history and the circumstances surrounding the present loss. You can consider the grief process to have come full circle when you have found a new balance in your life.

Though each person's grieving process is unique, certain elements are common to all. In what seems to be chaos, there is a certain order. To be aware of the stages of grief and the path to recovery can help grieving parents sort out their own experiences. As with most developmental processes, the stages of grief aren't well-defined. Progress takes a "spiraling" path upwards rather than "stair-steps." At times you will be sure you have mastered a stage, only to run into it again in a slightly different way. Sometimes the characteristics of all phases seem to be present at the same time. The first phase is the phase of shock and emotional numbness.

Shock and Emotional Numbness

Anyone who receives terrible news about their baby feels as though they have landed in a nightmare. It doesn't matter what stage of pregnancy it is or the age of the newborn. Many of us instantly retreat into ourselves, like a turtle ducking into its shell. Others react with emotional outbursts. At first it's impossible to comprehend the death. We refuse to believe it.

> *I so hoped that our child would still move a little, or that it hadn't been dead for too long, so it could be brought back to life . . . crazy thoughts!*

It's a struggle to grasp what happened. It's hard to think clearly. We may feel detached or "outside" ourselves. We may feel cold. Breath is reduced to a trickle. We probably couldn't deal with the whole truth all at once. For this reason, nature protects us at first with a form of natural anesthesia: shock. This stage can last a few hours, a few days or even a few weeks. Taking sedatives tends to stagnate us in this phase.

Adrenaline levels rise in response to shock, so thinking is impaired. At the same time we may have to make decisions we probably never thought about before. We don't know what's ahead. We don't know what responses are appropriate. We don't know our rights and obligations or our options. We don't have the perspective to know which actions will help and which will make processing the tragic event more difficult. However, *the actions and circumstances of these first hours and days determine how the experience will affect our lives in the long run.* This chapter provides practical advice for this initial time. The task of this phase is to come to accept the reality of the loss.

Help to Find Your Own Answers

In the last 20 years, the medical and paramedical professions have learned a lot about what kind of care is most beneficial to parents whose child has died and what tends to hamper their recovery. At best you will be under the care of someone who will not only administer medical help but also have your emotional needs at heart.

At first you will find it hard to make decisions because you will probably feel paralyzed. But letting other people handle everything only reinforces feelings of helplessness. In general, you will heal faster and better the more empathetic support you receive and the more you can live through this experience in terms of your own needs, values and wishes.

To create the best possible basis for integrating this loss into your life, you will need information from your caregivers on which to base your decisions. You need to know:

વ what to expect,

વ in which decisions you can take part,

વ the options you have, their advantages and disadvantages (including possible risks),

વ how much time you have to make these decisions,

વ what has helped others in the same situation in the long run, and

વ what they regretted in the end.

Surround Yourself with Good People

It is important that you have help and aren't left alone in this difficult situation. Sometimes you will come across caregivers who feel overwhelmed themselves in dealing with death. That's just the way it is. If you feel you aren't getting the support and answers you need from the professionals tending you, look out for yourself and seek out your own support, if at all possible.

I can ask myself:

☐ Who understands me best?

☐ Who would hold me and just be here with me?

☐ With whom do I feel free to show the "real me"?

☐ Who would help me confront my thoughts and feelings?

☐ Who listens well? Who might be a good sounding board and wouldn't try to tell me what to do?

☐ Who has the emotional and spiritual strength to be with me/us under these challenging circumstances?

☐ Who has lived through a similar experience and could give me/us some orientation, perspective and inspiration?

☐ Who can give me the information I'm not getting from my caretakers? For example, childbirth educator, midwife, grief counselor, SHARE National Office (see page 247), clergy.

☐ Who has taken a special interest in this pregnancy and can help me say good-bye to my dead baby?

Letting Go Is a Process

To most women, "having death inside them" is an eerie thought. Once death becomes a certainty, the child that just minutes or hours before had been loved as an extension of themselves now is perceived as a foreign body. When it is evident that a child has been dead for some time, many women fear they could be poisoned by it. This isn't true. If a child dies, the body treats it the same way it would any other *infarct* (dead tissue) (see also page 10, about twins). As long as the amniotic sac is intact and no infection occurs, no "poisons" can develop. Gradual decomposition begins only through contact with bacteria.

Very often the first reaction is, "I want this over with as soon as possible!" That's normal and it passes. If birth is induced and a baby is born while parents are still in a state of shock, they often don't want to see their baby. It remains a foreign body to them. But when they do have enough time to get used to the idea, and they can develop the right perspective and receive the right support, they can go through a real healing process. At the end of it, they can accept the baby as their own again, even though he or she is dead.

Parents at that point may go through a new phase, in which they don't want to let go of their baby. This is normal, and this too will pass.

In my experience, it is beneficial for parents to have time to get used to the terrible news before the birth or before any measure is taken. Often parents realize only much later how important it was to have "slept on it" at home for at least one night or to have talked half the night about the situation—especially if they find comfort and security in their relationship or have a circle of nurturing friends and family. Depending on where you live, midwives might also be called on to join you at home.

It takes time to acknowledge what has happened on a deep level, time to grasp it, and time to let it go. We need help for this job. If circumstances allow, take part in deciding about future proceedings and their timing, after you are properly informed of the advantages and disadvantages of giving yourself time, and after you are assured that you will be safe and well provided for at home.

I can ask myself:

- ☐ What are my fears about the dead baby in the womb?
- ☐ What questions do I want answered and by whom?
- ☐ Do I need time? What for? How much time do I think I need?
- ☐ What are my feelings towards my dead baby?
- ☐ Can I still let myself love this baby? What would help me?
- ☐ Can I let go, or what do I need to be able to let go of my baby?

Inching Forward, Taking Time

Waiting for the birth had its advantages. We could slowly come to accept our baby's death and were better able to consciously say good-bye than if we had still been in shock.

Decisions and actions must be dealt with on the spot in an emergency. Otherwise you don't have to rush. Whether a miscarriage is ended by a D&C (see page 38) or birth is induced, consider how much time you can and want to allow yourself. Your inner clock runs slower when you are in shock.

We need time and the permission to feel out our own needs and wishes. We should be able to inch our way forward and have the opportunity to change our minds at any time. Our wishes can be different from one hour to the next, even from one moment to the next, as the process unfolds. *In each and every one of us there is an inner voice that knows what we need and what will be right for us. We can rely on and trust that voice.* The decision we will make affects every part of who we are and who we will become.

I can ask myself:

☐ Which decisions do I need to make immediately? Which can wait?

☐ Am I aware of all my options, or with whom would I like to check?

☐ Have I made any decision I regret now? Whom do I want to tell that I changed my mind? What questions do I still have?

Getting over the Shock

Coming out of shock and gradually beginning to grasp what happened helps us move forward in the grief process. Some helpful ways to overcome shock are listed below.

ès Traumatic experiences bring us back to basic human needs, such as our *biological need for touch.* To be touched or held closely by someone can dissolve feelings of shock and numbness. In an embrace, breath can begin to flow again and energy returns. The free-flowing breath of the person holding us can be "contagious." You may need to ask someone to hold you until you have calmed down, because others may not know if hugging is appropriate.

ès Help yourself with *your own touch.* First "awaken" one hand by rubbing, patting and gently massaging it, applying a little pressure in the center of the palm and noticing any changes before doing the same to the other hand. Then place one hand, palm down, in the middle of the triangle formed by the ribcage and an assumed horizontal line at the height of your navel. That is the center of your body and your being—the source of your life energy and your essence, according to Middendorf Breathwork® (see page 131). Place the other hand, with the back of it against your body, exactly opposite the first hand, at the small of your back.

Be aware of the centers of your hand that you stimulated earlier, and position them along the median line of your body (on the spine). Then be very "centered" and aware of what is under your hands. Let your hands "speak" to the place you are touching and "listen" for a possible "answer" (reaction) from there. If you do this for a while, it will stimulate breath movement in your center. From there, the breath radiates to other parts of your body, bringing sensation back and making you feel connected to yourself again. You will slowly become calmer, and your mind will become clearer.

- Ask yourself at what other parts of your body *touch* may feel good (for example, shoulders, middle of the chest, forehead) and place your hands there. After a while, become aware of whether you feel movement under your hands—the up-and-down of your breath. You may also perceive warmth and a feeling of "coming alive" under your hands.

- Placing your hands in the same way on your abdomen and *"feeling" towards your baby*, as if speaking to it with your hands, leads you away from denial and back to the reality of the situation. This helps reinitiate the bonding that stopped so abruptly.

- It can help you think more clearly again if you *get moving*—perhaps outside or with your mate or a supportive person who is open to your needs.

- Just being able to *talk about what has happened*, about your memories, the death of your dreams and yearnings—being able to, in Glen Davidson's words, "tell your story" over and over again—brings you out of speechlessness, numbness and disorientation.

- In many cultures, people face death and loss with *loud crying*. People come from near and far to join the wailing.

When our first baby was on the way, we lived in Africa. When our neighborhood learned that our daughter had been born dead, the women around me started wailing loudly. At first it seemed strange, but it became contagious. And then it felt so good not to have to hold back my pain but to be able to cry it out. I was deeply touched to experience so much solidarity—others helped to carry part of my loss. Although my grief was intense, I felt much better rather quickly. Unfortunately, my second pregnancy back home ended in a late miscarriage. But here I can't wail. I'm suffocating from feelings that can't come out.

Maybe you can find your own private place to wail, where you can release your feelings by wailing, groaning and other sounds, instead of holding them inside.

&❧ You can also *sound tones* in a conscious way. Toning, especially if you do it repeatedly, will help various parts of your body feel like they have "opened up." Different sounds have different effects in your body and determine where "space" is created. Based on the principle that nature abhors a vacuum, breath movement is attracted to those specific areas. Your breath starts to flow again. A new quality of awareness develops.

Do the touch exercises described above as a good preparation for sounding. You may want to close your eyes. Focus on your breath: Let it flow in, flow out and wait for it to come in again on its own. Let it happen, don't *make* it happen! Next, only *imagine* yourself toning at first—chanting a given sound. As your breath flows in, *silently* contemplate a tone with it—perhaps an "m" (as in *mom*), an "o" (as in *so*), an "a" (as in *sad*), an "oo" (as in *mood*), an "ah" (as in *car*) and let whatever tone you chose flow into you and spread throughout your body.

As your breath flows out, imagine accompanying it with that same tone, at first silently, as long as your breath naturally lasts. After a few silent tones, begin to tone audibly if you wish, using your voice but without trying to be particularly loud. In time, you may observe that the different tones "widen" different parts of you. For example, the "oo" creates space in your pelvic area, the "o" widens your breathing center, the "a", your entire torso. Allow for a short, natural pause, after which the breath flows in again on its own with a tone, and accompany the exhalation with a tone again.

Try out the volume and pitch that feel best. Toning can become very meditative and centering. After you finish, stay centered on this feeling for a little while and take note of any changes in your body (especially a sense of more spaciousness and more "aliveness") or in your emotional state (more peaceful and calm). Toning can be very helpful during labor!

&❧ *Aromatherapy* can help you harmonize your feelings. (For detailed instructions, see chapter 4; for sources, see Appendix 4.) To reduce the feeling of shock, use neroli, mimosa and cedar. To think more clearly, use incense, juniper and hyssop. Mandarin and vanilla essences can help you reestablish bonding with your baby.

&ᴥ Another way to reduce the effects of shock on your energy system and help you clear your head is to use Rescue Remedy (No. 39) from the *Bach Flower Essences*. Information on other useful Bach Flowers can be found on page 134.

&ᴥ Of the *California Research Flower Essences*, Arnica (No. 2) helps relieve the effects of shock (see page 136).

I can ask myself:

☐ Who or what could help me slowly overcome my shock?

☐ What appeals to me? What is feasible and available?

☐ How and where can I create the space I need?

☐ Whom do I want to ask for help and support?

Initiating and Facilitating the Process

Certain actions can help move along and facilitate the grief process—especially when there is time between learning that the baby is seriously afflicted or dead and its birth.

&ᴥ You can *arrange time*, just for you or together with your partner, during which you won't be disturbed. You may light a candle, and place a flower or a symbol that represents your baby before you. Take sacred time to "be" with your baby in your thoughts, to "walk" your path together in your mind, from the very beginning (and perhaps even earlier) to this moment—affirming your bonding, acknowledging and honoring his or her precious little life.

&ᴥ Focus on your breath. You may wish to play calming music quietly. Allow questions to emerge from deep inside.

&ᴥ You may prefer to reflect on everything as you walk in *nature*.

&ᴥ *Writing* can help bring order to thoughts and untangle emotions. You might write a poem or a good-bye letter to your baby in which you express whatever bothers you.

&ᴥ Working with the medium of *colors* may help you. Arrange paper, paints or crayons in front of you. Close your eyes and place one hand over your heart, remaining attentive to the movement of breath under your hands. Let a question rise from your heart. When the question is clear, write it at the top of the paper. Then turn over the paper, pick a color and allow what is inside of you to flow onto the paper spontaneously. When you're done, look at the picture from across the room. Let it "speak" to you. Ask yourself what you see, what feelings it triggers and what thoughts come to mind. Without censoring yourself, write down your impressions below the question on the paper's reverse. After a moment, read it over in context.

Look at your drawing and writing from time to time. You may see something in it you hadn't noticed before, you might understand things in different terms, or the message might change. New pictures may evoke other questions. Through drawings, you can get in touch with your inner self.

❧ Getting bad news about your baby is like having the rug pulled out from under you. An exercise that I call *letting yourself be carried* can help you stabilize and help you experience in a tangible way that you are supported after all.

Lie down on your back with your head resting comfortably on a pillow (make sure your head isn't tilted too far back), your arms alongside your body, the palms of your hands facing down. Focus on your breathing without altering it. Tell yourself in your mind: "*I, (your name), am letting myself be carried.*" Start by focusing on one foot and wander through your body, taking time to experience deeply how in every part of you, you are being carried by the floor or whatever you lie on. "*I let my right foot be carried, I let myself be carried in my ankle* (even though it may not touch the ground) . . . *in my right lower leg, my right knee* (imagine the ground reaching up and gently wrapping around and "cuddling" your knee) . . . *in my right thigh . . . I let my entire right leg and foot be carried.*" Take a moment to perceive your leg and foot in comparison to the other side. Does it feel different? Perhaps bigger or warmer? Perhaps heavier or lighter? Now turn your attention to your left foot: "*I let my left foot be carried . . . my left ankle . . . my lower leg . . . my knee, my left thigh . . . the entire left leg and foot . . . .*" How does this side feel? How do both legs feel now compared to the rest of your body?

Continue: "*I let my pelvic area be carried . . . my sacrum . . . then the small of my back (the ground cuddles that part of me, too) . . . then the middle of my back, my ribs . . . my upper back with the shoulder blades . . . the shoulders. I let my right upper arm . . . my elbow . . . my right forearm . . . my right hand be carried* (compare arms . . .) . . . *then my left upper arm . . . my elbow . . . my left forearm . . . my left hand. . . .*" Continue on to the neck, letting the ground cuddle your neck as well. "*I let my head be carried and cradled by the ground and the pillow.*" Become totally aware of being carried by the surface that supports you, surrendering yourself to it. Has your breathing changed? Perhaps you feel more peaceful and calm. This is also a way to help yourself if you have trouble falling asleep or if you wake up during the night.

ໄ► You may feel isolated and alone after receiving bad news about your baby. The following visualization exercise may help you feel more connected again. (You may want to record the instructions on tape.)

Sit in a chair with your eyes closed and concentrate on your breathing. Feel it coming . . . going . . . a little pause . . . coming . . . going. . . . Be aware of your contact with the ground. Then, in the distance visualize a gleaming, golden light that slowly moves towards you until it is over your head. With each incoming breath, golden light flows into you through your highest point, the top of your head (your *crown chakra*). Each exhalation soothingly saturates your head—your brain, your sinuses, your eyes, your ears—from the inside with light and well-being. With each new breath, light continues to flow in. With each exhalation, the light gradually spreads farther and farther, eventually reaching even the most remote parts of your body, weaving through your body as though in a gentle dance, reaching every cell.

At first, light flows down the backside of your body, every breath moving it a little farther along—warming, widening, releasing tension, illuminating your body—into your neck, shoulders, upper back, under your shoulder blades, down the back side of your arms . . . spiraling along your backbone down to the small of your back and bringing warmth and radiation to the kidneys . . . permeating your sacrum and buttocks. *How does my backside feel now?*

Now it flows into your legs and down into your feet, rising from there in a spiral motion. Riding on the waves of your breath, the golden light begins to fill in the front of your body. It is as if the light gently, lovingly massages you all over. Then it flows into your womb—to your baby—bathing it with the greatest love and tenderness in a protective golden sphere of light. . . . It spreads to your solar plexus and to your stomach and liver, up into your chest, gently massaging your heart, creating light and lightness in your lungs. It warmly extends into your armpits and seeps under your collarbone, it widens your throat area and gently moves into your face—caressing your mouth, your cheeks, your eyes, your forehead. Spilling out of your crown chakra again, it forms a cascade of light that rains down on your head, enveloping you and creating a safe and protected space in which you can feel soothed and secure. *How do I feel in my "light veil"? How does it feel to know my child is enveloped in his or her sphere of light?*

I can ask myself:

☐ Which of these suggestions appeal to me the most?

☐ What is feasible in my situation?

☐ What would feel good now?

☐ What do I need to be able to grasp the reality of the situation better?

Know What Is Happening

A Miscarriage in the First Three Months of Pregnancy

If the baby dies in the uterus, you may be able to wait and let the birth happen naturally, if you want to and it won't endanger the mother's life and health. This choice may make it possible to see the tiny baby—from approximately the eighth week on—and to say good-bye (see page 45). (With a D&C this outcome is less likely.) Not rushing things can be an advantage, as 30-year-old Carol's report about the miscarriage of her first child shows:

> *I was in shock. Everything went so fast—the diagnosis, admittance to the hospital, the D&C early the next morning . . . the machine was set in motion, and I had to go along whether I wanted to or not. I drove to my husband's work to pick him up. It wasn't until I saw him that I started to cry. We drove home together. It was 11 in the morning—we were supposed to be at the hospital at 2 p.m. to be admitted, talk to the anesthesiologist and fill out the paperwork. The feeling of "not having time" made me afraid. There was no opportunity for us to talk about our feelings, cry, comfort each other, simply to be together . . . no time for the grief we were experiencing.*

> *I called Hannah and told her all about it. It felt so good to talk about what was going on inside me and to feel someone understood. She gave me the name of a gynecologist friend. He explained I didn't have to rush into anything, I could take my time, even over the weekend. Suddenly I felt so much better. "We have time, we don't have to rush." At 2 p.m., we drove to the hospital. I introduced myself to the anesthesiologist and explained that I didn't plan to stay overnight but would come back tomorrow, just before the operation. He didn't mind because there was no health problem and no technical reason to stay. I had to promise I wouldn't eat anything after 10 p.m. and I'd be punctual the next morning. My gynecologist was a little surprised, but he agreed it would be all right. I filled out the papers and left.*

My husband and I spent the afternoon together at home. We developed a closeness we'd never known by being together in this painful situation. In the evening our friends Rob and Hannah came over. We sat together in front of the fireplace a long time. It felt good to talk about what was going on inside us and to find understanding and consolation. I was really glad in this helpless situation to have friends who respected my feelings and gave me the support I needed not to violate them.

Looking back, I understand now how important it had been for me to pay attention to my own feelings. It was important not to let myself be forced to comply to a hospital routine that would have been convenient and standard procedure for the doctor and other people involved, but that would have overridden my emotions and needs. I believe I would have been left with an emptiness inside, of having missed something important, and I wouldn't even have been able to say what was missing. This way I came to terms with the loss of our child, and the wounds were able to heal well.

I can ask myself:

☐ If the situation offers a choice, what are my/our wishes?

☐ How much time would I like before labor is induced or a D&C is performed? What do I need this time for?

☐ What is important to me?

☐ Who would be good for me/us?

The Birth of a Dead Baby—a "Real" Birth

If your baby dies in the womb after the third month of pregnancy, you generally have to go through a normal birth. Depending on the situation, birth will either be induced shortly after the death has been confirmed, or, if you are close to the expected due date, your doctor may recommend that you wait for the natural onset of labor. The thought of giving birth naturally to a dead child is unbearable for some women.

I'm supposed to wait until labor begins! Just wait?! *My mind was racing. How does labor start? . . . The baby is decomposing inside me, and it will probably make me sick. . . . I still have to go through with the delivery, without getting a baby to hold in my arms. "Can't you just remove her somehow?" I asked. They replied that they wouldn't perform a Cesarean. That would be too risky and would only lead to unnecessary pain afterwards.*

It is common for women to want to have a Cesarean at first, but in retrospect they are usually glad they were spared it. Myriam (29), with her husband, gave birth to their dead baby in a supportive environment and said afterwards,

> *I couldn't believe it when I was told I needed to give birth to Sarah. But in retrospect I am so glad that I didn't have a Cesarean, because then Frank and I wouldn't have been able to participate in everything surrounding her birth and death, and maybe we would not even have wanted to see her. This way everything evolved so naturally. If I'd had a Cesarean, I'm sure I'd feel much worse than I do now.*

Women often experience the birth event as distinct from the fact that their baby is dead. Therefore it's all the more important to strive for a positive birth experience and to follow any birth plan that was devised in childbirth-education classes (for example, music, aromatherapy, massages, water, birth positions). The experience of the birth in a nurturing atmosphere can touch you very deeply.

> *To have given birth to my baby was a deeply moving experience, even though she was dead.*

Many women who have gone through a natural birth and were able to hold their child in their arms immediately afterwards report feeling euphoric at first, despite the baby's being dead. It seems we can only take one step at a time—first we react to the birth, and then, only days later, to the death. Seeing your baby while you are under the influence of birth hormones will usually not be as painful as seeing her for the first time later.

When birth is induced before the mother's body is ready to give birth, labor is frequently prolonged.

> *I was hooked to an intravenous drip for 48 hours before anything happened.*

> *Over 24 hours have elapsed since labor was induced. . . . The others are beginning to worry. I remain calm and certain that I will deliver our child in her own time. I know it can't go any faster. I still need a little time to say good-bye to her . . .*

Then again, labor is quick for some women. Near the expected due date, labor can be stimulated in various ways. Induced contractions are more painful than the wavelike contractions brought about by the body naturally. You can support yourself during labor through aromatherapy by using verbena, lemon or the semi-precious jasmine and rose essences (see page 133).

I can ask myself:

☐ What are my fears? What information or help do I need to reduce these fears?

☐ What are my needs and wishes for the birth right now?

☐ How do I think I may want the birth to be handled?

☐ If I change my mind regarding certain procedures and wishes, to whom would I feel most comfortable telling my new wishes?

Looking back on the birth, I can ask myself:

☐ How did I experience the birth?

☐ What questions do I have about it? Who can answer them?

☐ Whom do I want to tell about the birth?

Medication, Yes or No?

The majority of hospitals take the position that women who have a stillbirth should be spared the pain of labor. This concurs with the wishes of many laboring women, probably even most of them, but certainly not all. For some women, it is of utmost importance to go through the birth process fully aware and conscious. Katie, whose child died without apparent reason a day after the expected due date, said:

> *When I arrived at the hospital, the doctor tried to coerce me into letting him give me an epidural. "No way," I thought. I wanted to experience the birth! Andrew had died inside of me without my being aware of it, and I wanted to be sure that he would not be born that way too.*

It was clear to me, too, that I didn't want pain-reducing medication during labor.

> *I do not want to desert my child. But also, pain has a protective function for me. The excruciating pain of the transition-phase contractions, together with my involuntary fasting from food during the 48 hours of labor, catapult me into an altered state of consciousness. I feel as if surrounded by a "magic circle" of five feet. . . . There is only my child and my husband. . . . It is as though the experience of pain removes the dimensions of time and space, opening me up for a true encounter with my child. Without time and space there is eternity—and for God only knows how long or short a*

period after the birth, death does not exist for me. I gently hold Cara in my
hands and feel no suffering during that time. I talk to her, opening up my
soul to her, sharing everything there is in my heart—there is love and
tenderness . . . and yet after some time I am able to let her go.

Recently I attended a woman during labor whose child had died in the 27th week of pregnancy. She had received labor-inducing medication for two days while under the influence of epidural anesthesia. However, her labor wasn't progressing. After I had spent many hours at her bedside and the effect of the anesthetic was wearing off, I asked very gently if she might want to try—just for a little—to manage without the anesthetic so her body could help in her effort to give birth. She agreed. With her cooperation, her dead child was delivered in no time at all. She said afterwards:

I wouldn't have believed it could be better for me this way. My first child
was born by Cesarean. I have no memory of her birth. This time I have at
least experienced childbirth.

Barbara, a midwife, contributed another observation:

I've learned that it may be good for women—only if they want to, of
course—to be able to feel the pain of contractions at a stillbirth. Where they
would normally be numbed and silenced due to shock, they are able, during
the delivery, to scream out their emotional pain as well, and this has been
helpful to some of them.

When giving birth to a child who is dead, even more than when giving birth to a child who is alive, we need to be able to decide *for ourselves* what is best. We need others' support and understanding—even if we change our minds over the course of labor. Being drugged with sedatives or being under full anesthesia only delays the grief process and hampers its future course.

It's as if emotions are put on ice, "freeze-dried," so to speak. Then, when
sedation stops, feelings "thaw" and surface, full force—often at entirely
inappropriate times.

Rather than using medication during labor, you may want support yourself through natural remedies (see page 131). Aromatherapy (verbena and lavender) may help.

For a loss in early or mid-pregnancy, especially when the birth was induced with prostaglandin, a D&C (*curettage*) is usually performed after delivery to make sure no placental tissue is left in the uterus. It may be done later if examination of the placenta shows it isn't complete. This operation is usually performed under general anesthesia. However, this procedure reinforces the feeling that the birth was just a bad dream. A D&C may be done under epidural or spinal anesthesia, so that you can perceive dully what is happening. That idea may be unpleasant to you but you won't feel any pain. Both options have their pros and cons. Deciding one way or another is a matter of individual personality.

I can ask myself:

☐ What are my wishes about using medication during the birth? Why?

☐ What are my wishes about using anesthetics during a possible D&C after the birth?

☐ What are my wishes regarding tranquilizers?

☐ Whom do I want to inform of my wishes?

A Cesarean Birth

When your child is born by Cesarean and then dies during the birth or within the first hours afterwards, you are in a special situation. You may only learn about your child's death or serious condition when you awaken from the anesthesia. Mary Ann's child was delivered by Cesarean in the 31st week and died some hours after birth:

It felt strange to have a flat stomach when I awoke from anesthesia. I was in great pain. "At least I know why. I'm a mother now." At 8 o'clock in the morning, a woman doctor I had never seen before walked in and said she had sad news, that my child had died at 1:30 that night. "But you're young, and I'm sure you'll get over it quickly," she said. Then she was gone.

My husband came at 9 o'clock. We were asked whether we wanted to see our baby. When I said yes, they wheeled me in my bed into another room, where the attending physician was. He explained that our son had died because his lungs were not mature enough. At my request they placed our child, Patrick, on my bed in a portable bassinet and left us to ourselves. I was still in intense pain, with drips attached to my left and right arms. I couldn't move at all and couldn't hold my baby. My husband stood by, also feeling rather helpless, so we had them take the baby away.

I am very sorry that I couldn't hold my son, and I'm sorry I was so drugged that I don't remember much. I was very sorry I'd had general anesthesia. Otherwise I could have seen my baby alive. At least my husband heard him cry right after the delivery and had a look at our son as he was lying in the incubator. He had an advantage there. I really missed out on that.

Very rarely, a Cesarean becomes necessary when a vaginal delivery would be dangerous for the mother (for example, in the case of blood-coagulation problems) or for anatomical reasons (for example, in the case of a transverse presentation).

General anesthesia will make your experience of the death seem all the more unreal. It's almost impossible to scream out one's pain or even cry shortly after an operation—it can cause additional physical pain. So emotions can be released only in very small doses.

After the operation, the mother's movements are restricted for several days. If the baby has been transferred to a children's hospital, she won't be able to see her right away. If a child dies in a U.S. children's hospital and the mother is still unable to leave the hospital, then officially a funeral director must bring the dead baby to its mother. (This isn't the case in Canada.) But there can be exceptions. This special situation requires the good will and cooperation of both hospital staffs. This is apt to happen naturally if both sides are aware of how important it is for a mother to see her child under these circumstances.

If the situation allows, I can ask myself:

☐ Would I rather have general anesthesia and be unconscious when my child is born or remain conscious with an epidural?

Our Child is Born Alive and Is Very Sick

When our child is born alive but is in serious condition, we may need to make certain decisions immediately. We may be asked for permission for operations that may prolong the child's life only a few days or keep it alive indefinitely with the possibility of lifelong, severe disabilities. We may even be asked to participate in the most difficult of all decisions—whether to turn off life-support systems. These decisions seem beyond our capabilities. We hardly feel fit to make them in the best circumstances, let alone in a state of shock.

What you can do now:

☙ First, in order to think more clearly, check on page 28 to see what might help you get over your shock.

☙ Spend as much time as possible with your baby, caressing and holding him as best you can, talking to him and maybe even putting him to the breast. He can be administered oxygen outside of the incubator and kept warm by a sheepskin or a heated blanket while you hold him. Your love will "nourish" your baby and be important for him even if he does not survive.

ê∍ Touching your baby the way you may have experienced touch yourself (see page 28) will stimulate the baby's breathing and body functions and can be beneficial, perhaps even life-saving, for him.

ê∍ If your child is taken to the neonatal intensive care unit, visit her as often and as long as possible. You may have to go in a wheelchair.

ê∍ Take as many pictures as you can, including pictures of you or others holding the baby.

I can ask myself:

☐ Which people would be good for me/us now?

☐ Who should have a chance to "meet" our baby, if possible?

☐ How can I show my baby my love?

☐ What decision are still to be made, and how do I/we want to make them?

The Hospital Stay

After a miscarriage or a stillbirth, just as after a normal birth, the mother's body needs time to return to normal. There may be milk in the breasts as early as the 12th week of pregnancy, but definitely by the 20th week. Often the flow of milk is suppressed by using lactation suppressants. These have strong side effects. You can ask your healthcare professional for natural alternatives if you prefer.

Pain caused by engorgement can often be relieved or minimized by placing ice packs on your breasts. This way, the milk gradually dries up on its own. Very rarely women have reported to me that milk was still present weeks or months after the birth—perhaps a sign of the body's longing for the baby. To have your milk come in will make you painfully aware that your body was prepared for the coming of a baby that is not here now. Susan said:

> About five days after the abortion, my milk started to come in. My breasts were hard-like-rocks and sore, and I developed a fever (mastitis, I presume). That day and the next were two of the worst days of all. I've happily nursed two babies, and getting milk seemed like just the cruelest possible reminder of what was not going to happen. I couldn't stop crying.

In addition, your uterus must return to its normal size and shape, and blood vessels where the placenta had been must close. Following a delivery in an advanced stage of pregnancy, you can have intense contractions, particularly if this was not your first pregnancy. Blood vessels at the site where the placenta had been implanted will start to heal. The healing process will be accompanied by a uterine discharge called *lochia.*

After a stillbirth in an early stage of pregnancy, bleeding (particularly if a curettage was done), will usually stop within a week. In contrast, after a full-term pregnancy, the bleeding can persist in an ever-diminishing amount for up to six weeks. An unpleasant-smelling discharge is a sign of infection and must be treated medically. If an episiotomy was done, it must be sutured.

A woman with Rh-negative blood must be treated within 72 hours with RhoGAM after a miscarriage or stillbirth. RhoGAM eliminates antibodies that may have developed in her blood and that could harm an Rh-positive child in later pregnancies.

At the Hospital

> *After several hours we were taken to a private room off the maternity ward. They had set up a bed for my husband. Being able to stay together was very, very important to me. I didn't want to be alone under any circumstances. But then we heard a baby cry, and I saw the expression of excruciating pain on my husband's face. I knew we couldn't stay. I got dressed, we summoned the doctor and then went home, only hours after our baby had been born and had died.*

It's a good idea to have a say in how and where you want to be accommodated in the hospital. Many women prefer that a private room be turned into a "family room," letting bereaved parents (and perhaps young children) remain together, receive other family members and friends and say hello and good-bye to their baby. Others may decide to return to their original room, especially if they have formed relationships with roommates who can support them. Members of support groups will often visit bereaved parents in the hospital if they are asked. Hospital staff need to inform the parents of this option and the comfort it can bring.

Most bereaved women leave the hospital within 24 hours of giving birth. Some want to leave as soon as possible after the delivery if there are no medical complications, particularly when at home they can anticipate the support of family members and friends.

I can ask myself:

☐ Do I want to stay in the hospital or would I feel more comfortable at home?

☐ If I stay in the hospital, how and where would I like to be roomed if the situation allows it?

☐ If I want to go home, is there someone who can stay with me and help me?

☐ Would I like a call or visit from a member of a bereavement-support group?

Saying Hello, Saying Good-Bye

Attachment and Loss

As human beings, we have an inherent need to form strong emotional bonds. This stems from our instincts for safety and security. John Bowlby in his book, *Attachment and Loss*, has written about this concept comprehensively. We live our lives to the fullest only if we can form bonds and not pull away from attachment because we are afraid of possible loss. Love and grief are closely related. The more we allow ourselves to open up to love and really enter into a relationship, the deeper the pain when we lose the loved one.

Other people can't fathom the grief of parents who "haven't known" their child because they have no idea of the depth of that attachment.

> *How can anyone cry so much over a bunch of cells?*

Long before becoming pregnant, we start bonding with our baby-to-be. Even as small children we start preparing ourselves for this in little ways when we play games like "Mother, Father and Baby." The thoughts we devote to our children before and during pregnancy are the fibers of the fabric of our attachment.

> *Last week I thought I was pregnant. I had hoped, as I had many times before, that the child that I wanted so much was about to find his way into this world. I resolved not to drink a single drop of alcohol, let alone take any kind of medication, and I started treating my body with great care. A bit of that deep love a newborn triggers in us had already begun to pleasantly spread throughout my body.*

When my period came after all, I noticed how many feelings and thoughts
I had already invested in that anticipated baby. I had pondered the nature
of this little being, giving thought to when it would come into the world,
how big the age difference would be between this child and my older
children, how my life would be changed by him or her, and what I would
be willing to give up for this child.

When pregnancy is confirmed, we might see our baby on ultrasound
and hear her heart beat. As mothers we feel her movements inside us.
We begin to accept her as a separate being and to recognize her in her
essence.

Susan (40) (see page 14), who was overwhelmed by the intensity of
her pain at the loss of her baby in the 19th week of pregnancy, reflected
on it in this way:

The issue . . . is depth of attachment and commitment and love for the
baby. It's how far the pregnancy has "knitted" itself into you. I picture the
pregnancy starting in the uterus and slowly . . . spreading into the
woman's body and mind and heart. It sends out tendrils and cords that get
thicker and go deeper every week. The later she loses the pregnancy, the
deeper the pain and damage to the woman.

Reading Susan's comments, one might easily conclude that parents
could be spared this pain and grief by preventing an attachment to
their child. Perhaps this was one reason hospitals used to "spare" parents the opportunity of seeing their dead child and didn't even talk
about him or her—acting as if nothing had happened. Unfortunately,
the price was high.

Attachment exists, to a greater or lesser degree, whether we want it
to or not. Through conversations with women who once had a miscarriage or stillbirth, I learned it's wrong to believe that if mothers "have
nothing to do with the experience" they will soon forget it. Twenty
years or more later, these women still suffered under uncompleted grief.
When attachment ends abruptly, without giving us a chance to resolve
it, disquiet remains.

Rounding off the process of bonding, which began during pregnancy, initiates the process of letting go of your child, at first on a
physical level, then on an emotional level and finally on a spiritual
level. It is the best basis for healing and later, for being able to make
yourself available for new relationships. "Letting go" is not to suggest
that you should forget your baby. Memories help you along on
your path of mourning and facilitate meaningful processing for the
entire family.

Getting to Know Your Baby—Completing Bonding

*We sensed our doctor was reluctant to show us our baby. But we were
sure we wanted to see our son. This was very important to us.*

Some mothers may be afraid they won't be able to cope with such
an encounter.

*Right after the birth my physician asked whether I wanted to see our
stillborn daughter. I thought, "I'll go crazy if I see her now." One or two
hours later, after she had already been sent to the pathology department, I
wanted to see her so much, but I just didn't have the courage to ask.*

In the many encounters I have had with bereaved parents, I have
never met anyone who, in retrospect, wished they hadn't seen their
dead child. But almost all parents who did *not* see their baby still
expressed regrets or were resentful of their caregivers years later for
having deprived them of the opportunity. A restlessness lingered on
that stemmed from unfinished business—something that could never
really be "solved."

We need concrete memories of our child—what she looked like,
what was special about her, what effect she had on us. To have touched
and held her in our arms—or in our hands if she is very small—and
maybe even bathed and dressed her will create impressions that will
remain in our hearts forever. Our baby will thus be able to take her
place in our lives and in our family. Despite her death, this way no
"dark spot" will remain to churn around deep inside, seeking to be
brought to light.

You'll need time to really be able to register your child's uniqueness.
It is healing for you to talk with him, to tell him everything that you
feel from deep in your heart. You will need intimate time together.
Maybe the hours or even just minutes after the death will be enough
for you. Maybe later you will want to have him brought back to you so
you can spend more time with him. It will be your only time together
and only *you* can decide when enough is enough. To have been able to
experience your child, to whatever extent possible, will bring you
peace.

Nobody would think of asking a mother if she wanted to see her live *baby.
It is the most natural thing in the world for a mother to see her child—
dead or alive.* (Marina Marcovich, M.D.)

When parents receive matter-of-fact support from their caregivers, whether or not to see the baby isn't a question. With the birth of dead babies I have observed the same patterns of bonding that I have observed with parents encountering their live baby—first looking, carefully touching the baby with their fingertips, then with their palms, and finally picking up their child. To have missed this creates regret. That's how it was for Esther, who is still wrangling with these issues:

> *At the time I didn't want to see her . . . Now I'm so sorry I never saw her . . . Oh, God! How can you carry a child for nine months and really know her—you know her patterns, when she's active, when she's not—and then not see that baby! I will always, always regret that . . . !*

Some parents will need extra help and possibly advance preparation for the encounter with their baby. It will help make your baby real and reduce your fears if someone tells you a little about what your baby looks like, gives you a lock of his hair or shows you his footprints first.

If you are still afraid of viewing your baby, then ask someone to describe your baby to you in an accurate and loving way when you are ready. Beverly, a single mother, was terrified of seeing her daughter because she had been dead in her womb for six days. She couldn't overcome her fears. Having been under extremely strong medication during labor, she had barely been aware of the birth. Her own mother took the responsibility of looking at the baby in her daughter's place, in case Beverly had questions later. In any case, ask that photos be taken.

Sister Jane Marie Lamb has dedicated 16 years to accompanying bereaved parents on this path and may have the most experience in this field. She recommends seeing even the tiniest baby after a miscarriage, once it is recognizable as a human being and if it has not been noticeably damaged by curettage. (By the end of the eighth week, the baby has already taken on distinct human forms.)

Not long ago, I was called to visit Lucy, whose daughter Christina, weighing 1 pound, 2 ounces, had been delivered by Cesarean the day before in the 24th week of pregnancy. Without the Cesarean, Lucy would have bled to death. Christina survived only one night. Her father Peter got to be with her while she was still alive. He really suffered when he saw his tiny baby attached to tubes and other life-support equipment. It was clear to Lucy that it was a good idea to see Christina, and she wanted to, but she was terrified. The funeral director was asked to bring the dead baby to her mother in the hospital.

Before I went into Lucy's room, I looked at her daughter and tried to see her with the eyes of a mother, with the eyes of love. In Lucy's room, I endeavored to describe the tiny baby lovingly and as accurately as possible to her. Lucy absorbed each little detail with every fiber of her body. When I wheeled the little covered bassinet into her room, she almost died of fright and wanted to be left with her husband for a few moments in order to compose herself. Then she wanted me to stand by her side again.

Viewing the Baby

Oh, she is already a complete, perfect child! And she was in me!

With deep pain engraved on their faces but also with great intensity, Lucy and Peter peeked into the bassinet and absorbed their child's looks, just as Lucy had absorbed my words. They noticed the similarity to their living child. They were fascinated by the beautiful coloring of Christina's face, by her delicate mouth and chin and fine facial features, by the little nails already completely formed on her tiny fingers, by the little earlobes, by the hair on the fine skin, and they were surprised by such large feet on such thin little legs.

When babies are very small or have been dead in the womb for a while, their tissue and skin are very delicate. Their skin may show *maceration*, peeling off a little here and there, just as skin sometimes does when we skin a knee. Often the skin also has some darker spots at first, as if it were bruised. Water retention in the tissue can make it look a little puffy. The baby's lips are often raspberry-red.

Parents often are afraid to look at their baby if it has been dead in the womb for some time. Cornelia's son was born in the 19th week of pregnancy, after he had been dead for about three weeks:

> The midwife took our tiny baby in her hand and arranged him a bit. He was very soft, almost as if there were no bones inside him. I was surprised how much facial expression this tiny being had, even though he was only 19 weeks old and had been dead in my womb for the last three weeks and had become a little bit flabby. I am so happy that we got to see him.

When babies are born with malformations, there is always the question of whether parents can cope with seeing him or her. Experience has shown that the reality is never as bad as the fantasies parents develop in their minds if they do *not* see their child.

Sister Jane Marie related to me that in all these years *only once* did she feel that it might be better for the mother not to see her child—and even then she questioned this decision retrospectively! She said, "Parents see their baby with the eyes of the heart and not with clinical eyes." Parents often hardly notice the malformations, or these are at least not the focus of their attention. Parents tend to dwell on that which is beautiful and unique about their child and retain those images in their hearts.

Medical personnel sometimes seem leery of showing parents a child who has been dead for a few days. A funeral director told me that he feels dead babies sometimes look better on the third day than they did right after birth because many of the spots disappear and tissue swelling goes down.

If you think family or friends might want to see your baby later, tell the staff. A baby who has died can be kept in a cool room in the hospital. This also applies if the desire to see your child again (or for the first time) overcomes you after the baby has been taken away. If an autopsy is conducted to determine the baby's cause of death, she may have already been taken to the pathology department, but that does not mean that it's too late. She can be returned to you after the pathologist is done, or you can tell the funeral director that you want to see her again. To view your child once more, after your hormonal system has returned to normal somewhat, can help you grasp the finality of the death.

Many parents are afraid to encounter their child in a state of *rigor mortis*, the stiffness of the body that occurs in adults after death but usually not in stillborns. Stillborns have no intestinal bacteria, which normally speed up the process of decomposition after death and promote rigor mortis.

It's natural to be afraid to say what you want. Most of us shy away from asking questions. We fear that our worst fantasies will be confirmed. We may have inhibitions about retracting decisions made at first. *But later will be too late!* Becoming fully aware of that fact may give you the strength you need to act now.

I would give anything to have been able to hold our child in my arms.

જાજાજા

I wanted so much to be alone with my child and my husband, but I was afraid to ask the nurse to leave the room.

I can ask myself:

☐ What are my fears, and what will help me reduce them?

☐ About what am I afraid to speak out?

☐ Whom would I like with me at the birth?

☐ What are my wishes regarding the burial of my baby?

☐ What are my wishes concerning my partner or our families?

☐ What do I think I may want to do, but will play by ear?

☐ What help do I need and from whom?

☐ What environment and setting would I like for saying hello and good-bye to my baby (for example, candle, flowers, linens)?

☐ Is there a specific piece of clothing I would like to dress the baby in? Is there someone who could make a tiny gown for our baby?

☐ Is there anything I want to place with her?

☐ How much time do I and my partner need with our baby?

After the encounter I can ask myself:

☐ Was there enough time and were my wishes fulfilled?

☐ What has remained unfulfilled? What can I still do, if possible?

☐ What did I find special about my child?

☐ What do I want to retain forever in my memories?

☐ Has a symbol come to me that represents my baby?

☐ Have special words or thoughts come to me during my "talks" with my child?

☐ What is it that I want to record in my diary in words or in drawings to help me keep the memories of this experience alive?

☐ What did I have problems with? With what and from whom do I need help?

☐ What questions do I still have?

Family-centered Stillbirth

> As I entered the room, I sensed an atmosphere of peace. In one of the two beds rested the mother, in the other the 6-year-old was sleeping peacefully. The father was sitting on the bed close to his wife. The grandparents and two close friends were also there . . . and in the middle of the room was the little bassinet with the baby, who was born dead in the 20th week of pregnancy. It occurred to me that these parents wouldn't have to say, "Nobody got to know our baby." These parents would not have to mourn their child in isolation as so many others do.

It is very painful, especially for mothers, when they feel as though their child was only real for them, that nobody else has known their baby. Even fathers often have trouble consciously conceiving the reality of their baby until they've seen it. Brothers and sisters can often only really grasp what has happened when they have been able literally to "grasp"—touch—the baby. Children usually deal quite naturally with the death of a baby (see page 94). However, to be in touch with their parents' feelings only from a distance makes them fearful. Nor should this grandchild remain abstract for the grandparents. When family and friends are allowed to see, hold and build a bond to the dead or dying baby, they are much more likely to grieve along with the parents. They will be capable of much greater empathy, enabling them to better support the mourners.

Parents must have the opportunity, if they want it, to be with the people who are important to them. They need the chance to say hello and good-bye to their baby in an intimate and dignified setting, for as long as they wish.

I can ask myself:

☐ Who should and would want to get to know our child?

☐ Who would like to hold our baby?

☐ What are our other children's questions? In what form, depending on age, do they need preparation and answers?

☐ What ideas can I give my other children for saying good-bye to their littlest sibling (pictures, letters, dolls, gifts)?

☐ Who should appear with our baby in the pictures we take?

Saying Good-Bye

At this point, we realize we have moments and opportunities at hand that will never come again. Give yourself the necessary time and peace to experience these moments. If need be, assert yourself in order to get your needs met.

Lucy and her husband experienced their encounter with daughter Christina as a great gift. The peaceful expression on her little face brought them peace. They couldn't take their eyes off her. The father took a little cross from his neck and placed it on their child. Step by step, Lucy was able to come closer to her tiny baby, looking at her intensely as she was lying in the little bassinet, and eventually next to her on the bed. Then I placed the baby on her lap so Lucy could see her more closely. The parents looked and looked. They knew they had only these very short moments to capture a whole lifetime—that every second, every glimpse was of monumental importance. Then the parents timidly began to touch Christina. Finally they cradled their little child in their hands, close to them. I left them alone then, giving them their privacy.

The same applies to parents whose child is dying. Witnessing their baby's suffering, perhaps attached to many tubes, can be very, very painful. It is so natural to want to protect our child from pain. But here we are, in a situation where we are totally powerless. All we can do is just "be there," knowing that this little soul can feel our presence and love. To have touched, held, and perhaps even nursed our child may ease our grief. The hours or days and nights spent by the side of such a tiny person hold in them the potential of transformation.

> *It was so comforting to me that my baby was allowed to die in my arms. Somehow or other I believe that perhaps it had a positive effect on her little soul that she was not totally alone in dying. I was able to envelop her with all my love, and my tears blessed her on her journey "back home."*

Naming and Baptizing/Christening

Recently I attended a couple who were just suffering their third pregnancy loss, this time in the 28th week of pregnancy. The two past experiences had been nightmares for them, and the parents had never really processed them. During labor I asked them whether they had thought about naming their child about to be stillborn. Both looked at me with surprise. Then the wife said to her husband,

> *Yes, it really would be better if we could refer to the baby by name rather than talking about our third miscarriage.*

Giving the child a name can be very beneficial for grief work. It helps give him his place in the family, ensuring that he will be remembered. This is particularly important if there are other children. Many parents want their child's name to be confirmed through baptism. Even parents who may have felt remote from church recently are urgently drawn to baptism in the face of the death or imminent death of their baby.

Any person who is baptized can perform an emergency baptism her- or himself. If a child lives for a short time, a pastor or priest can administer a baptism. When a child is stillborn, some clergy come into conflict when confronted with parents desiring baptism. Some of them interpret church regulations to mean that baptism is a sacrament only for living children. But clerics can also baptize out of their pastoral responsibility to bring comfort and consolation to parents. In any case, they can place their hands on the child and bless him. If a baptism is important to you, then look for a clergyperson who is understanding and will perform it.

Others may feel the need to develop their own ritual to recognize this child as a person, its life and its death.

I can ask myself:

About naming:

☐ Is this child to have this name (if you had chosen a name previously)?

☐ Or, if necessary, who should name the baby?

☐ Or, do I want to listen inside and see if a new name comes to me?

If yes, then listen to your breath until you become completely centered. Don't hold onto thoughts. Let them come and go. Then turn to your baby, be it real or in thought (you can do this during the delivery or later), and open yourself to your child, taking your time. Ask silently, "What is your name?" and listen for an answer. When you receive a name, you may want to ask, "What does your name mean?" Again, listen for an answer. It may be that the answers coming from your soul will move you deeply.

About baptism or rituals reinforcing the baby's existence:

☐ Do I want my baby baptized?

☐ If my clergyperson won't baptize, can I think of someone else who might?

☐ Or, who would know of someone?

☐ If necessary, who could administer an emergency baptism? Who should be our witness?

☐ Have we already chosen godparents? Do we want to include them?

☐ Would a blessing bring me/us peace?

☐ Would we like to develop our own ritual?

☐ If so, what ritual or what action could help make our child real in a way that would be meaningful for me/us?

☐ Who could help me develop such a ritual?

☐ Whom would I like to have present at the ritual?

Letting Others Know

A *birth-death announcement* can help friends and acquaintances deal with the situation and also make your child real for them. With such a notice you can signal what you need right now. You might want contact, or you may need time for yourself and will contact them later, when you're ready.

I can ask myself:

☐ Do I want to notify friends and relatives with an announcement?

☐ If so, what do I want to convey?

☐ What should the announcement look like?

☐ To whom do I want to send it?

☐ (If no announcement is desired) Whom do I want to notify about the death of my baby and in what way?

> *Every life is a gift that will live in our hearts forever.*
>
> *Sue Ellen Johnson*
> *Born and died on*
> *May 31, 199-*
> *5 pounds, 3 ounces, strawberry-blond hair*

A possible birth/death announcement

Collecting Mementos of Your Baby's Existence

It's difficult to remember later what happened while you were in shock. If you see your child while still under the protection of birth hormones, you may feel you won't ever forget her looks, but as time passes memories do fade. Sometimes this can cause panic later. Especially if you didn't see your child, you may find it hard to accept her death. A desire for photographic proof often comes months later.

> *I thought I wouldn't need photos because after the delivery, I couldn't comprehend my daughter as dead. Later I regretted not having any mementos of her.*

Having mementos of him or her has proven to be very important for healthy mourning and for the healthy integration of the child into our lives. Keepsakes of your child will make it easier for you to focus on your feelings about her. With photos, you can see for yourself and show relatives and friends, "This child is real! I'm not grieving over a dream,

I'm grieving over *this child*." It also helps your other living children. They may be too young now, but they will ask many questions later. With a photograph, you can say, "This was your sister," or "This was your brother."

> *Our baby was stillborn 4-1/2 years ago. Lately our children have started to ask all kinds of questions about Laura. To my regret, I couldn't tell them what she looked like. I only knew that she must have been a very beautiful and peaceful-looking infant because the funeral director had said so to my mother. Then it occurred to me that photos might exist somewhere. I started calling various places—the doctor, the hospital, the pathologist, the funeral director—but no one had taken a picture . . .*

You, or whoever takes the photographs, should be aware that this is a one-time opportunity. Therefore, take them in a loving, dignified setting. Perhaps you'll want a picture of your child in your arms or in the arms of the grandparents or your other children. Most hospitals now have their own cameras ready, some of which take self-developing pictures. Or you may want to use your own camera and have the pictures developed immediately. If the photos aren't satisfactory, you can retake them. Most hospitals now take pictures without being asked and keep them on file for several years. Experience has proved that years later, parents need to look at photos to resolve their grief.

Hand- and footprints (made with an ink pad) or a lock of hair are also direct mementos of your baby. Or perhaps you want to make the hand- and footprints from plaster-of-Paris. You could revive the ancient tradition of creating a mask of the baby's face. You can ask for the baby's identification band or a crib card containing information about your child, the baby blanket in which she or he was wrapped, the little gown or bonnet—anything that touched the baby's skin— when these aren't automatically offered by the staff. Many hospitals have designed their own Certificates of Life to verify that your baby was real. If you are temporarily stuck in your grief process, anything that reawakens the memory of your baby can be helpful.

I can ask myself:

☐ What mementos do I want?

☐ How do I want the pictures of my baby taken?

☐ Do I want photos taken with my own camera? Do I want them developed immediately in case they don't come out, so I'll have another chance to take them?

☐ If I don't have any concrete mementos, what symbol or symbols could help me and how do I want to use them? (see page 80)

What Happens to Our Baby?

Autopsy—Yes or No?

We will be asked to make decisions for which we are unprepared. One such decision concerns autopsy. Most parents will be advised to consent to an autopsy in order to determine the cause of the child's death. Laws regarding autopsy vary from state to state and province to province, so check with hospital personnel if you have questions. In many states, except in cases of sudden infant death syndrome, where an autopsy may be required by law, it's up to the parents to ask for, consent to or decline such an examination. Parents may retract their written consent within a specified time.

What exactly happens during an autopsy? We often imagine that babies are dissected. This isn't true. Incisions are made, tissue samples of organs are removed, and the body is sutured again, exactly as it would be for a living person undergoing surgery. Following this, the child is released for burial.

> When we saw our baby again the day after the autopsy, she was dressed and had on a bonnet. You couldn't tell anything had been done to her.

You usually receive a preliminary autopsy report within a few days. The tissue samples are stored in a preserving liquid for more exhaustive tests at a later date, just as they are for a baby miscarried at an early stage when no burial is desired. For this reason, it often takes a while before the parents receive final autopsy results.

In many cases it is good to find out the exact cause of death. In other cases, where the cause is self-evident, an autopsy or post-mortem examination may be superfluous. Many parents fear that they are acting contrary to their church by having an autopsy done. What is customary varies among religions and even among denominations, so it may be a good idea to find out from your own place of worship if you aren't sure. Some of us may find it easier to accept our child's death as fate and not explore its reasons medically.

I can ask myself:

☐ Would the information obtained by an autopsy be meaningful to me?

☐ Do I/we want an autopsy for our baby, or is it more in tune with our values and the situation not to search for the cause of death?

☐ Did I consent to an autopsy but now realize I don't want it done?

Thoughts and Information about Burial

The Legal Situation

Burial laws vary from state to state and province to province. In the United States, they are also regulated by the cemetery regulations of individual cities, communities and possibly the place of worship. Therefore, no general information can be given here. If caregivers in your hospital don't have detailed information on the local situation, you can obtain it from a funeral director.

Awareness on lawmakers' and society's part regarding perinatal loss has increased. The efforts of many have affected legislation regarding rights of burial for babies as well as burial options. These legal changes take into account the newer psychological research on the importance of burial for the grief process, as well as progress made in perinatology. But most of all, they meet the needs of many bereaved parents.

> *If we want our child to be buried, then it must be possible—regardless of size, weight or term.*

Babies considered miscarriages by law generally do not *have* to be buried (officially it is the responsibility of the hospital administration to see to the disposition of the remains). But in the United States they *can* be buried if the parents desire. Doctors can issue a death certificate for such small babies. If problems arise, you may want to get in touch with the SHARE national office.

For babies that need to be buried by law, the doctor issues a stillbirth certificate. Check with hospital personnel for procedures about having a funeral postponed; for example, when a mother can't leave the hospital for medical reasons. The funeral director can arrange that. Mortuaries will keep the child for viewing until the mother can also attend.

Experiences and Wishes of Many Parents

It's natural to want our child handled with respect and dignity. When parents have had the opportunity to get to know their baby, most want to have their child buried. A father who wasn't at all sure whether he wanted to open up emotionally to his child said afterwards:

> *There was no question I had to see Laura, and there was no question that she had to be buried.*

Experience shows that, as difficult as a funeral may be, it is a milestone along our path of grief and helps us move forward. For most people it's a comfort to know where their child is buried and to have a place "locate" their grief.

It took all the courage I had to say that I wanted to have our tiny child buried. I was told it wasn't possible to bury a baby her weight. Later I learned that wasn't true. We didn't have to have our baby buried, but we could do so. But by then it was too late. I needed a long, long time to get over this. I kept wondering, What did they do with my child? Where is she now? And the very worst thought was that she may have ended up somewhere with the garbage.

Many parents I talked to had similar fears. Dignified handling of their child was very important to them. Parents who weren't able to bury their child, but had wanted to, suffered from that for a long time.

What am I supposed to do with my grief? There's no grave or other place I can take it.

The more you become involved in helping to create a funeral ceremony that is meaningful to you, the more helpful it will be to your mourning (see Rituals, page 59). Well-meaning people may want to "protect" you by offering to take care of "these things" for you. Don't be talked out of it if you've made up your mind to do something.

My sister-in-law tried to convince me not to burden myself with the funeral, that she'd be glad to handle everything for me. She meant well. But for me, it was important to be there and to help arrange for and create the ceremony. It was my last act of love for my little angel and my final farewell to Allison.

It may be meaningful for a mother to place her child in the casket herself. In the Australian film *Some Babies Die*, the mother of little Cosma, who died after birth, had her baby brought back to her for several days in a row and got to really know the child in the presence of her other three young children. In the end she placed her personally on a soft sheepskin in a small casket, attended by her own mother and a caring hospital-bereavement team.

Burial Possibilities

Many people purchase a separate burial plot for the baby or use a family plot. Parents may find comfort in having a baby placed in the grave with a beloved family member. Many cemeteries in larger cities offer a special baby's section. There are also anonymous burial fields.

> *In the church hospital where I work, part of the grounds is being used to honor miscarried children. At the official opening, a large stone was dedicated to all children who have suffered an untimely death.* (Sister Jane Marie Lamb)

If you wish, the funeral director will help with the formalities. But whenever possible, you as parents are encouraged to help to create funeral rites that are meaningful for you, because they will help you resolve your grief.

The Cost of a Funeral and Burial

In light of a child's death, it may seem banal to speak about funeral costs. But in some cases, parents' wishes weren't fulfilled because they felt too inhibited to address material matters.

> *When our stillborn child was delivered, we had financial difficulties. I would have liked to have a funeral but I was afraid it would be too expensive. I felt ashamed to ask about the cost. In the end, to my regret, we gave up our child to the hospital routine.*

Depending on circumstances, the cost of a funeral can run anywhere from nothing to more than $1,000 (including the burial site). (Some funeral institutes don't charge for the burial of a stillborn and in some places the cost of children's burial sites is borne by communities or churches.) Prices differ around the country. If you have financial concerns, check with the hospital social worker to find out what resources are available. Some mutual-support groups have also pooled together to support families in need.

When Burial Isn't Desirable or Possible

Having a funeral with a gravesite isn't what everyone wants. Some parents would rather distribute their baby's ashes in a place of beauty (see page 61). You may want to check with your funeral director for the regulations in your community and state.

Some people have gotten faulty information regarding their right to bury their baby. They find out only after it is too late that they could have had a personal burial. A substitute ritual can console parents in this case.

> *The idea of having a ritual appealed to us. Before we moved, we went to the anonymous burial plot where Philip had been interred and dug up some*

*dirt. We used this to plant a tree at our new home in his memory. Since I
don't have a grave, I need some place I can always go.*

I can ask myself:
- ☐ What are the regulations regarding the burial of my baby?
- ☐ What burial possibilities are offered in my community, and what are my choices?
- ☐ What are my wishes for burial or funeral?
- ☐ Which funeral director do I want to work with?
- ☐ Where can I get more information?
- ☐ (If my baby doesn't need to be buried by law) What might I want to do instead?
- ☐ (If I will/did not arrange for a burial) What might I want to do instead?

Rituals—Help for the Living

The need for rituals seems to come from deep within our collective spirit. Rituals produce a sense of belonging to a society or community. Society is sustained by rituals. When the meaning of rituals is lost within a culture, the culture may become disoriented. Rituals help us emphasize the significance of a situation and to give it proper attention and dignity. Rituals make our inner processes visible through outward actions. The silent language of symbols promotes understanding at a deeper level and helps us integrate the changes—the transformation—into our being.

All cultures have rituals—*rites of passage*—for all major transitions from one important stage of life to another, to facilitate the necessary adjustments. Letting go of the old often isn't easy. What is new and unfamiliar can create tension. A little help from rituals is appropriate and useful. All fruitful transition rituals look at whatever has been, acknowledge what it brought, say good-bye and let go to make room for what is new. Good rituals work through repetition and patterns but also leave room for spontaneity and individuality. In your situation, two of the most fundamental passages in the life of a person come together—birth and death. This demands an awful lot of you as individuals or couples.

Many parents who have lost their baby in pregnancy need others to acknowledge and validate their baby's existence. Especially when your baby has not lived and is not known to others, a funeral can say,

"Look—we had a child, and this child is no longer alive." "Fathers and mothers who, for whatever reason, weren't able to bury their child or say good-bye through a ritual have a hard time finding peace of mind and processing their grief," says pastor Dorothea Bobzin, herself a bereaved mother.

Sometimes dead babies are buried before the mother is able to leave the hospital. But it is good and important for both parents to be present at the funeral. With a burial you give the body of your dead child (or his ashes) back to the earth. Although this step can be extremely painful, it helps you grasp the finality of your baby's death—the first task on the way to healing. Only later will you be able to assess what this dead child has meant and brought to you.

> *Sometimes I go to a funeral to honor the dead person. Other times I don't even know the dead person and go to the funeral anyway to signal to a friend, "I'm here because of you. I want to show that you can count on me on your way through your mourning."*

Rituals exist to help people with living, and it is good to keep them up. Where rituals have become meaningless, we can perhaps give them new meaning or create new rituals. They can help us deal with death. The more the rituals are individualized to your own feelings and experiences, the more helpful they will be to you.

If you belong to a congregation, church or temple, you will probably want to hold a religious funeral service. Let your wishes be known and help develop a ritual to suit your needs. You can select songs, poems, readings and symbols that console you. Look in Appendix 3 for some suggestions. Even more are available in the excellent book, *Bittersweet . . . hellogoodbye*, available through SHARE (page 247), and in *Good Grief Rituals* (Childs-Gowell 1992).

Sometimes, if your child was stillborn or not baptized, clergy may deny an official ritual (see chapter 9). If you don't feel understood or well cared for by your pastor, priest or rabbi, don't hesitate to seek out another person who will comprehend its significance for you. You can also have a religious funeral without a minister by reading selected biblical texts, saying prayers and singing songs that are meaningful and console you. A simple secular interment in complete silence or within a circle of loving friends and family members is also possible. Perhaps you have empathetic friends who can help create a farewell ceremony that is meaningful to you and adapted to your own special needs. Martha, with her husband, a priest friend of theirs and a group of teenagers in their care, put together a church service for their son Sebastian Moses, who was stillborn full-term:

Our friend led the church service. In the middle of the circle, on two blankets, I laid everything we had prepared for the birth of Sebastian: diapers, little T-shirts, a blanket sleeper, toys, books on pregnancy, childbirth and nursing, and so on. After a reading from the Bible, we told our friends and relatives a lot about our time with Sebastian—how we had looked forward to him, what our thoughts had been, and what meaning his birth would have had for us. I talked about the time when I had felt the first movements, how surprised and pleased we had been when he reacted for the first time to the organ music. . . .

When we got to the part when the doctor told me our child was dead, Martin symbolically placed a black cloth over the baby's things and we sat for a while before this cloth—before death . . . It was an attempt to make the incomprehensible comprehensible. Then Bill, Martin and I sang a song.

Then we talked about what keeps us going—which words, thoughts and gestures were able to break through our pain and make us open for something new. As an expression of our hope we placed colorful flowers on the black cloth—flowers and symbols. The very strong feeling that we were not separated forever but would be together some day filled us with a deep joy.

The young people had prepared readings to help them express their shock and grief at what had happened. After the service we celebrated an Agape ceremonial to express that God is omnipresent in the midst of the community that gives us support. This celebration was very, very healing and comforting for all of us.

Sandra's sixth child, happily anticipated by the entire family, was stillborn. This is the ritual she chose:

Daniel was cremated. My twin sister flew in with her family from San Francisco. We drove to a trailhead at Mount Rainier, a breathtaking, beautiful mountain 45 minutes away from our home. We spread the ashes up on the mountainside. My 11-year-old daughter recited a comforting poem about a stillborn baby, my 9-year-old niece played a lovely song on the flute and all the other children picked daisies, which they threw after the ashes. It was a meaningful ceremony for me.

At the burial of Rebecca, who died of sudden infant death syndrome (SIDS) at 11 months of age, balloons were released into the sky as this letter, written by her mother, was read:

Dear little Rebecca Leah Andrea,
Softly and gently, so contrary to your nature, you left us, for you were boisterous and passionate even before your birth. Then your birthday came—exciting and turbulent. So it began, and so it remained for the span of your short life.

For us, who remember you with such fondness, you were something special! You were simply you. Already aware of your charms, you thrilled each of us. Without language, you brought smiles to every face. Without knowing many words, you spread your joy of life. You little rascal!

We will gladly recall all your little pranks, and remember your eyes, so wide and curious. And your unusual voice, so deep and raspy, sounding like the autumn wind in leafless trees when you laughed at our jokes.

Yes, you will live on in our memory, even though we are now standing here—grief, anger, despondency and longing inside of us—and many questions on our minds. For eleven months you have shared with us your joy of life. We thank you for every moment of it.

We will never forget you! Take care, little rascal!

Often a funeral takes place too early, when parents are still in shock. Sometimes a mother doesn't have an opportunity to participate. Or, the parents don't want anyone else present because they are afraid they'll break down in public. It is appropriate to hold a memorial ceremony at a later date. One couple sent out the following invitation:

When our son Jonathan was stillborn, we just didn't have the strength to have a lot of people around. We know we hurt the feelings of some of you. Our mourning is not over, but we are ready to face the world again. At this point we would like to let you share in our loss and make up for what wasn't possible for us in the beginning. We kindly request that you meet with us at our house on ____ at ____ o'clock so we can jointly walk to Jonathan's grave, and we invite you to join us afterwards for a memorial service for him at the chapel.

If a funeral wasn't possible, you certainly can hold a ritual at a later date among a circle of chosen friends and family:

> *With the help of the slide series* (author's note: by Julie Fritsch, see page 252), *we created a service for our little son Alexander. It was ceremonial, and it really helped us cry . . . This was a fine substitute for not being able to have our son buried.*

At a service, we look back on and recall the life of a person. It may be healing for parents whose child has died after birth to hold a commemorative ritual after some time has passed. In the presence of close friends and family, or even just as a couple, you may want to reflect on what this child would have meant for your life and what he or she continues to mean for you. In many cultures, official ceremonies occur at a later point and serve as milestones in the bereavement process.

I can ask myself:

☐ Would I like to have a funeral or other ritual?

☐ If so: What are my wishes for a ritual? What actions, texts and readings, poems or symbols would be meaningful for me?

☐ What would best meet our needs and reflect the significance of our child?

☐ Do I want to write my child a farewell letter that I or someone else can read aloud or that I can place in his coffin?

☐ What clothing should our baby wear? Do I want to dress him myself?

☐ What would comfort me/us?

☐ What would help us peacefully let go of our child's physical body?

☐ Which family members or friends do I want to ask for help to create a ritual?

When some time has passed:

☐ Do I want to hold a memorial service for my child?

☐ What form could this take?

☐ Do we want to be alone right now, or do we want to include friends and family?

Here is an excerpt from a letter that Barbara wrote to her son Tommy. It was read at his funeral service:

My dear little son,

I had actually planned to write all along during the time we had together . . . for your sake, for later . . . I wanted you to know how much I enjoyed every day, how I loved to feel you in my body and talk with you. Yes, I could feel that you were a son—somehow I knew. And what did you feel? . . . I am sure you could sense you were wanted, and that your Mom and Dad were waiting and longing for you with all their love. We loved you with all the strength of our two hearts.

We awaited you with tenderness and affection. You were the result of the greatest event of love between your father and mother . . . Now, after 32 weeks inside me, someone or something has decided that you should die inside of me. I hope you did not suffer too much. You know, I'm afraid of dying. And you, little person, had to take this difficult path all by yourself. Or perhaps you felt my need to be near you. I hope with all my heart that it helped you. But I won't ever know.

My son, please excuse us for deciding to have an autopsy done on your body, but we needed to know what made your little heart stop beating.

We are now going to put you in the cool earth—my loved one, whom I would so much rather have put to my breast. Your Daddy got you a pair of warm booties so you won't freeze. Your Daddy is so loving . . . there are moments, hours, when I can hardly comprehend so great an ability to love. But you could not experience this yourself. Believe me, little Tommy—your name—the hearts of your parents have so much capacity—and you are in our hearts with a very gentle, and at the same time sad, feeling. If it is all right with our loving God, you will someday have a healthy living brother or sister. We will tell him or her all about you, how wonderful it was to carry you inside of me, how your Dad and I loved to caress you and feel you with our hands on my round tummy . . . Though we are in despair now, you have brought us much happiness for almost 32 weeks.

And now, beloved son, sleep in peace and go on in the arms of our loving God, go to the place where it is certainly warm.

We have loved you more than anything else in this world.

Your parents

3

A Time of Searching and Yearning

I've dreamed repeatedly of walking down hospital corridors searching for my child.

After the first shock subsides, we meet hard reality. We begin to comprehend, little by little, what has happened. This is the time of searching for what we have lost, of painful, insatiable yearning and of brooding over seemingly unanswerable questions. Swiss therapist Verena Kast (1982) describes it as the "time of emotional outbursts"—pain, anger, guilt, fear, despair, failure, jealousy and other powerful feelings we must live through in order to heal. Researcher Dr. Glen Davidson (1984) found that this phase usually lasts four to six months.

Powerful Thoughts and Feelings

The experience is a little like coming out of anesthesia at the dentist's. As the effect of shock—a natural anesthesia—wears off, we feel more and more pain over what was torn from us. Emotional suffering also causes real physical pain. Other underlying feelings come to the surface, raw. *To allow and experience these feelings, to find an expression for them and deal with them, is the main task of this phase and paves the way for healing.*

Love for our child may be felt as a strong yearning. This is often an especially difficult time for parents who did not see their child.

For months I looked into every baby carriage . . . Perhaps my baby would have looked like this? Or like that? No, she definitely wouldn't have looked like that!

Some mothers dream of wandering through long hospital corridors, searching for their baby. Other common feelings after a loss are feelings of guilt, regret, sadness, loneliness, fear, failure, self-doubt, lack of self-esteem, jealousy, discouragement, despair—even hate and bitterness. It's natural to resist what has happened and to be keenly disappointed for a time. These feelings may be expressed as anger that is difficult to control. Anger may be directed at the doctor, nurses, your partner, God, an unfair fate, others who have healthy babies, your own body for failing you, or even at your baby who left you, especially if there is no explanation for why it happened. Deep down, you may hope you'll get your child back if only you rant and rave long enough. Aggression may also be the expression of unidentified pain. Anger may be a way of expressing helplessness over the realization we can't control some things in life. Anger that isn't vented or transformed in some way can turn into guilt feelings or psychosomatic problems.

I would love to have cried, but I couldn't. The few memories I had wouldn't come on their own. There were no mementos. Only after seeing a pregnant friend was I finally able that night to scream out my pain into my pillow. All at once, the hardness and tension in me melted away, and my body became soft again. Deep peace overcame me. That's when I understood! Pain that can't find an outlet builds up until it discharges as aggression. One way or another, the pain must come out or you will explode!

Some mothers, for a short time, even wish to die themselves so they can be with their baby.

If your baby has lived and then dies, you may believe you still hear her crying. You may dream she is still alive. If you once felt your baby kicking inside you, you may think you still feel her movements. Or you may suffer from an inner emptiness.

If I could have painted a picture of myself, you'd have seen someone who looked entirely normal on the outside. But inside I would be hollow.

I can ask myself:

☐ How does mourning express itself in me?

☐ Where am I in the mourning process?

Wanting to Understand

This is also the time of many questions and reflections. Parents who didn't see their baby may ask, What did my baby look like? Whom did she resemble? Was she in any way disfigured, and did they try to hide this from me? Where is he now?

It is also a time of brooding. What went wrong? Could I have prevented his death? Am I to blame? Did she leave because I asked myself so often how I'd manage with two small children? Did his death have something to do with our marital problems?

> *I was told Laura's death was caused by a detached placenta. I went over the last two or three days in my mind and kept thinking, What did I do? Did I work too hard? Did I take any medication during the last nine months? I believe I am a good person, and I'm confused. What am I being punished for?*

It is also a time of investigation. What happened? Why did the pregnancy end in a miscarriage or stillbirth? What problems did my child have? Did he suffer? What can I find out about his disease? Was this a one-time thing, or could it happen again? What was the birth like, again? I remember it but is that the way it *really* happened?

During this phase, parents often need to talk again with those people who attended them at the hospital and experienced everything with them first-hand. To get answers to questions that remain, parents often want to hear an account of the events from doctors, nurses or other staff. This is explained by our human need to put experience into some kind of comprehensible order.

This is also the time when parents read everything they can find. They rummage through libraries and book stores in search of anything that will give them more information. This stage can last months.

What Can Help Now

It may help you to know that your condition is normal and that other people in your situation have felt the same way. Beyond this, it's sensible to take steps to facilitate your mourning process, at least to help prevent overtaxing your physical health, which can be greatly compromised by grief. This chapter, like the previous one, provides concrete suggestions and direct questions intended to help you along.

Processing your loss and resolving your feelings takes time. You can help yourself by dedicating undisturbed time to this effort.

You may want to look for a spot to turn into *your special place*—one that radiates tranquillity and well-being to you; a place where your breath deepens and becomes more peaceful, and where you can be without distractions for a while. There you can listen inside and feel close to your innermost self. It's nice to have such a spot in your home. But also try to find a nearby place outside where you feel nurtured and safe, perhaps a secluded spot in a garden. To enhance the atmosphere of the place in your home, you might decorate it with a flower and light a candle whenever you go there or, if you wish, use scents to increase your well-being, clarity and depth (see aromatherapy, page 133). You may want to keep a journal or diary at hand, a drawing pad and colored pencils, oils or chalks that come in a wide spectrum of colors. At times you'll want to surround yourself with symbols or mementos of your baby. Occasionally you may want to invite your partner or a supportive person to your special place. Arrange it so you can sit upright comfortably (maybe also lie down), and relax.

> *I set up a cozy place for myself in the sunniest part of our bedroom, with a pale blue wool throw and many, many pillows. On a blue silk scarf I arranged candles, crystals, stones and shells I'd collected at the beach, as well as a photo and always a fresh, delicate pink rose, which was the symbol that had come to represent my daughter to me. There I drew, cried and wrote all the pain I felt in my soul. I felt a very strong spiritual connection with my child.*

But sitting quietly isn't right for everyone. Many people find it easier to work through their feelings while walking.

> *I was completely unprepared for the magnitude of the loss, the depth of the wound. . . . I eat little and sleep less. I cry unpredictably. I take showers and cry. I walk—3, 4, 5 miles—and cry. . . . At night I walk up and down the house while everyone else sleeps—and cry. . . . I can't sit still. I keep moving around, even when eating or talking to someone. (Hodge 1995)*

I can ask myself:

☐ How do I process things best—through reflection while sitting quietly, by moving around or in some other way?

☐ How have I worked through difficulties in the past?

Be Aware of Your Feelings

To become healthy again, it is important to permit *all* feelings to surface. To repress them hurts you, body and soul. To acknowledge feelings is a sign of strength. Some adults still have problems expressing sadness and grief because as children they felt accepted and loved only if they were laughing and happy. Some were punished for crying, or a parent turned away and abandoned them when they expressed unhappiness and pain. We were taught to be tough, and we learned well.

But grief, with all its accompanying feelings, is certain to make itself known again and again, one way or another, until you have acknowledged it properly. Feelings that are acknowledged and processed gradually lessen or transform themselves.

I can ask myself:

☐ Which feelings am I aware of in myself?

☐ How are they expressed?

☐ Which feelings don't I allow myself to have? What could the effect be?

☐ Which feelings am I only guessing at?

☐ Who could help me discover and become clearer about my feelings?

☐ Which feelings can't I reach? Who or what could help me?

☐ What is my relationship to my feelings, in general? What has helped me express them before?

☐ Is there some unprocessed loss from my past that is coming to the surface now? Do I see a way to deal with it now?

☐ In whose presence can I express *any of* my feelings?

☐ With whom can I talk about my feelings? Of whom may I ask support?

☐ In whose presence do I feel as though I have to hold back my feelings?

☐ Who tries to soothe my feelings and prevent me from expressing them?

☐ Thinking back to my childhood, what messages did I receive with regards to feelings? Which feelings were considered OK, and which might have been considered undesirable?

☐ How did the important persons in my early life respond to my sadness, pain or other "unpleasant" feelings? What did they "say" with words, facial expressions and actions?

☐ How does this affect me today? Is it helpful, or do I wish to choose new reactions?

☐ What do I expect regarding my partner's feelings? What are the consequences of that?

☐ What expectations does he or she have for me? How am I affected by that?

The following discusses some of the most common feelings connected with mourning.

Expressing Pain and Grief

What can you do to help yourself?

Crying is healing. Emotional pain is felt as inner tension, which is temporarily released when you cry. Scientists have discovered that tears help restore physiological and emotional equilibrium (Frey 1985). Unshed tears can make you ill. Let tears well up from your gut (not just from your head). *Let your crying be connected with your breath* (or else you will feel drained afterwards)! If crying wears you out rather than relieves you, it may not be "connected" crying. Cry as long as you need to. Eventually, the periods between crying spells will become longer. At some point—when your time has come—you will have "cried it out" and the tears will (almost) stop. Susan reports:

> *When T. says, "Mommy, I just hate it when you cry," I tell her I have 10,000 tears to cry about the baby, and I can cry them now or I can cry them later, but they* have to be cried. (Green 1992)

ॐ There may be times when you would like to cry but cannot. *Telling your story* over and over again brings back memories. With them, emotions surface and dissipate, bit by bit. It's a good idea to remind the people who are listening to you that your tears feel good and help you heal.

ॐ You may want to *attend a self-help group* where you meet with people who understand what you are going through, can help you over rough spots and give you hope for recovery.

ॐ *Reviving memories* helps connect you with your feelings. Having mementos is very helpful for this.

ॐ If your child has been buried, you might be in touch with your grief at the grave. Or, *create a substitute memorial place* that you connect with your baby.

ॐ *Scream into your pillow.* Consciously notice your breathing pattern afterwards and observe any change.

ॐ *Watch a sentimental film.* This can be a catalyst for crying and releasing inner emotional tension.

ॐ *The Anguish of Loss,* (see page 268) by Julie Fritsch, may help you. In the book, Julie expresses her feelings after the death of her son, Justin, in the form of 22 sculptures, which are pictured along with poetic texts. Looking at the book and reading the poems can put you in touch with your own emotions.

ॐ Some bereaved couples have been inspired by this book to *draw pictures* that depict their own grief.

ح You may also want to *play with some art clay* and see what happens when you work with it.

ح If you try to appear as though you are happy when in fact you aren't, you may want to try the Bach Flower Remedy *Agrimony* (No. 1) (see page 134).

Finding Comfort and Relief

ح *Touch* (from yourself and others). Also, closeness to your partner. Use nurturing touch on those body areas where you feel pain and other emotions.

ح *Vocalizing and toning* can help you express grief well and also helps create a sensation of openness within you. In addition, use toning to center yourself, harmonize your breath and feel more peaceful.

ح *Writing.* Write down whatever thoughts come to you in a journal (this can be an important outlet for somewhat-introverted people), write poems, write to others about yourself and what you are experiencing.

ح *Drawing,* as described on page 31. Or, give yourself a specific topic and then draw 7 to 10 pictures as they come to you. For example, "my journey through mourning," "pain," "feeling anger," "forgiveness," "what I've lost," "finding comfort in my grief," "love."

ح *"Let yourself be carried;"* see page 32.

ح *Listen to music* that moves you (possibly with earphones), whether it is classical, meditative or a special song, such as Eric Clapton's *Tears in Heaven,* which he wrote after the death of his young son.

ح Have a *holistic body-therapy treatment* to promote your inner equilibrium and stability (for addresses, see pages 253 and 254).

ح An *aura massage* by yourself, your partner or another close friend can be soothing. Whoever does this massage needs to first "awaken" their hands by gently rubbing them as directed for the touch exercise (page 28). Pay attention to the centers of the hands. With the hands held at a distance of 2 to 4 inches away from your face, feel warmth coming from the hands. Once you have become familiar with this energy, the energy field of your body can be caressed very slowly (at a distance from the body) concentrating on and remaining for a while especially at those areas that radiate coolness. Let your breath flow.

ح With your eyes closed, *stroke your face and your head* with your "awakened" hands in a way that feels right for you. Or, with your index fingers held vertically against your face (alongside your nose) and your thumbs underneath your chin, stroke your face outward towards your ears. Do this repeatedly, perhaps in the rhythm of your breath. Then place your fingertips on both sides of the middle line of your forehead (the fingers held in a horizontal position, the index fingers positioned near the hairline, the pinky finger near the eyebrows) and stroke with an even pressure towards your temples and then down to and behind your ear. To finish, look at your face in the mirror and, this time lightly, gently and lovingly stroke out every line in your face.

જ You may want to *hold a soft pillow* or a stuffed animal while you sleep. Or you may want to cuddle up to your partner.

જ You may be consoled by visualizing your baby bathed in light, or by creating other images that comfort you.

જ The Bach Flower Remedy *Star of Bethlehem* (No. 29) is considered the "comforter of the soul." It can help soothe pain in this kind of emotional emergency (see page 136).

જ *Aromatherapy* (see page 133) can be another natural help, particularly rose, geranium, balm, cedar and lavender.

જ *The recommendations for the body given in chapter 4* will improve your well-being and create a good basis for working with your feelings and thoughts.

If You Did Not See Your Baby

For parents who didn't get to know their child, this phase is often the most difficult. Wondering what their child may have looked like often keeps them from finding peace. They may get stuck in this phase of the grief process. What can be done?

જ *Check with the hospital for photographs.* Most hospitals now take photographs automatically and keep them on file for years.

જ If the pictures appear too clinical, you can *have a good artist draw a loving picture from them.* (Inquire locally; for addresses, see page 252.)

જ If no pictures were taken but someone can describe the baby, an artist might be able to *sketch a picture from this description.*

જ *Draw a picture of your baby from your heart.* We carry within ourselves an image of what our child probably looked like. Some mothers have kept on drawing and drawing pictures until they felt, yes, this is what my baby could have looked like!

જ *Look for a doll* that looks the way you think your baby might have looked. One mother found such a doll and carried it around with her in a totebag for a long time, and this transitional object helped her work through her grief. (She shared her doll with us at a bereaved parents' workshop.)

§ Another mother looked through magazines until she found a picture of a baby that corresponded with her inner image of her child. You might also *look through family albums*.

I can ask myself:

☐ Which do I need more, help expressing my pain or ways of soothing my grief?

☐ What could help me get in touch with my painful feelings now?

☐ What would I like to try to soothe and comfort myself without cutting myself off from my feelings?

☐ Do I feel guilty because I can't cry?

☐ Does my crying not bring relief?

☐ What would be good for me now? What do I need now?

☐ Which of the ideas above do I like best?

☐ Whose presence and support would I like now?

☐ Do I regret not having seen my baby or having no mementos? If yes, what do I want to do to help myself now?

☐ If I have regrets, am I sure it is really too late, or with whom would I like to check?

Expressing Anger and Aggression

Often, after a person dies, he or she is practically declared a saint. So what do you do with feelings of desertion and anger, which are also justified? You may wonder, "How could I be angry at an unborn child?" The answer is: *Of course* you can be angry at your child! Your anger isn't rational, but emotional, which has its own dynamics. Anger is a normal component of the grief process. Sometimes it isn't directed at a particular person or thing but just expresses pent-up pain. It's important to find ways to release or transform these feelings without becoming destructive to ourselves and others.

How can you deal with aggressive feelings constructively?

§ When you sense anger and aggression boiling up, admit it to someone. Admitting you are angry often defuses it.

§ Describe your feelings in a journal. Honestly ask yourself (allow irrational feelings here):

§ With what persons, institutions or principles am I angry?

§ What circumstances have triggered my anger? In what way was I perhaps hurt?

❧ Perhaps you can find an outlet for this aggressive energy that is appropriate to the circumstances (maybe in someone's presence who isn't afraid of your feelings and who can hold you afterward). Always stay connected with your breathing. Some ideas:

☞ *Scream* into a pillow or somewhere where it won't scare or alarm anyone.

☞ Release your anger physically by *pounding on a pillow or a mattress*.

☞ *"Shadow box,"* and release a loud sound ("hoo") with each punch.

☞ *Hit the palm of your left hand* with your right fist (again accompanied by a tone), gently practicing how to fit your hands together first, so you won't hurt yourself. The row of joints between the palm and fingers of your right hand should touch along the middle line of your left hand, and the lower joints of your right hand hit flat against the palm of the left hand (the left hand doesn't resist but moves along with the force). (This description fits right-handers. Reverse for left-handers.)

☞ *Thrash and snap a rolled-up towel.*

☞ *Stomp on the ground* until your energy changes and you become calm inside.

☞ Stomp around the yard or through the woods and *kick up leaves.*

☞ *Rhythmically beat a drum or a cardboard box.*

> *I sat in front of our son's grave for hours, picking up lumps of dirt and hurling them on the ground, hard.*

❧ You can transform your anger and give it a constructive direction. For example:

❧ putting it in motion (jogging, running, aerobics, bicycling, swimming . . .)

❧ dancing

❧ working hard physically (as long as you do it consciously): gardening, kneading bread dough, chopping wood . . .

❧ drawing with colors that express your mood (get a big piece of paper, pick the color that fits and draw until you feel calmer)

❧ working with soft art clay and seeing what you create (at first you may only want to pick up the heavy clay and slap it around on the table).

❧ If you believe someone has failed you or has treated you badly and increased your sorrow, you may want to write a letter to, or talk with, that person.

❧ You can put your aggressions down on paper and then burn them in a ritual. Or crumple the paper into a ball and throw it into in a river, to be carried away by the water. This kind of ritual can bring you an astonishing amount of relief.

To admit anger and to find reasonable ways of expressing or transforming it is the prerequisite for forgiving. Sometimes forgiving is not easy, but it is absolutely necessary for healing. Not to forgive can destroy us spiritually or prevent us from finding happiness or peace.

I can ask myself:

☐ What aggressions am I aware of in myself?

☐ Do I understand them?

☐ How do I want to deal with them constructively? How can I transform my aggression?

☐ Do I need support for this and whom do I want to ask for support?

☐ Is my anger only connected to the present situation or is there unresolved anger from my past contributing right now? If yes, how much?

☐ What might be underneath this aggression? Could my aggressions stem from tension from other unexpressed feelings, and if so, how I can I help myself?

Dealing With Guilt Feelings and Resentment

No one can live on this earth without making mistakes and thus "collecting" a lot of guilt. Only those who never try anything new avoid making mistakes. To make a mistake means that at a certain moment we lack the knowledge, the qualities, the possibilities to act in a "better" way for all concerned. Or, it means that what is right for me is not good for someone else. These situations occur throughout life. Forgiveness is a necessary, creative human process for handling them.

The feeling of having "gone wrong" can range from minor, superficial things, to subtle inner attitudes, to truly significant issues. Guilty feelings can help us develop and mature. We can put them to use if we honestly admit mistakes and feel true regret over them. Forgiveness happens if we "do the right thing" in the spirit of honesty, civility and strength, not out of weakness or fear. At best, this realization changes our future behavior for the better. It's good to talk about this inner process with at least one other person.

Many of us have grown up in an environment where, for whatever reason (such as lack of self-confidence or fear of punishment), it was hard to admit mistakes. Perhaps someone else's feelings of failure were projected onto us. Or perhaps guilty feelings were used to control others in an unhealthy way. If this experience was common, we may feel responsible for all sorts of things for which we are in no way to blame. If you are experiencing guilty feelings, look inside. Become aware of their true nature so you can use them constructively—to throw light on your own behavior and to further your development. Here are some suggestions that might help:

ॐ If you have created a special place (see page 237), go there to look deeply and honestly into yourself. Listen closely to your breathing for a while. Then place your hand over your heart, connect with the feelings in your heart, and ask:

☐ Where do I believe I have gone wrong? Whom and how do I feel I have failed?

☐ Are my guilty feelings justified? Could I have acted differently?

☐ Do I tend toward unjustified guilt feelings, and how did they develop?

☐ Are my guilty feeling based on my past family history, and if so, how have these affected me?

☐ Do I want to let go of unjustified guilt feelings? What would help me do this?

☐ If I am unclear on the nature and origin of my feelings, with whom would I like to talk through my feelings?

☐ Who has a clear perspective and wouldn't just pacify me?

☐ About what do I need additional information?

☐ About what do I have regrets, and what does that do to me?

☐ Am I resentful of others?

☐ Toward whom, what for and in what way do I want to make amends?

☐ Can I, do I want to forgive myself and others?

☐ If not, what do I need to be able to forgive myself or others—to find forgiveness?

☐ Have I won new insights that will have consequences for my life and my future? What do I want to do differently?

Some people will want to look into these questions while walking. It also helps to write your thoughts in a journal. The answers you find will initiate the next step in your healing process, more than likely with far-reaching consequences for your life.

Here are a few more ideas for dealing with guilty feelings, for those who are interested in doing exercises as a form of self-therapy. Be warned: They may release strong emotions. You may want to try them in the presence of a person you trust and who will hold you if you need it. (These exercises are intended for a mentally healthy person who has a clear sense of reality.)

~ If you can't let go of guilty feelings towards your child, you may want to have a "talk" with him or her. As usual, when you go to your special place, start by focusing on your breath for a while. With each out-breath, let your tensions fall away. Let your thoughts come and go. Perhaps you will "only" become more calm and centered. But you may also slowly come to feel that you are reaching a different dimension within yourself. Regardless, realize that something inside is changing. Ask your inner self for a picture or a symbol of your child or perhaps a connection with his or her soul. Admit you feel guilty and examine these feelings. Say what hasn't been said or clarified yet. Ask any questions that you would like answered. Then listen to the thoughts that come to you.

> *After our daughter Allison's death, I felt guilty for three years. The evening before she was strangled by her umbilical cord, I had broken my promise not to drink alcohol during the pregnancy. Three years later, I still had not gotten over her death. My life was still chaotic. I decided to see a therapist who gave me the idea of "talking" with Allison. It really worked. After that "talk" I felt redeemed. I knew with certainty that nothing I had done caused her death, and even if it were the case, my daughter would have forgiven me a long time ago.*

~ Sit on a pillow on the floor, and place another pillow symbolizing your baby in front of you. After centering yourself with eyes closed (see above), speak to him as if he were there and could talk. Ask questions that concern you. Then trade places so you can talk from the baby's perspective. If you can completely open yourself to this exercise and listen to yourself talk, you may be surprised by the insights and true healing that can come to you.

You may receive messages or insights for your life that extend beyond the question that you started with. In closing, say thank you, and after concentrating on the flow of your breath for a while longer, notice any changes.

~ You can also have these talks at your baby's grave or memorial site.

~ You may receive answers and clarification through meditation.

~ If you are heavily prone to guilt in general, you may want to try the Bach Flower Remedy, *Pine* (No. 24) (see page 136).

Choosing the Right Time

If you had already prepared the baby's room or purchased baby things, clear them away only when the time is right for *you*. This act, too, is a milestone. To be sure, facing a room with all you had prepared for your little baby will be extremely painful. But experience shows that you will do better if you decide yourself what should happen to these things, rather than have someone else remove them.

I can ask myself:

☐ Do I want to put away the baby's things yet?

☐ What do I want to do with them?

☐ Do I want anyone with me while I do this? If so, who?

Getting Help and Care at Home

For a while you may find it hard to cope with everyday chores. At times you may need help meeting the little and big demands of everyday life. That's just the way it is. Do ask for help if you can't manage.

Where practicing midwives are available, you may want to consider hiring one for the time immediately after you leave the hospital. Midwives are well trained in birth *and* postpartum care. In the early days, midwives were called "wise women" because they were (and still are) in close touch with the mysteries of life and death. This vocation generally attracts women who have much depth and great empathy and love for others.

Midwives take a lot of time for their patients and look at the whole picture, not just the medical elements. In the privacy of your own home, they are better able to get a feeling for your personal situation. Often a very close and nurturing relationship develops. You may also enlist the help of a doula. (*Doula* means "serving woman." A doula is trained to give emotional support to women during birth and the time after.)

I can ask myself:

☐ What do I have a hard time handling on my own, and what could I use help with?

☐ Whom do I want to ask for help?

☐ If midwives and doulas are available, do I want to look for one?

Giving Yourself Breaks from Grief

If you allow all of your unpleasant emotions to surface, it is likely you will also experience unexpected moments of intense joy. This can be confusing and even make you feel guilty. Joy is sorrow's opposite. Don't be ashamed of it! Just accept it gratefully. As Kahlil Gibran has said, "The deeper the sorrow buries itself within your being, the more joy are you able to grasp." It is perfectly fine for there to be times of laughter in the midst of grieving. Allow yourself these breaks from mourning.

I'm glad you told me there would be times where I would feel real good, too—that it was normal, that grief would come in waves. I did wonder at times: Is it all right to feel good, or don't I really love my child? Is it OK that I no longer have to cry every day—only once in a while? When we went out to a restaurant for the first time and some neighbors saw us, I felt guilty, like: How can we go out to eat if our baby is dead? I realize now I really needed those breaks away from grief to gather strength for this really intense work.

It's hard to admit, but we found so much to laugh about, and sometimes a hearty laugh is really helpful. Even when we were the saddest, we found something to laugh about. Humor can be found in most anything. I always felt a little better after a good cry, and I always felt a lot better after a good laugh.

ஃ You may want to consciously try an inner smile. Beforehand, stroke out your face from the nose towards the chin bones. Close your eyes and smile as if from the inside out. Observe how this affects your body and your breathing.

ஃ You may want to get away for a vacation, even just a weekend, to give your mind something besides your grief to think about.

ஃ Let yourself be. Accept yourself as you are right now.

I can ask myself:

☐ What do I want to do to consciously give myself breaks from grieving?

☐ Do I feel guilty when I have happy moments? With whom do I want to talk about this?

Finding Answers to Your Questions

Occupying yourself with questions that arise is part of assimilating what has happened and will help you move ahead. You will probably need a lot of information. You may not find answers to some questions. To others, you will only receive answers with time, in a different way than you may have expected. Some answers only lead to new questions.

I can ask myself:

☐ What are my questions?

☐ Which do I think can be answered? Which probably can't be?

☐ To whom can I turn for information, or how and where can I find it?

☐ Do I wish to talk again with any of the caregivers who attended me at the time of the loss? If so, with whom?

☐ What do I want to ask them or what do I feel in my heart that I need to tell them?

To help clear your thoughts, you may want to try the Bach Flower Remedies *White Chestnut* (No. 35) and *Clematis* (No. 9) (see pages 135 and 136).

Finding Consolation

Many parents develop visions or thoughts that console them, which happened for Suzy:

> *Two persons who recently died came to mind, and I said to myself, "Those two will look after our child." I developed the idea that there is a place where all people who have died meet again, which I didn't believe before.*

Some people are comforted through music. Others feel consoled because they received a coded message of the impending death in a dream, which now helps them to accept it. Others feel a strong angelic presence after the death of their child, as related in Cathi Lammert's book, *Angelic Presence*.

Consolation Can Come through Symbols

Symbols can bring solace to the soul. Parents who have lost a child may be comforted by special symbols. Some mothers temporarily need to hold or carry around something that is the approximate size and weight of their baby. That may concern some people, but it is actually quite common. Many bereaved are comforted by metaphorical symbols and visions coming from their subconscious or dreams. Other symbols, such as rainbows or roses, can bring comfort also.

> *When my baby died during birth, I envisioned her as a light that continuously moved away from me, becoming smaller and smaller, until it had found its place as a star far away in the universe, where it always greets me.*

ೞೞೞ

> *On the way home from the hospital, we saw a triple rainbow in the sky. A feeling of happiness overcame me despite my grief. It was like a promise that I wouldn't fall apart from this experience, that all would be well.*

ೞೞೞ

> *A delicate pink rose became my symbol for my baby. This image came to me suddenly. The first weeks and months, I always had a rose on our dining-room table. It symbolized the love I had experienced through my lost child. I dried all the roses, and as the dried bouquet increased in size, the pain receded. Now, the dried roses, decorating our living room, and a fresh rose on special holidays or the anniversary of her death, remind us that our dead child will always be a part of our family.*

Others are reminded of the continuous cycle of life and death through the use of living plants, flowers or trees. Especially where people are unable to take their grief to a grave site, the planting of a tree or of flower bulbs that bloom anew each springtime can soothe an aching heart.

I can ask myself:

☐ Which images comfort me?

☐ Have symbols appeared to me that remind me of my child?

☐ What symbolic act might console me and help me cope better with this loss?

☐ Have I had dreams that seem important? Would I like to I find someone knowledgable in dream interpretation?

New Dimensions of Being

People often have experiences in connection with death and dying that don't seem to make sense in terms of their everyday lives. It's as if in encountering death, we may come to know other dimensions of being. In the many conversations I have had with the bereaved, a number reported paranormal experiences around the time their child died.

> *Two days before our baby died, our 6-year-old daughter drew a rainbow on a piece of paper and then covered it with black crayon. Then she began to scratch out crosses with scissors. The crosses appeared in gleaming colors.*

The mother of Rebecca, a little girl who died of sudden infant death syndrome at 11 months of age, reported that:

> *We were new in town and I took my three children on a walk to acquaint ourselves with the place. Somehow we ended up at the local cemetery. Rebecca was in her stroller. When passing the grave of a baby, Anna, my oldest, stopped, pointed at the grave, and said: "Look, mom, there's still room next to this baby's grave. When another baby dies, this one will have a friend, right?" Rebecca crawled out of her stroller and sat down square in the middle of that site. A week later, she was buried there.*

Marie-Louise von Franz, an associate of the famous Swiss psychologist Carl Jung, stated that deep in the subconscious mind, where time and space seem to dissolve, prevails "a sense of eternity and a relative state of 'unseparatedness' from other souls—a oneness with them." This could be an explanation for the soul contact that so many women report having with their children. In our dreams we may receive information in an encoded form.

> *During my pregnancies, I saw all of my children in my dreams. I saw David and Thomas as boys, and I saw their faces. Timothy, who was later stillborn, did not reveal a face at all.*

Naturally we should be careful about interpreting our dreams. Not all dreams about death refer to actual death. Dreams about death may also bring us a message from our subconscious mind, urging us to change our lives. These dreams can also be a way for our subconscious to let us know that our lives will or must change. Or, they may provide a way to work through fears that could otherwise hinder birth and parenthood. Also, dreams often show us symbolically that the unconscious does not view death as an end, but just as a different dimension.

We don't always dare talk about paranormal experiences because we are afraid others might consider us crazy or strange. It's conceivable that medical professionals, unfamiliar with such phenomena, could classify these experiences as hallucinations—in their opinion, a possible sign of mental disturbance that requires medication or psychiatric treatment. **For a healthy grieving process, it is tremendously important not to have to keep these experiences secret.** Bereaved parents need to find people they can trust and who will take *all* their experiences and feelings seriously. To be listened to nonjudgmentally and accepted unconditionally can help them move on. (Lindstrom 1983)

If a person experienced in the interpretation of dreams or "extraordinary experiences" can work with these phenomena and help us through therapy, they can enrich our journey through life. This was the case for Cornelia (30):

> *With the help of a therapist I established soul contact with my child, who had died during the 19th week of pregnancy. Someone who hasn't experienced anything like that probably won't believe it. For me these encounters were as real as those at her stillbirth in the hospital. In response to my question, why she had stayed with us so briefly, the answer was something like, "That was necessary for you. You were so 'closed' and rigid before. We looked at your strengths and weaknesses together. You had to learn to let go." This "encounter" really transformed me.*

I can ask myself:

☐ Have I experienced "extraordinary" experiences or dreams of this kind?

☐ What feelings did/do they create in me?

☐ Is there anyone I can share these experiences with?

☐ Do I need further help with this? How could I find such help?

Attending a Support Group

To communicate is human nature. (Goethe)

Even if you received your relatives' and friends' support in the beginning, their willingness to listen often wanes relatively soon—long before your mourning is over. Despite their best intentions, people who aren't personally affected can't understand what is going on inside you. (Think how you felt before your loss.) Nobody understands grieving parents better than those who have suffered the same fate.

In many parts of the country, mutual-help groups exist for parents who have lost a child through all kinds of pregnancy or post-pregnancy situations. The friends you find in such a group can become closer to you than your own relatives.

We felt much better after our first visit with the group. After each meeting I felt a little less sad. I felt it was OK be myself. There, people understood me, even if I said nothing, and they became close friends to me and my husband. Some had lost their child two or three years earlier. It gave me courage to see that they had not only survived but were leading normal, fairly happy lives again. Each month new people come. You can see how they get better as time goes on and, although they still have bad days, these steadily decrease. I also liked to hear the men sharing their stories.

These groups are a place where feelings can be shown unmasked. However, sadness is not the only feeling that prevails there.

When I came to a support-group meeting for the first time, I couldn't take the laughter. I felt I was the only one in the room who had known tragedy. Then, as people began to speak, I heard that each of them had lost at least one child. I still couldn't believe it. With each meeting, it became increasingly clear to me that all of these smiling people meant hope to me and the certainty that I, too, one day would be able to laugh again, and that this wouldn't mean I had forgotten my child.

Your hospital or doctor may give you the address of the support group nearest to you. If there are no support groups in your vicinity, you may correspond with other bereaved parents through Pen Parents or, on the Internet, through Hygeia, an interactive journal for pregnancy losses (addresses, see pages 246 and 247). Or you can ask your gynecologist or your hospital if they can help you contact other bereaved parents. A hospital might offer you their facilities as a meeting place. SHARE publishes a book on how to establish a support group, but some basic guidelines can be found in chapter 10. Applying energy to something positive that will benefit others can help you heal.

The Compassionate Friends is another support group for parents who have lost children at all ages, including after birth. Parents who have lost a baby from sudden infant death syndrome (SIDS) can turn to the Sudden Infant Death Alliance for information and fellowship. There are also many independent local groups. Women who learn during pregnancy that their baby is not healthy may turn for support and guidance to A Heartbreaking Choice or other similar organizations listed starting on page 245.

I can ask myself:

☐ Could visiting a support group be helpful to me?

☐ Do I want to communicate by letter or telephone with someone who has "been there"?

☐ Can I accept the fact that my partner may not feel that this way of processing grief is the right way for him?

The Forgotten Grief of the Father

It takes a man to cry. (Elisabeth Kübler-Ross)

In our Western culture, people find it hard enough to respond to a woman who has lost her child. But they find it even more difficult to find an appropriate way to react to a man. Maybe we are afraid of seeing a man cry. Men do not have "cultural permission" to grieve.

Men carry a double burden. They feel their own grief and at the same time suffer because their wives suffer. Many men even feel they have to take away their partner's pain and try to answer all of her questions.

> *My husband is used to knowing the right answer in every crisis. If I say, "Why me?" then he feels under pressure to come up with an answer. I know that he doesn't know either; I don't expect an answer from him.*

Men in our culture frequently have no source from which to draw strength. They seldom form intimate friendships in which they can bare their soul and receive empathy. They usually haven't learned to talk to others about their personal lives, feelings and thoughts. My observation has been that, therefore, men are at even greater risk than women of not fully healing from a loss.

> *Sure, I can understand that my wife suffers more from the loss because she had a deeper relationship with the baby and was more immediately affected. And I am willing to give her more love and attention. But she doesn't seem to realize that I am suffering too. This is a dilemma for me—I don't know where I can turn for comfort. In the long run, I'm developing all kinds of "deprivation" symptoms, like moodiness and depression.*

Then again, one father posed the legitimate question: "Where would we be if both of us fell apart?"

People generally ask only about the condition of the bereaved mother. The father is frequently ignored. He is often encouraged by other men and the gynecologist to "be a tower of strength" for his wife. He holds back his sadness so he won't burden his wife with his own pain. Women can easily misunderstand this as indifference.

Ideally, says Stephanie Matthews-Simonton, who is experienced in working with the dying and bereaved, people in mourning should be able to get up to 25% of their support from their own inner resources. Twenty percent of the support should come from their partner. Fifty-five percent should be derived from other sources.

Having to go right back and be productive at work can be particularly hard on a bereaved father when he, too, needs time for mourning. Because of work, most men can't afford to be affected by grief in the same way as women. With stillborn or newborn death, fathers usually take a couple of days off. After an early-pregnancy loss, the father must be back the next day. A grieving man in the working world doesn't often meet with understanding and compassion for his situation.

On the other hand, the job routine can help men extricate themselves from their grief faster. Maybe it is true that men can cope with their grief by transforming it into creative or active work.

Facing up to grief can help you become more complete as a human being. You have the opportunity to unfold inner qualities that, until now, may have been little developed—perhaps your more sensitive and gentle sides. This time of suffering can be a time for you to learn new ways of relating to others. In the midst of this crisis, you might find a real friend, someone who will listen patiently when you tell your story and who is not afraid of human closeness, and who can bear your tears. During this time of suffering and transformation, you may find support by visiting a self-help group for bereaved parents.

I can ask myself:

☐ Do I, as a man, feel responsible for my wife's well-being?

☐ How much support do I find in myself? How much comes from my partner and how much from other sources?

☐ Do I have people with whom I would like (and am able) to share the depth of my experience, or how could I go about finding someone to talk to?

☐ What effect does my work have on me?

☐ Have I taken enough time for grieving? What is a good way for me to deal with my grief?

Grieving Couples

Fathers and mothers usually react differently to the death of their baby. Many men seem outwardly less affected by a miscarriage or stillbirth than their wives. Perhaps it only appears that way. Some men have told me they felt they were at a disadvantage because they couldn't live through the experience as directly as their wives.

Since the intensity of pain after a loss is closely related to the intensity of the preceding attachment, it wouldn't be surprising if bereaved fathers didn't grieve as deeply or as long as bereaved mothers. There is a natural difference in the degree of attachment. Women experience the loss of a baby very directly. The baby is a part of our body. Losing our baby, especially if we have felt the baby move, feels like losing a part of ourselves.

As a man, you can see the baby on ultrasound and hear its heart beat in the beginning, but you aren't physically and hormonally connected to it. That is part of nature. Often your work makes it hard to dedicate thoughts to your developing baby. Only in the latter part of the pregnancy, when you can feel your baby move and kick by placing your hands on your partner's abdomen, do you usually perceive your child as a separate being. Many fathers only form a real bond with their child at birth and thereafter. Experiencing labor and stillbirth with their partners can help men increase the level of bonding and love. This can help build bridges between both partners, potentially reducing relationship problems.

> *John put all his anguish and sadness in a box, closed the lid, and said, "That's the end of it." I, on the other hand, leave my box open to pack and unpack over and over.*

Most of us have chosen a partner whose personality is different from our own. Our personality influences how we deal with grief. Extroverted people have a strong need to share their sorrow and gain energy through contact with others, while introverted people are more inclined to work out their feelings of grief in silence and gain energy from within themselves. "Thinkers" process things rationally, while "feelers" react emotionally. "Sensors"—the more pragmatic types—come to accept things quickly as unalterable facts, while "intuitives" need to muse over the meaning of an experience for a long time. "Planners" need control over their environment and tend to bring things quickly to a close, while "perceivers" take life as it comes and can live easily with open questions. Men in our society are often pressed into the roll of "thinker," "sensor," "planner"—roles in which there is little expression of feelings. Women mostly take the opposite role. By gradually coming to accept and integrate both the masculine and the feminine side nature puts in each of us, we can move towards wholeness. (Keirsey & Bates 1984)

Your tears flow within your heart,
Mine flow down my cheeks.
Your anger lies with thoughts and movements,
Mine gallops ahead for all to see.
Your despair shows in your now-dull eyes,
Mine shows in line after written line.
You grieve over the death of your son,
I grieve over the death of my baby.
But we're still the same, still one,
Only we grieve at different times
Over different memories and at different lengths.
Yet we both realize
The death of our child.

—Pam Burden
(Used by permission from The Compassionate Friends, Oak Brook, Illinois)

Differences in mourning behavior seem to be the main reason for misunderstandings and crisis after the loss of a baby. It takes a great deal of maturity to understand and accept the other as he or she "is."

Stress—and the loss situation is *stress in the extreme*—brings out our "shadow sides," those sides we do not cherish in each other and that may have rarely surfaced before. Unexpressed grief may end up being directed at our partner as aggression.

The life of a woman usually changes more by becoming a mother than the life of a man changes upon becoming a father. This too can contribute to problems.

With our baby's death, I was bereaved of my entire existence. I had given up my position as a teacher. From day to day my appearance changed. I slowly became a different person. For my husband, nothing changed. After our baby's birth, he would still have been a successful attorney. He would have continued to play tennis on Mondays and Wednesdays. But my whole life was radically altered.

I can ask myself:

☐ Where was each of us in our bonding process with our baby? Did I, the man, get to "catch up" on bonding at birth?

☐ Are my partner and I opposites, and how does this affect our grieving?

☐ Which of us tends to be more extroverted and which more introverted? Who is more a thinker and who more a feeler? Which of us is more the sensor and which uses a more intuitive approach to problems? Who needs more to have control over his or her environment and who takes life more as it comes?

☐ How have we both changed since our baby's death? What previously hidden sides have been revealed?

☐ As a woman, do I interpret my husband's lack of bonding as indifference to our child?

Relationships Change

The loss of a baby can put a relationship to a great test. In some cases it leads to serious crisis. Divorce rates among grieving parents are high. In other cases, relationships are strengthened. Dr. Susan Hodge and her husband grew closer after the loss of their baby due to a pregnancy termination after amniocentesis. Susan wrote about this process to her genetic counselor:

> *The unhappiness has brought my husband and me closer together, even though we've reacted to the loss so differently. I've been amazed, in fact, at our wisdom in accepting each others' differences in this difficult time. I don't reproach him with, "If you cared, you'd be carrying on and crying like I am;" and he doesn't say, "Enough already! It's time to put it behind us!". . . I know he feels sadness and loss; he feels cheated because we've lost our baby. But unlike me, he has not been pouring out his emotions. At first I was mystified that my husband could go on with his daily life, concentrate on his work, et cetera. Later, as the weeks have worn on and my grieving has taken its toll, I have been grateful that one of us was functional. Although he has not grieved in the physical, uncontrollable way I have, he has understood and accepted me unreservedly.*

> *Sometimes on a good day, I say to him, "Gee, I'm feeling a lot better now." He just sort of raises an eyebrow. Then when I crash, he's there to hold me again. My husband and my closest friend (also a geneticist, like me) are infinitely patient. They know I'm not stuck in molasses for the fun of it, and that I'll extricate myself as soon as I can. They quietly "cover" for me*

and take over my responsibilities when possible. Even though they're "running free" with the rest of the world and are not in the molasses with me, still they reach into it periodically so that I am not abandoned here. When I stare off into space, my husband leaves me alone. When I cry, he wordlessly puts his arms around me. When I talk and talk, he listens. We're kind to each other. All sorts of little things we used to squabble about melted overnight into the obscurity they richly deserved.

We can guess what may have caused a positive outcome for this couple. Although both partners grieved differently, they did not try to change one another. Their love grew through their mutual acceptance of and respect for each other. With Esther (39), whose first child was stillborn, the gap between her and her husband grew wider:

We have had many problems in our marriage since we lost Dorothy. My husband doesn't want to talk about "it." That's a big problem. His attitude is, "It happened. I'm sorry. It's over. Now let's get on with our lives." He said she was not really a baby yet; she was only a "hope" for us. He had only felt my abdomen once in a while. He didn't know this child. He hadn't loved her. He sees everything unemotionally, analytically. I never saw him cry. That was bad. I needed to talk about it, but he always cut me off. Nor did he want me to talk to others about it. My husband seriously believed that if he returned to his routine, I would follow suit. Because I loved my husband, I tried to act as if everything were all right, but it didn't work. The more I tried to bury my pain, the more it came out. The rational part of me knows that my husband's behavior is his coping mechanism, but the emotional part of me says, "Please share my feelings."

Esther's relationship threatened to fall apart not only because her husband didn't show his own feelings but also because her emotional reactions were unbearable to him and therefore he couldn't allow them. On the other hand, she couldn't accept his distancing, defensive behavior and interpreted it as indifference. Each wanted the other to be different. Their love was being buried by their mutual inability to accept and understand each other.

I can ask myself:

☐ How has the loss of our child affected our relationship?

☐ Can I allow my partner to grieve in her or his own way?

Sexuality after the Loss of a Child

By coming together sexually after the loss of a child, a couple can briefly put aside their brooding and feel close to each other, connecting themselves to the flow of life again. Susan said:

> *In the two months since the abortion, my physical desire for sex is still depressed, but the emotional support I get from it is terribly important.*

It may be that women especially, for a while, will only need tenderness. The palette of sensuality is large.

> *We often sat without talking, but we always had physical contact with each other. Peter put his arm around me, or I snuggled up to him.*

Closeness to one another and love for each other can temporarily cover pain. But the total openness of an orgasm can also lead us to feel the pain of loss more intensely.

> *My husband and I made love on the night before . . . I cried the whole time . . . This was inexpressibly tender and life-affirming.* (Hodge 1995)

Sexuality and physical closeness are biological needs that seek balance. Releasing tension with an orgasm, or from masturbation, can help reestablish normal breathing again, dissolve muscle tensions throughout the body and increase a feeling of well-being. As we know from Taoism and Tantra, both practiced in Asia, an orgasm increases energy in women but tends to deplete it in men.

Some women or men have an aversion to sex at first because they feel their present agony had its beginning there. We can become afraid of a new pregnancy and by extension, the possibility of another loss. Sometimes we use sex to cover up feelings of grief so we don't have to face them. Guilty feelings may interfere with enjoying one another.

If you are depressed, you may temporarily feel cut off from all sexual desire. Temporary sexual disturbances in both men and women are normal. Talk openly with your partner about your feelings and anxieties so that your reactions won't be misinterpreted. With patience, mutual tolerance and understanding, the problems will resolve themselves as healing progresses. Getting away to be alone together may help. If problems persist far into the second year of grieving, seek professional help.

I can ask myself:

☐ What are my needs regarding closeness, sensuality and sexuality? What would be good for me?

☐ What is it I don't want at this time?

☐ Do I allow myself sexual feelings, or do I think that wouldn't be OK?

☐ Am I afraid of sex because theoretically it could lead to a new pregnancy and another loss?

☐ Can I talk openly with my partner about my feelings and my needs and also about what may not be possible right now?

☐ If we haven't been able to talk with each other, do I want to try again now or write down my thoughts and feelings in the form of a letter to him or her instead?

☐ If we aren't sleeping together, how does this affect me? What can I do to prevent too much tension from building in me?

☐ If our relationship is troubled right now, with whom do I want to talk about it?

☐ Are our difficulties serious enough to warrant professional help?

Suggestions for Couples

These thoughts may help you face the loss of your baby as a couple in a healing way:

&❧ Let your relationship be your number-one priority.

&❧ Be patient with yourself and your partner.

&❧ Try to accept that your partner isn't at the same place in the grief process you are.

&❧ Strive for openness, honesty and kindness in your communication.

&❧ Allow your own feelings. Communicate what goes on inside of you and give your partner the chance to express his or her pain.

&❧ Also, give one another room to grow in the relationship.

&❧ Work at increasing your affection, caring and respect for each other. Discover ways to nurture and express these feelings.

&❧ Enhance one another's healing through physical closeness and touch.

&❧ Encourage one another to enjoy life and each other. Laugh together, cry together. Discover things to do together that bring you joy.

&❧ Find support from sources other than your partner.

&❧ Nurture the thought together that, as precious as your child is to you, there is still much worth living for.

Sister Jane Marie Lamb encourages fathers to let others know that they, too, are grieving.

> *When someone asks you how your wife is doing, tell them and then add, "And I'm doing . . . ."*

Men often suffer because of assumed demands from their wives. They feel heavily burdened by this perceived responsibility. In talking to women, Sister Jane Marie says:

> *Tell your husband, "I don't expect you to take away my pain. I don't expect you to give me answers. All I want from you is to listen to me, because I have to be able to talk about it. If you don't need to talk about it, that's all right. I would like you to just hold me in your arms so I can feel your closeness.*

When conflicts reached the point that partners no longer can talk to one another, writing to each other may provide a way out of the crisis:

> *This has been the worst period I have experienced for a long time. I have felt deep despair, loneliness and abandonment. The turning point came when, after a week of despair, I sat down and wrote a long letter, putting down all the thoughts and feelings I was experiencing. Although I wrote the letter for myself, I handed it to my wife.*

When one partner has trouble listening to the other, it may help to agree on a definite, limited time each day when each is willing to give his or her full attention to the other.

You will need to seek professional help when:

- constructive communication is no longer possible,
- anger towards your partner (which may be normal for a little while) doesn't subside,
- one partner has begun an outside relationship to escape confrontation with grief, or
- even good friends can no longer help build a bridge between you.

It would be good to find a couples therapist or family therapist experienced in working with the bereaved.

I can ask myself:

☐ Which of the suggestions above could help me?

☐ Do we both feel we can overcome our present difficulties ourselves, or do we need help?

☐ How do I go about finding help?

Sibling Grief

Children may react to a death in the family with loss of appetite, stomach pains and diverse physical complaints. Children can become anxious, whiny and withdrawn, or respond with aggression, anger, hyperactivity, irritability, moodiness, greater dependency, thumb-sucking, stuttering, regression, school problems, bed-wetting and nightmares.

Children grieve in "small doses." Normally their souls heal faster, just as their bodies do. Most turn toward life again soon, with comments like, "When will I get a new baby brother?"

Children and Death

For us as adults, death is mostly very painful and distressing. It is understandable to want to shield children from an encounter with it. Often we transfer our anxieties to our children. But children, especially those under nine years of age, usually have an entirely natural relationship to death. They are shockingly open and direct in the company of adults whom they trust and in whose presence they feel they can be themselves.

Here is an excerpt from a father's account of his experiences with his 5-year-old daughter, Corey. Daniel's second daughter, Elizabeth, was born with congenital birth defects and died 24 hours after birth.

> *If anyone had asked me a hypothetical question about how one deals with a child in regard to the birth and death of a sibling, then perhaps I would have answered that one gently tells her the truth, but should protect her from traumatic sights and experiences. Corey taught us a great deal about the capacity of children to deal with death, about their awareness of life and death, about their needs and much about ourselves and our needs. She also taught us to listen better to children.*

Corey, who had actually wanted to be present at the joyous birth of her baby sister, arrived at the hospital shortly after Elizabeth—born with a cleft palate, low-set ears, and possibly other less apparent disfigurements—had been rushed to the intensive care unit.

> *. . . After a little while, the uncertain Corey asked about her sister and we told her that Elizabeth was very sick. "I want to see her." It was clear that Corey expected from us that we deal with her in a direct and straightforward manner. Kate, our labor and delivery nurse, made a quick assessment of Corey's needs and what she was capable of handling. She*

suggested that we let Corey see the baby through the glass window about 15 feet away, so that the birth defects would not be so apparent . . . Corey looked for a moment then said, "Those tubes on her look just like E.T.'s before he died. Is Elizabeth going to die?" We told her all we knew at the time: "Elizabeth is very sick, and it is possible that she will die. We don't know yet."

Elizabeth was still alive the next day. Corey insisted on seeing her although we tried to talk her out of it. "We'll see what can be arranged, Corey, but her face will look strange; it didn't grow together right." Quietly and filled with sadness we talked about what Elizabeth looked like, why she would die, and about our feelings. In the afternoon Corey was permitted to see Elizabeth, who was now free of all the tubes, as she sat on the lap of her mother, Susan. "Oooh, gross!" she said as she saw her sister's face. She turned to Susan, "May I touch her?" Susan nodded. Corey reached inside the bassinet and began to stroke Elizabeth's arm. "Her skin is so soft! Look, she has curly red hair! It's soft, too!" Corey turned again to Susan and said tearfully, "She's going to die." Turning back to Elizabeth, Corey began to talk to her. "Your skin is so soft, Elizabeth. I wish you didn't have to die. We love you." Elizabeth began to move her arms and legs in response to Corey's voice and touch. Corey turned around with an expression of delight on her face. "She loves me. She knows I'm here!" For a long time, Corey stroked Elizabeth and talked with her, holding her hand and caressing her hair. Then it was time to go. Corey repeated over and over, "We love you. We'll never forget you." The nurses standing behind us wiped the tears from their eyes. "I want to stay with Elizabeth. I want to see Elizabeth die." We were shocked. See Elizabeth die? How morbid! "No, Corey, we can't do that. We don't know when she will die or how long it will take."

In the evening we received a telephone call that Elizabeth had died. A pediatric nurse told us that she had been with Elizabeth as she died, had caressed her and talked to her, and she had gone to the other side peacefully. Suddenly we regretted that we had not been there with her. "Corey was right."

I had to go to the hospital to fill out papers and Corey insisted on coming along. At the nurse's station, she burst out with, "I want to see my dead sister." The nurse, who had just attended a seminar about children and death, thought Corey should be allowed to see Elizabeth one more time. She told her Elizabeth's face was somewhat blotched and purple. Corey didn't seem affected by the description; she simply wanted to see for herself.

Elizabeth was wrapped in a blanket. Corey was sad and fascinated at once. She looked once more at the physical disfigurements that she knew already and reminded herself that Elizabeth had other problems she couldn't see and that couldn't be fixed. She touched her several times, repeating that we would never forget her, and how sad it was that she had died, and how much we loved her. After several minutes we left the room and went home.

In the weeks that followed, it became clear to us how valuable it was that we let Corey take her own lead as to what she needed. There were no nightmares about a disfigured baby. The reality had been seen and accepted. That misshapen face was only one aspect. There was also the delicate skin, the soft hair, and the memory of how Elizabeth had responded to Corey. We did not have to conceal our grief from Corey, we are able to share it with her . . .

(Reproduced with permission from *Journal of the American Medical Association,* volume 251/6 (March 1984), pages 732-733. Copyright 1984, American Medical Association)

Children have very good "antennas." It's impossible to keep a secret from them. Even when we don't tell them what has happened, they know when something isn't right. When they don't understand what is going on around them, they become insecure and develop fantasies about what may have happened. They know very well when people are being insincere, and they sense when adults do not want them to ask questions or show their feelings.

If death becomes a taboo and children are excluded from it, they can't be helped to sort out their feelings. They feel isolated. Corey lived in an environment in which her reactions and feelings were permitted. When children are allowed to share their wishes and thoughts openly, they won't be harmed by an encounter with death. How this first encounter with death is handled can affect their future relationship to death and grieving. Many have their first experience when a beloved animal dies. There, too, a child's grief must be taken seriously.

I can ask myself:

☐ How do (or did) we respond to our living children regarding the death of their brother or sister? Can we let them take part and accept their reactions?

☐ Is there still something we need to do for our children? Do we need help with this and if yes, what is it we want help with? Who can help?

Different Age Groups

Children's reactions to death depend on their stage of development and how they perceive death. Children who have already been confronted with death and dying directly can grasp the meaning of death earlier than others (Jampolsky 1983). Children are often not aware themselves of what is happening to them, or they cannot put their experience into words. For that reason it's good to have an approximate idea of what goes on inside children at specific ages. That makes it easier to guess at and respond to their unexpressed questions, emotions and needs and correct any scary fantasies.

Children under three years of age cannot picture death. They live in the present and have no reference to time. At this age they only sense that something around them has changed. They are aware of adults' grief and anguish and react more to our emotions than feel sad themselves. They may have anxieties about being abandoned because mother is in the hospital. Little children may develop sleep or eating disturbances. Children who are breastfed may even refuse to continue nursing and wean themselves.

What is true for grown-ups is also true for these little ones. They need a lot of physical contact. Especially at night, it is good for them to be physically close to mother or father. To feel mother's or father's skin, their warmth, the movement of their breath, helps them relax and feel secure.

For children between three and five years of age, death is like a journey or sleep—life under other conditions. In their minds, one can come back from there. Our world and the world beyond are two sides of the same coin—an image that frequently shows up in adults' dreams, too. Children of this age group live in a magical world. In their fantasy, they can create their own world, one in which they are all-powerful and are able to make things happen or "unhappen," even death.

At this age, a child might say or think to himself, "I don't want a baby . . . then I have to share my toys . . . the baby should go away." When a sibling dies, a child in the magical-age stage may believe that his thoughts or a jealous blow to Mom's tummy caused the death. He is afraid of being punished. He will need reassurance that nothing *he* did caused the death, and he must feel he is protected and loved. Children often misinterpret what is said to them. Therefore, choose words carefully and thoughtfully.

Between the ages of six and nine, most children begin to understand that the dead do not return to our world. They still can't imagine that death will strike them or their family personally. Typically, they still live in their innocent world. Eight-year-old Anna comforted her mother when a dear friend of hers died of AIDS: "Oh, Mommy, I know you're sad but I know for sure that Tom is much better off where he is now." Often at this age, children envisage death as a person who comes to take people away. Some children at this age believe that death is contagious and need to be told that this isn't true.

Six- to 9-year-olds still need assurance that nothing they said or thought is responsible for the death.

> *One day before I was admitted to the hospital, I had an argument with Natalie, my 6-year-old. In her anger she had hit me in the tummy. I was genuinely mad and told her to stop it—that she could hurt the baby. I think I also sent her away. A few weeks after my miscarriage, it became clear she believed the baby died because of her blow.*

Nine- to 12-year-olds recognize that death is irreversible and become aware that their own earthly life will end too some day. Children at this stage are very curious about the biological aspects of death and are very interested in the sober, verifiable details of death and burial. To us they may seem quite unemotional and matter-of-fact about death. My own grandmother told me this story:

> *During my childhood it was customary to lay out the dead at home until the burial. When I was eight or nine years old, I was sent to take a wreath to the home of the deceased, as was the custom. When I think about it now, I find it strange, but I always wanted to see the dead person. I believe I was investigating for myself, "What does death look like? How does it show itself? What is death?"*

Don't hold a child's factual interest in death against him or her, though you may be appalled at their reactions. Whenever possible, give in to their wishes.

> *Our then-9-year-old said over and over again that he wanted to see our baby. We thought it would be too much for him. Even years later he reminded me with reproach and regret in his voice, "I wasn't allowed to see my sister."*

Starting at this age, children can be in touch with and can reflect on their feelings. Anger, guilt and sadness may be particularly pronounced. A child may also be afraid that something will happen to her or that she will become sick: "Will this happen to me, too?"

Teenagers perceive death pretty much in the same way adults do— inevitable and irreversible. At this stage of life the topic of separation is a prevalent theme as they strive to detach themselves from their parents.

They have an ambivalent relationship towards separation. Many questions and emotions seethe inside, preoccupying them and often overwhelming them. They struggle to find their place in life, to develop their individuality and to search for values by which to live. Often they withdraw within themselves and tend to work out things inside, including the topic of death. Their hormonal system puts them on an emotional rollercoaster.

Teenagers usually find it hard to take others' sadness or tears, for fear their own turbulent emotions could erupt. They often repress their feelings. Their peers, now more important to them than their parents, are occupied with their own development and usually don't have sufficient maturity and life experience themselves to give real assistance. Under conditions like these, grief may be suppressed, only to reveal itself in unhealthy ways. School problems, eating disorders and acting-out behaviors are frequent. An understanding school counselor might become their grief mentor and help them develop coping skills. In some places, teenage grief groups exist (for example, a TAG group; see page 247). During this stage of increasing autonomy and self-reliance young people need support, particularly in understanding and dealing with their own emotions. Often an empathetic adult outside the immediate family can help more than their own parents.

I can ask myself:

☐ What have I learned about my child's possible reactions to this situation with regard to age? What do I understand better now?

☐ What do I want to pay special attention to?

☐ Have I observed reactions that suggest our child misunderstood something? If yes, how do I want to handle that? How can I help?

Practical Help for Responding to Siblings

Each child is different. If you have more than one child, speak with each one separately so you can respond to individual needs. In talking with your child, take her on your lap, hold her hand, put your arms around her or simply be close to her. First address things that your child may have already noticed: the pregnancy, the fact that Mom was in the hospital, or that Mom or Dad may have been crying. Talk honestly with simple words about what has happened, adapting yourself to the child's age level. Choose words thoughtfully and avoid expressions that could be misunderstood (see above). Children can take what you say literally. When they don't understand something or know something is missing, they will make up something to fit.

It's a good idea to keep checking to see what your child has understood (particularly if he or she shows inexplicable reactions or anxiety). Gently make sure they haven't drawn false conclusions. When children feel sure of your time and attention, they will ask questions. Don't provide more information than they ask for specifically. Younger children will comprehend best if you speak to them in images or offer them comparisons from nature, fairy tales or stories.

I can ask myself:

☐ How do I want to present the news to my child or children?

☐ What images or comparisons come to mind?

☐ If we find it hard to tell our child or children, who could help us break the news?

or, looking back:

☐ How did it go? Do we need to add anything?

☐ How did our child or children react?

☐ Is there anything else we need to do?

Help to Grasp What Happened

To begin with, you might ask yourself if your child, too, should get to know his brother or sister who is dead. The positive accounts of wonderful professional women caring for bereaved couples—Ann Coon, Chris Pfeffer, Pat Stauber—whom I met in southern Florida some years ago encouraged me to include siblings when I began working as a *doula*, a labor guide for the bereaved.

Two-and-a-half-year-old Janina and her precocious twin sister had already bonded with their baby brother "Charlie"—that was the name the family had given the expected baby—by listening to his heart beats with an empty toilet-paper roll pressed on Mom's tummy. When they came to visit Mom in the hospital after she lost the baby around the 22nd week of pregnancy, the girls kept asking where Charlie was. Mom didn't know herself, but she explained he was dead because he had come out of her tummy before he was big enough to be able to drink from her breast. We decided jointly to arrange for the children to meet their brother. "Oh, it's true," Janina exclaimed, looking from the baby to Mom's breasts. "Charlie couldn't drink from your 'buttons' yet."

When children see "their baby," they can "grasp" death. In later conversations with them, we can then refer to concrete memories. A natural bond with "their baby" develops.

Our 4-year-old son, who had gotten to see, hold and say good-bye to stillborn Stevie at the hospital, wanted very badly to have a photo in his room of himself holding his brother. When we went for a walk, he would pick wildflowers and put them in a vase in front of the picture. It wasn't morbid, just very natural, very tender. He talked lovingly and with pride of "his brother."

When children aren't included, death remains abstract. Children should be prepared for what they can expect with regard to the baby before coming to the hospital and also that Mom will be very sad for a while. In addition, it's good to review with them what they have experienced. Children usually want to touch or hold "their" baby (depending on what subtle messages they get from the grown-ups). That's natural. Even 2-year-olds can handle a baby with love and reverence. However, an 11-month-old rascal who was along when Janina and her twin sister came to look at their brother almost snatched away the blanket I had carefully wrapped around the baby. "Stop! You can't play with Charlie!" the startled mother cried. Even she had to laugh after it popped out of her mouth. The humor of the situation broke the tension and brought normalcy back into the room.

In the touching Australian film, *Some Babies Die* (see page 252), we see that children relate to their dead little sibling with ease and naturalness if they are supported by the adults around them. If you are afraid yourself or feel unable to support your child, find another empathetic person who can be by his side as he gets to meet his little sibling— someone the child trusts and to whom he can address all his questions. If your children weren't able to see their brother or sister or were too small at the time, you may want to show them a photo sometime later, or possibly a sketch or painting that may have been made.

At first I wasn't sure whether we ought to show the photos of stillborn Lisa to our 4-year-old son Christopher, but our experience was positive. He reacted naturally and casually to the pictures and now freely talks about going to visit Lisa at the cemetery. "Will you go to the hospital again, to Dr. Eldering, when our next baby comes?" he asked. That led me to believe that he had worked things through all right, otherwise he would probably be apprehensive.

I can ask myself:

☐ Do or did my other child or children have the opportunity to "grasp" the death?

☐ Is there anything we need or want to do retroactively?

☐ What are my fears?

☐ Do I need support? If so, who can stand by me (or us)?

Saying Good-Bye

Children say good-bye in their own way, just as Corey, quoted earlier, did so spontaneously. Corey's experience exemplifies what we can do when the baby is born alive but is expected to die. Children deepen their bond with "their baby" if they are allowed to give the baby a gift—and their choice (a favorite doll or toy, a drawing or a little letter) is often touching.

Funerals are important family affairs, "something as normal as a family meal," says Elisabeth Kübler-Ross. They help everyone concerned accept the reality and better comprehend death. If children are excluded, they may be left with the feeling that they aren't an important part of the family.

> *When I was three years old, my great-grandfather died. I wasn't allowed to go to the funeral because I was so little. To this very day, I remember feeling excluded and I just could not understand it.*

On the other hand, children should not be forced to take part. Explain exactly what will happen (you may need to find out yourself) and let them decide whether they want to come along. Someone capable of putting themselves into a child's shoes should be designated as their caretaker and be there to respond to their questions. This person should also be prepared to leave in the middle of the ceremony if the children so desire. Perhaps children can take part with their own rituals at the burial.

In a brochure of the organization Bereavement Services/RTS (see page 246), a mother reports:

> *We did have our children there. This just seemed right to me. My daughter just stood by our side and patiently watched and observed. My son got bored. He went down right next to the casket. He drove his little car right over the casket. I thought this was very strange, not reverent, not proper, but then, I thought this is a child. This was his way of coming in contact with what was going on.* (from *Parents' Booklet*, page 19. La Crosse, WI: Gundersen Lutheran Medical Center. Reprinted by permission of Bereavement Services/RTS)

I can ask myself:

☐ Do I have any thoughts as to how our child/ren could say good-bye to their sibling?

☐ Would our child or children like to be present at the funeral or burial? Depending on age, how could he or she take part in it?

☐ Which sensitive person could be there for our child or children?

Daily Life With Children after Bereavement

Many children, in the time that follows, chatter naturally about the event and ask questions, while others keep silent. That depends on age and personality, but also on how much they had been involved. Some react only superficially at first and, as for some adults, grief may resurface years later, when another loss occurs.

Children's reactions to loss vary, with each child needing his or her own type of support. In every case, however, *they will need additional attention.* Unfortunately, the anguish and self-absorption of mourning, and even feelings of anger and rage, frequently make it difficult for us as parents to be able to respond to our children's immediate needs. We may even feel aggressive towards them because they remind us of what we lost. We may unsettle them if our behavior and routines have changed, which give them security. Or we may smother them by being overprotective. Sometimes other people, perhaps loving grandparents or close friends, can help us respond to our children's needs. It's a good idea to have a grief mentor for children available in this situation.

> *Unlike in the first week, when I was so grateful to have them, I have now become irritable and distant. It's as if I was gearing up for a helpless infant and suddenly don't know how to handle two big, independent, demanding children.* (Hodge 1995)

On the other hand, children comfort us greatly while we mourn.

> *The girls do comfort me. My younger daughter, particularly, seems to sense when I'm feeling bad, even before I start to cry. She'll reach out and take my hand, while she's still chattering away about something else. My older daughter no longer begs me to stop crying. When a friend called one night . . . to tell me she'd just had her baby a month early, I congratulated her, put down the phone, and cried more intensely than I had in weeks. My older daughter said, "It's OK to feel jealous, Mommy. It's OK to cry." This really helped.*

❧❧❧

Our little son David was quite important to us because he personified life for us. He soon had us laughing with him in spite of our grief.

It's good to talk with your children about your own feelings.

I tell the children that the way I am acting now is normal, and that it will end—(though sometimes I hardly believe it myself). (Green 1992)

It's not a good idea to move after a loss, because children need the comfort of a home and surroundings they are familiar with at a time when, in many ways, their world no longer seems stable. They need to be assured that in the midst of these unfamiliar events, everything is basically all right.

To give the child who has died a "halo" puts a heavy burden on surviving children. Left unresolved, these burdens may have repercussions much later.

I can ask myself:

☐ How are my children reacting to the loss? How do they mourn?

☐ How am I reacting to their feelings? What do I feel? How can I deal with my feelings?

☐ What may unsettle my children? How can I help maintain some stability for them in the midst of my grieving?

☐ Can I attend to my children's needs? Who else might help us and perhaps mentor them for now?

Helping Children Process What Happened

Children can best sort through the event and their inner conflicts through play: role-playing, playing with dolls, hand puppets or toys and the like.

At one point David molded many frogs out of clay. He sat one on a chair and said that one was sad and crying. We kept the frogs for weeks, and I'd ask David now and then how the one frog was doing. After a few weeks, he said the frog was happy again and didn't need to cry any more. That was his grief process.

❧❧❧

For weeks our son played "dying and funeral" with his friends. At first I thought it was morbid, and it scared me until I understood that this was his way of working it all out.

With the help of dolls, stuffed animals and puppets, you can communicate with your children at their level. This is a good way to find out what is going on inside them. For example, Sister Jane Marie used a hand puppet, a small stuffed rabbit named Thumpy, to talk with kids. (Thumpy is also the main character of a children's book, which is accompanied by a helpful workbook for children who have lost a sibling.) When parents don't know how to support their children on their own, they can get and give guidance with the help of books like this one. Check with SHARE or your library.

Children can express themselves well through painting and drawing. With the help of paintings you can obtain information about what might still be unresolved. Thus you can gently guide them on their way. It will do your children (and you) good to swim, take a walk in the fresh air, hug them or give them a massage. They need times of fun and play to maintain their mental and physical balance. Physical activity of any kind is beneficial.

It's possible your children will ask you about life after death. If you have a clear opinion, tell your children, but also let them know that there are other people who think differently. This gives children the psychological "space" to come to their own answers and convictions.

Also, be prepared to help your children understand that the world around us at times responds to our problems awkwardly or with little empathy, and that this isn't their fault.

> *On the day our baby died, our older son, then nine years old, handed in an almost-blank piece of paper after a test saying, "I could only think about our baby." His teacher who, as we found out later, had repressed his own grief over the earlier death of his wife, couldn't bear this. He insisted on giving him an "F" for the test, although we explained what had happened.*

If anxieties and depression persist—if your child acts out or does poorly in school, if he is accident-prone, expresses self-destructive tendencies or even a wish to die, and you can't make headway by talking with him or supporting him in other ways, definitely seek professional help. Preferably seek a therapist experienced with children and young people. Be sure that he or she also has an understanding of grief processes!

I can ask myself:

☐ What outlets does my child have for processing what has happened?

☐ Has she found her own ways, or what suggestions can I give her?

☐ If there is more than one child, how do their needs differ?

☐ Is there enough opportunity for play and fun?

☐ What could I do with and for my child or children that would also be good for me?

☐ What are my views of death and life after death, and how do I want to answer my children's questions in this regard?

☐ Does my partner's view in this respect differ from mine, and how do we want to handle this with regard to our children?

☐ Has our child exhibited reactions that trouble us? If so, do we feel that professional help is called for?

Interacting with Others

The Grief of Grandparents

For grandparents, grandchildren signify the continuity of life and are a source of joy. Grandchildren offer the older generation a chance to make up for what they may have missed with their own children—whether caused by inexperience, lack of patience or lack of time.

When a baby dies, it is usually a great loss for the grandparents, too. They have the pain of seeing their daughter or son suffering without being able to help. The grandparents' grief is usually overlooked. Many still belong to a generation where they were taught to be strong and silent. Many have not learned to express their feelings or to seek solace and support.

> *My father came to the hospital just after we had decided to see our baby, who had died that morning. We asked if he would like to come along and he said yes, but probably out of a sense of duty toward me. I think he suffered terribly from the sight, because he rushed out of the room without a word. I had the feeling the loss affected him more directly than the rest of us.*

For other grandparents, it may be comforting to be allowed to "bond" with their precious little grandchild despite his death—to cradle him in their arms, perhaps to discover the resemblance to one or the other side of the family. This and perhaps photos taken with their grandchild in their arms might be a precious memory for them.

Sometimes grandparents, in their own need and helplessness, cannot find a helpful way of interacting with their children. When our own parents or other people important to us react to the death as if nothing had happened, or respond in other inappropriate or painful ways, we may perceive this as a double loss.

> *I called my father from the hospital and told him what had happened. His first reaction was, "I wasn't quite ready to become a grandfather anyhow."*

I can ask myself:

☐ Would the grandparents also like the chance to meet their grandchild? If it is too late, what can be done retroactively?

☐ How are our families reacting to our loss? What feelings might be behind their reactions?

☐ Do any of my parents' or in-laws' reactions to the loss now stand between us? If so, what can we do to help clear it up?

☐ With whom could I possibly talk about my hurt feelings?

Others around Us

Unless they have experienced a loss themselves, people around you may not know how to treat you after your loss. In their awkwardness, many of them will make inept, appeasing remarks that hurt more than they help. Others don't dare speak of the loss for fear it could cause you pain and make you cry. They don't want to add to your suffering.

> *After our baby died, every time we saw our neighbor, pregnant with her third child, she grabbed her two children and vanished into her house. I'm sure she was afraid I'd be hurt at the sight of her and her kids.*

People need clear signals and straightforward guidelines from you as to how you would like to be treated and what your needs are. This goes for grandparents, too.

> *I told them it was OK to talk about the death of our child, and that I would cry but the tears were good for me. I told them I needed to talk about what happened, and I didn't want anything in return except that they listen to me and perhaps, now and then, hold me in their arms.*

> ༺༂༺༂༺༂

> *I've cried out for help. I have said to people at work, "Please come for a cup of coffee with me." I've called friends around the country, and said, "Something bad has happened, and I want to tell you about it."*

Here are Susan's reflections and experiences regarding her relationship with her neighbors and friends after her loss.

> *During the sleepless nights I go over the comments and reactions again and again. I replay the scenes in my head, and I reread the cards and letters. I feel so grateful to each person who said something or cried with me, and I wonder how I could ever have hesitated to express my sympathy when others I know have suffered a loss. . . .*

The other side of the coin is that when people don't say anything, or assume that it's over and that we're "all better now," or tell us how "lucky" we are—that's like denying our anguish. Then there's a little piece of pain that does not get drawn out. With these people, I now feel that there is something unfinished, left dangling between us, and that unless we resolve it, our relationship will never be the same again. (Green 1992)

Even though we sometimes don't want to admit it to ourselves, *we are all part of a greater whole*. Our life is good to the extent that we allow ourselves to feel we are part of the greater whole, which involves participating, giving and taking. We don't need to be afraid to ask our friends or relatives for support and nurturing. Some time or another, we will have the opportunity to return what we have received to the community.

I can ask myself:

☐ How do I want to be treated by the people around me?

☐ Can I give clear signals to others about what I need exactly?

☐ Can I accept help from others graciously? If not, why not?

☐ Are there any people I have a grudge against because of how they reacted to me?

☐ If so, can I admit I'm disappointed and let them know what I need?

☐ Can I forgive them? If not, what do I need to be able to do so?

4

Grief Continues

Human beings are equipped to sustain a large amount of stress. We have the ability—after a period of intensive mourning—to heal on our own and then turn back to life in a new way. But getting there is hard work. Grief can take us to the limits of what we are capable of enduring, both emotionally and physically.

A Time of Disorientation and Transformation

The period around the half-year mark after the death of a loved one, and the months following, is the hardest for most. We have grasped the reality of the death on a deeper level, and we have lived through many raw feelings. Now we grope to create a new life out of the shambles of the old one. It is as if the person that we once were falls apart so that a new person can emerge.

Now you start to adapt slowly to a life without your baby. Most of us eventually manage to give our baby a place in our lives and hearts and yet also to let go. Sooner or later we let the love we felt for our baby flow into new relationships or tasks. We can best come out of the experience if we find meaning in it. Our values will have changed. The length of this phase depends on one's individual situation.

Grief Is a Personal Experience

Although our journey through grief follows a general pattern, each situation is unique and each person reacts differently.

> *I was plagued by the thought I couldn't have any more children. "I'll kill myself." "I'll jump out the window." I don't believe I really would have, but that expressed the despair I felt at the time.*

෯෯෯

> *I consoled myself that I was only 26 and that I had at least until age 35 to have a second child.*

෯෯෯

> *With each miscarriage, my faith increased that I would be able to cope with my fate. I thought, "Even if I cry tomorrow, I will have laughed a lot today, and nobody can take that away from me." After eight miscarriages and a stillbirth, I now have two wonderful children, and I live my life to the fullest, with great intensity and depth and an unending gratitude.*

A grief experience is determined by many factors: the meaning this pregnancy had for us, the depth of attachment, the circumstances of birth and death, possible previous losses and grief processes, and the length of time we waited for this pregnancy. Other factors include personality styles, the quality and form of our relationship with each other, patterns of communication, inner resources, personal philosophies and beliefs, levels of maturity and, most of all, whether or not we are supported by a social network. In addition, the motivation for having a child can affect our experience of grief.

> *Now I realize I wanted to have a baby because I couldn't stand my job any more. I wanted this child for self-centered motives—as compensation. That made me feel tremendously guilty when I miscarried.*

Our basic philosophy of life and death influences the experience. Those who believe that death is the absolute end have more difficulty losing a child than those who believe that the soul continues to exist, be it in the sense of Christian religions or Eastern philosophies. Those who believe in reincarnation, feeling that each soul has a task on this earth, seem to have the least trouble integrating the experience into their lives. Trudy (47), a physician, said:

> *When I had a miscarriage 20 years ago, I viewed life only from the intellectual side. I considered my miscarriage then as just a terrible accident*

*without meaning. My spiritual side was not well developed. I was left with
a tremendous feeling of emptiness. In retrospect, I regret my lack of
spirituality then because I couldn't process the experience for my own
growth.*

Grief is more intense when people think they might possibly have
prevented their child's death. Grief can also be more complicated
when a parent was ambivalent at the beginning of the pregnancy—
often the case. Anita (27), who lost her child in the fifth month of
pregnancy, shares her emotions one week after her stillbirth:

*My daughter told everyone that our baby didn't like it in my tummy.
During pregnancy I was often pretty nervous. Some days I felt pretty
worn out. We had just started building a house. Perhaps I took on too
much. I regretted that my husband was so busy with the house and that we
weren't able to enjoy this baby as intensively as our first child. If I knew I
really was to blame for her death, I'd never have another child . . . (crying)
I would always think that this child didn't want to stay, that it was my
fault, and then I wouldn't deserve to have another one."*

In those cases where a woman rejected the baby from the start, she
often feels guilty if she miscarries.

*This pregnancy didn't fit into my life at all. I had thought about abortion,
but didn't go ahead with it. . . . Then, when I had a miscarriage in the
11th week, I was overcome with guilt. Even though I felt great shame and
it was difficult, I started to talk about it with several people. I believe,
because I allowed myself to experience this guilt, I received something like
forgiveness. It's all right now.*

If a woman has had an abortion previously, a subsequent miscarriage
or stillbirth is often experienced as punishment. Repressed grief from
the first loss can magnify the new grief. Susan wrote:

*Over the years since that earlier abortion, I had suppressed my feelings and
memories so well, that I couldn't remember even what year it had been in.
Now . . . I had to face that pain and regret. I dug out old calendars and
reconstructed when that abortion had taken place. And I cried and cried
and cried for the sadness I hadn't fully faced at the time about that earlier
abortion and the sadness at waiting so long to have a third child.*

With losses that some may consider taboo, mourning is often
even more complicated (see page 11). If several aggravating factors

accompany the present loss, professional help to sort out your feelings may be in order. This is especially important if you are planning subsequent pregnancies. With the help of the questions in Appendix 2, you can think about your particular grief situation, including its personal and social factors. Depending on your individual situation, you will experience the following phenomena to varying degrees.

Thrown Out of Equilibrium

I felt as though I were in a deep hole. I had no energy left. I could sit for hours, stare into space and do absolutely nothing. I had no motivation. I couldn't imagine ever finding my way out of that hole again.

Myriam's story is typical. Lost in thought, you can find it hard to make decisions. It is hard to remember things or concentrate.

I drove through red lights. I saw them but they didn't register. I went from one room to another and forgot what I wanted there. In the mornings I'd come to work and see I'd left lights on all night.

In general, you'll have very little drive and endurance at this time. You may suffer from sleeplessness and a loss of appetite, or just the opposite, from an overpowering need for sleep and an uncontrollable appetite. You may be nervous and irritable. You may be in a depression-like state. You may feel insecure. It might help to remember that others under the same circumstances feel very much as you do.

Before our child's death, I had been a fussy housekeeper. For some time afterwards, I became the opposite—hanging around in my nightclothes all day and staring out the window. On the outside, I must have seemed paralyzed. But on the inside, I think, my entire life, my entire being was in the process of transforming itself into something totally new.

Perspective and good judgment may be compromised right now. Therefore, the first year of mourning is not a good time to make major decisions. It's not a good time to move, especially if you have other children. Big life changes would mean more new information and conditions would have to be assimilated on top of grief-related burdens.

Yes, overall I do feel better in any given week than I did the week before, but not necessarily on any given day. More to the point, I don't want to feel "all better now." It's not time yet. I'm grateful for the good days, but when the bad days come, they're necessary, too. If I had a pill that would make all the bad feelings go away, I wouldn't take it. That would be denying the importance of what has happened. I even resent it a little when friends say, "I'm glad you're looking cheerier today." Yes, I'm cheerier today, but tonight I may be up all night crying. Don't rush me! I also think, "If it makes you uncomfortable, tough—I'm the one who lost a baby, and I have a right to grieve!" (Hodge 1995)

Just when we feel the worst, friends and relatives often intimate that, by now, we must certainly have gotten over our grief. Not everyone is capable of trusting their feelings and standing behind their needs the way Susan was. Because society does not allow us much room and time for mourning, we may think we "aren't normal" or that we're "going crazy." Although actually we still need a great deal of support, many of us tend to isolate ourselves from others for fear that they might see we're not really "getting over it by now." Susan said:

Paradoxically, as I talk about how helpful the support has been, I've also come to realize how lonely grief is. . . . At the deepest level, no one can "share" this pain, not even my husband.

Grief can tax health. Resistance is lowered. We become predisposed to physical illness.

Six months have passed since Sarah's death. I've been sick a lot—a bad bronchitis, a fever over 104 degrees, followed by a drawn-out bout with chickenpox. This is totally unlike me—I used to get a little cold once in a while, but nothing like this . . .

I can ask myself:
☐ Which of the symptoms described above can I relate to?
☐ Can I give myself the time I need, even if it doesn't agree with what others feel is right?

Mourning: Prolonged Stress

A high-level adrenaline output increases the pulse rate, raises blood pressure and keeps muscle tension high. If our eating pattern becomes irregular during mourning, as it often will, our nutritional state suffers. Our metabolism can gradually go awry. Keeping a body running in high gear over time requires an immense amount of energy.

Prolonged stress—which can be generated by mourning—weakens the body's immune system (Bartrop 1977). Research has shown that, in a healthy person, the level of *lymphocytes*—cells responsible for our body's resistance to disease—range around 2000. In a grieving person, they were found to be 1100 after one week, 700 after four months, and even as low as 400 after seven to eight months. So it isn't surprising that, after a loss, some people are much more vulnerable to illness. It's not a bad idea to schedule a general medical examination between the fourth and sixth month after the loss.

Less serious conditions can also plague us: headaches, breathlessness or shallow breathing, pains in the neck, the feeling of a knot in our stomach or throat, pain around the heart, back pain, lack of sexual feelings, muscular weakness, dizziness, tremors, oversensitivity to noise, chronic colds and flu, chronic fatigue and sleep disturbances. *Doing something for your body, mind and spirit* (see page "What Can Help During This Time," starting on page 115, for ideas) *can help alleviate these ailments and, above all, make you more resistant to more serious health problems.* It's important now to nurture yourself. Treat yourself kindly.

I can ask myself:

☐ Through what physical symptoms does grief manifest itself in me?

Finding Deeper Answers

The state of grieving is a state of regression. Grief forces us, perhaps for the first time in our lives, to push everything else aside and dedicate ourselves to what goes on inside. We are led to deeper and deeper realizations about life and ourselves. Buried yearnings and needy feelings rise to the surface. Maybe you will become aware of how often you've treated yourself unkindly and uncaringly and decide that from now on you will treat yourself with more love and respect. Possibly you will become clearer about where you haven't lived up to your own potential, and where you owe more to your own life. Or you may view your interpersonal relationships with greater clarity and honesty.

You may gain the wisdom to know what behavior, thoughts and actions may have hampered nurturing relationships in the past and decide how you can contribute more love and harmony to them in the future. You may become aware of where amends are called for and decide to make them. Or, you may realize where you need to create healthy boundaries. You may have the power to make necessary changes.

Questions pertaining to the meaning of life may preoccupy you now. You reassess your beliefs and values and possibly come to new convictions and priorities. The question, "Why did my baby have to die?" will gradually take on a completely different quality and lead you to new and deeper spiritual dimensions. If you use the potential of this phase and consciously grant yourself time for this intense process, you'll come out of this terrible experience as a transformed, more mature, perhaps more spiritual person—closer to your true nature.

But this effort takes a lot of energy. It's no wonder you often don't have energy for other things. Because you are doing really hard work inside, don't demand too much of yourself on the outside, if possible. Practice listening more to and following your inner voice and not being so caught up in others' expectations. Listen inside, and then do what feels right *for you*. It is good enough if you are somehow able to cope with your daily life. If you need help, ask for it.

This process, even if you really give in to it, will not move quickly. The pain over what you have lost usually intensifies again around the first anniversary of the death. For some, this time is a turning point, after which they start feeling noticeably better. Others, depending on the situation, gradually start to feel better in the second year. For still others, especially when many aggravating factors come together (see page 233), the road can be long. Some need to seek professional help.

I can ask myself:

☐ Have I given myself adequate time to work through mourning?

☐ If not, how have I distracted myself from taking the proper time, and do I want to make time in the future?

☐ If yes, how have my values, convictions and priorities changed? What do I understand better about myself, my relationships, about life?

What Can Help during This Time

What helps? Crying a lot. Reading about pregnancy loss. Talking to people. Crying some more. Long walks. Playing the piano. More crying. When I say these things "help," I don't mean they cheer me up or help me forget. They just help, maybe by keeping me from exploding. (Hodge 1995)

Our bodies, emotions and thoughts are closely interwoven, and they all influence our spirits. When we make a beneficial change in one area, we also bring about healing in the others.

Being Attentive to Your Body

Your body is the home of your thoughts and emotions, and suffering manifests itself most concretely there. During mourning, it is especially important to nurture your physical self. Each of us in the course of our lives (hopefully) has discovered effective ways to renew ourselves. Our body actually knows what it needs. But at times we may feel cut off from ourselves and can't come up with the simplest ideas. We may be grateful for helpful suggestions. Some of the suggestions below can be amazingly effective if you give them your full attention. You might make a list of the ideas that appeal to you most. Put it on your mirror or the refrigerator to remind you and inspire you.

A Healthful Life Style

In our sorrow we often forget to care for ourselves adequately. But self-care is extremely important. *Keeping a steady rhythm going in as many areas of our lives as possible is very beneficial.*

ॐ *Sleep* has a healing effect. But the sleep patterns of bereaved persons are usually irregular. The more you try to fight so-called *sleep disturbances*, the more they are likely to appear. If you can welcome the "awake" times, you can use these nighttime hours. At that "in-between time" between waking and sleeping, we may be capable of deeper insights than we are with our daytime consciousness.

Try to maintain a balance between rest and activity. Don't eat a heavy meal before bedtime. Don't give your mind anything that is hard to digest, either, such as an upsetting TV movie. A glass of hot milk and honey with a sprinkle of nutmeg enhances sleep. Walk around the block before you go to bed, or take some fresh air by a window.

If you can't sleep, it's still a good idea to lie down. Whenever possible, lie down for at least 10 minutes mid-day as well. "Let yourself be carried." On page 120, you will find exercises that can enhance sleep or at least make your sleepless state more pleasant and peaceful. In many cases, these can preempt the need for medication. Use medication with great caution, because the regular use of sleeping pills hinders or stops the emotional healing process. Some medications are addictive besides. If you can't sleep by natural means but badly need a good night's rest now and then, see whether you can limit your intake of such medication. Don't use it more than two or three times a week.

ॐ *Smoking* robs us of important vitamins and has a negative effect on circulation.

&❧ We may tend to escape our situation and emotions by taking *tranquilizers* or ingesting *alcohol*. They may bring temporary relief, but the side effects *aren't* beneficial. It's easy to develop a chemical dependency that can turn into a real disease. Besides, tranquilizers and alcohol interrupt the grief process. When you stop taking them, you'll be at the same point emotionally that you were when you started.

I can ask myself:

☐ Do I need to change any of these elements in my life? If so, in which areas would I like to make changes?

☐ Can I do so on my own, or do I need help? If so, from whom?

Nutrition

It's easy to slip out of good eating habits when grieving. You may not feel hungry or have the energy to shop for or prepare food. But not eating properly can cause nutritional imbalances that aggravate already-vulnerable health. A balanced, wholesome diet of fresh, unrefined and unprocessed food products—rich in vitamins and minerals and as close to their natural state as possible—is especially important to your health now. In particular, pay attention to getting enough C and B vitamins. At times of great stress like this, your vitamin C requirements are higher than normal, and B vitamins will help steady your nerves. Also, follow a regular mealtime routine. Ask your doctor for sensible nutritional guidelines to follow or check out what's available at your local library.

It can be hard to have the strength or motivation to shop and cook while grieving. It would be wonderful if a tradition developed in which those visiting bereaved parents, even after the early periods of mourning, bring along a nourishing meal—a casserole made with fresh vegetables, a nice salad or at least some fresh fruit. If you feel you can't manage cooking or shopping, feel free to ask specifically for what you need help with. Friends and relatives usually are glad to know exactly what they can do for you. It helps them overcome their own feelings of helplessness. If you know your diet is completely out of balance, you may want to consult a nutritionist.

People in mourning also tend to forget to take in enough liquids. Drink at least eight large glasses of liquid a day (such as water, juice, milk, herbal teas). To help you remember, you may want to prepare the day's ration each morning. Drinking coffee and black tea is not advisable because they contain a lot of caffeine (coffee contains more than tea) and are not good for your body—not even to help remedy your lethargy! After drinking coffee, your energy level drops sharply. Also, coffee inhibits the absorption of vitamin C.

I can ask myself:

☐ Do I manage to eat a fairly balanced, wholesome diet? What do I need more or less of?

☐ In which ways could my diet be more healthful?

☐ Do I have the energy to look after myself and my family in this respect? If not, who could help us?

☐ Do I drink enough fluids, and are they the kind that won't add stress to my system? What would I like to cut down on? What would I like to cut out?

Movement and Exercise

Physical movement restores a healthy breathing pattern and also helps restore "inner balance." Movement distributes more oxygen throughout the body; it stimulates heart activity and helps get rid of depression. In addition, under certain conditions, *endorphins*, hormone-like substances, are released that counteract depression and create a sense of well-being. Through lively exercise it's easier to attain the opposite—stillness and rest.

🐾 *Stretching* is the simplest exercise and very useful. At times throughout the day, gently and naturally stretch and extend yourself, as a cat would. As you stretch, become aware of how movement enables your breath to flow in all by itself, and as you let go of the extension, your breath flows out. After allowing a natural, short pause, let your body spontaneously lead you to the next extension.

What other parts of your body can you stretch besides your extremities? Your joints—hands, elbows, shoulder joints, your jaw joint and ankle joints—often need special attention. The back, shoulders and neck are usually especially needy in anxious and grieving persons. Stretching parts of your face and even widening the inside of your mouth might feel good.

Be careful not to overextend yourself, because that causes parts of your body to become hard and rigid, which is counterproductive. After stretching, allow yourself a moment to "harvest" what you gained through stretching. Pay attention to breathing changes and how you may feel "wider" (less constricted) and more alive in some places. Is your body telling you to pay attention to other areas? If so, follow these instincts. Don't suppress a yawn. Allow it to rise from your abdomen and let your mouth open wide. Yawning is a natural way to release tension and feels good.

ঈ *Bicycling, hiking, walking, jogging, playing tennis, swimming, gardening*— all provide exercise and at the same time take you outdoors, which in itself has healing powers. Rhythmic activities are particularly good.

ঈ It can be hard to find your "get up and go" at first. You might line up friends who would like to exercise with you. Or you might overcome your inertia through a *visualization exercise.* Sit in a relaxed posture and visualize yourself in detail performing whatever exercise you have chosen. (What do you look like? Where are you? What are your surroundings like? Feel the movement of your muscles, be aware of your breathing, feel your heartbeat, notice what your body feels like. Feel the wind or the water. Be aware of your contact with the ground, the bicycle or exercise method you've chosen. Try to perceive with all your senses.) Simply imagining the movement sends impulses from your brain that cause physiological changes in your body. If you continue to do these pre-exercises several times a week, you will prepare your body for the actual motion and facilitate your getting started with regular exercise.

ঈ *Walking* helps you focus and feel grounded. Be conscious of your feet touching the ground, and of how walking changes your breath.

ঈ *Bouncing* on the balls of your feet stimulates your circulation and feels good. Stand with your feet about a foot apart, relax your knees and let the weight of your body shift forward a little. Gently and rhythmically bounce up and down on the balls of your feet, with your heels lifting off the floor while the balls of the feet remain on the ground. (Important: If you get cramps in your calves, be sure your heels return to the floor after each bounce.) Shift your weight from one side to the other as you bounce rhythmically. Be aware of your joints. Try to let go of tensions in your ankles, your knees, your hip joints, your spine, your shoulders, your neck. Make large and lively or slow and meditative movements, depending on your mood. When you stop, pay attention to how you feel: *Do I feel lighter? Have I shaken off something that was bothering me? How is my breath now?*

ঈ *Free-form dancing*—moving your body (perhaps with your eyes closed) to meditative music or other music you like—feels good. In dance you can express pain and suffering, anger, rage, despair, fears—but also power, yearning, love . . .

> *I danced out my feelings until I was dripping wet. I thought, what I sweat out now, I won't have to cry out later.*

I can ask myself:

☐ What exercise and activity has made me feel better in the past? What would work in my present situation?

☐ Which exercises or activities do I want to try? Which outdoor activities?

☐ What rhythmic activity comes to my mind that I like?

☐ If I'm not motivated to exercise right now, can I resolve to visualize myself exercising to help motivate me?

☐ Can I think of a friend who would enjoy exercising with me?

Relaxation, Calm, Help with Sleep

The following suggestions are helpful if you have trouble falling asleep.

❧ Don't hesitate to sit quietly whenever you need to. You might rest in a hammock on a deck, in a comfy chair in your den, or in a rocking chair inside or on a porch. Or, rock yourself gently and rhythmically while lying in bed or on the floor. (Some massages include this rhythmic rocking motion.) If you can't relax, try more vigorous movement first (see above). That will help you work out the kinks so you can rest more easily.

> *I put up a hammock in the room we built in the attic, and I spent many productive hours there staring at the ceiling, rocking myself, thinking about my life. It was the most nurturing thing I did for myself.*

❧ The exercise "Letting Yourself Be Carried," (see page 32) can help you feel secure and calm so you can fall asleep more easily.

❧ Water, the maternal element connected with emotions, can also help you let go. You can let water "carry" you by enjoying a candle-lit bath with essential oils (see page 133) and soothing music. A hot shower can give you the feeling that, for a moment, your sorrows and burdens have been washed away. An alternating warm-cold shower (hot-cold, hot-cold), a traditional European remedy, can relax and invigorate you simultaneously. This works even better with a hand-held massage shower head. Start at the point on your body farthest from your heart and work upwards.

❧ Another water remedy (hydrotherapy) for tension is a foot bath. Fill a small tub with lukewarm water, spiced with essential oils if you prefer, and put your feet in it. Bring up the temperature to about 105F by gradually adding more water. Soak your feet for 10 minutes or as long as it feels comfortable. You can also purchase professional foot spas with massage features. A foot bath can help your whole body relax and feel better. This too is a wonderful remedy for insomnia.

❧ After a footbath, you may want to massage your feet. Place one leg on top of the thigh of the other and then massage that foot tenderly and attentively with your hands, being very focused on what you are doing—kneading, stroking, patting, caressing or just calmly leaving your hand in one place. When you finish, wrap your ankle with both hands, the center of one hand located on the ankle, the thumbs alongside each other. Enjoy how it feels for a moment. Then put your foot back on the floor. Ask yourself: How do my feet feel now? Do I feel more secure? More "grounded" and literally in touch with the floor? Have my emotions changed? Do I feel more in balance?

❧ This exercise can help you sleep also. It involves your feet and hands. Lying on your back, legs uncrossed, flex one foot so your toes point as much as possible in the direction of your head. Keeping the foot in this position, move it several times to the left and the right . . . left . . . right . . . each time coming as close as feasible to the bed or the floor—as if you were slowly waving sideways with your foot. Relax and feel the effect before you repeat the "sideways waving." After enjoying this feeling for a bit, proceed with the other foot.

Now continue with a hand. With your arm extended along your body, the base of the hand (which stays close to the bed or floor) stretches in the direction of the foot while the rest of the hand, with your fingers extended, flexes at the wrist and exerts a gentle backward pull toward the arm. Making sure that the base of the hand stays down, move the hand left and right several times, again as if waving sideways. Then relax and feel the effects. Repeat before you proceed to the other hand. Sometimes I can't finish this exercise because I fall asleep while I'm doing it!

❧ During intense mourning you may become focused on your anguish to the exclusion of everything else. It can be healing to go into your yard and simply *look* at what you find there, however briefly. To explore a flower, a twig, a blade of grass, or watch a butterfly, bug or an ant with total concentration can help you become more "open-minded" and placid inside.Try to use all your senses. Visit a wilderness area or park where you can see the horizon and contemplate that for awhile. If you can't do that, you may want to contemplate a photo of a beautiful vista or a nature scene, an appealing painting or a house plant, noticing every tiny detail.

❧ Listening to a cassette of birdsong or other sounds of nature, maybe with earphones, can put you in another place entirely and take your mind off your sorrow for a while.

❧ In chapter 2 (page 30) I described "sounding tones." This powerful activity is deceptively simple, but you may only realize how helpful it is after practicing consistently for several weeks. It can change you in a deep way. However, it only works if you enter into it fully, with your eyes closed. Do not willfully control your breath but let it happen in its own way. The sounds "oo," "mm," and "oh" can help you fall asleep or calm yourself.

❧ Singing can lift and lighten your spirit, calm and enliven you all at once. Singing repetitive, simple little melodies and rounds, over and over again, such as *Dona Nobis Pacem* (Give us peace) or *Kumbaya* can be especially comforting. You might find comfort in a gospel or spiritual song. Singing in a circle with other people can be particularly uplifting. You might make up your own words for known melodies.

As I was lying there unable to cry or feel anything, all of a sudden the song "I am sailing" came to mind. I began to sing this song to myself, but with new words that just came to me. "I am sorrowed, I am sorrowed because my baby now is dead, I am sorrowed, I am sorrowed, and my body feels like lead." Tears began streaming down my face. One verse after the other spilled out. "I am crying . . . I am angry . . . I am praying" . . . on and on. I must have sung for half an hour. Meanwhile my husband came into the bedroom, held me quietly, and understood on a much deeper level how I felt. The energy in me changed. When I finally came to a stop, I felt a deep peace. My song—totally unplanned—most words of which I don't even remember, had been my individual way through mourning, and it took me miles ahead on the road to peace.

❧ Numerous scientific studies (for example, those of cardiologist Herbert Benson of Deaconess Hospital in Boston) have confirmed the far-reaching positive physiological effects created through a state of meditation, as well as through relaxation exercises.

I can ask myself:

☐ Which of the suggestions above appeal to me?

☐ Can I rest or am I too restless to relax? Do I need to exercise vigorously first?

Grief Continues   123

Healing Warmth

Grief and pain constrict the body. Warmth helps relax an aching, tense body.

ह➥ Take one or, better yet, two hot water bottles to bed and rotate them among the different painful or heavy-feeling parts of your body.

ह➥ Traditional European folk medicine suggests using a "potato pack." Boil potatoes in their skin until cooked, flatten them slightly, and tuck them into a few layers of a dishtowel. Place the pack on any part of your body that hurts. A natural ingredient in the potato also makes this pack useful for relieving some inflammations.

ह➥ If the weather is warm, let the sun warm and energize your body (but avoid overexposure).

ह➥ How about a visit to a pool or a sauna with a hot spa or a Jacuzzi® whirlpool bath? Let the water support your body.

I can ask myself:

☐ Do I believe warmth could be helpful? Which of the above would I like to try?

Holistic Treatments and Massage

Holistic treatments are based on the idea that "preventing is better than curing." Curing illness can be hard on the body—certainly harder than keeping the body well in the first place. Some preventive health-care measures may be covered by some health plans.

ह➥ *Physical therapies* (for example, therapeutic massage, rhythmic massage, hot packs) can restore your sense of emotional equilibrium. If you have a holistically oriented family doctor or osteopathic doctor, he or she may be able to treat you or refer you. A chiropractor may also help you feel better.

ह➥ There are many forms of *holistic body therapies or practices* aimed at helping the entire body system to work in a harmonized way. You will certainly find some form offered in your area, including but not limited to: Shiatsu, Reiki, Feldenkrais, polarity massage, acupuncture, Middendorf Breathwork, Trager bodywork, CORE massage, Rolfing, yoga, foot reflexology, dance therapy and movement therapy. An example of how holistic body therapy works, featuring Middendorf Breathwork, is given on page 131.

ðŸ•¯ Outside help doesn't always have to be professional. A reciprocal *intuitive partner massage* enables you and your partner to touch each other in a loving and healing way. This activity can help you bridge gaps caused by disorientation, confusion and speechlessness surrounding the loss. Maybe a friend can give you a massage. Many excellent massage books are available.

ðŸ•¯ It's nice for someone, perhaps on an exchange basis, to lightly tap your back with the palms of the hands or with their fists (relax at the wrists—snap them just before your hands make contact with the back). You don't need to remove any clothing. Have the other partner begin more vigorously at the sacrum (low on the back), be more gentle in the kidney area, and then stronger again in the region of the upper back. Using the fingertips works too: Again, with relaxed wrists, lightly and rhythmically tap the back (moving from the lower to the upper back), as if light raindrops were falling on it. In finishing, the "giving" partner can gently and sensitively place one hand on the sacrum and the other hand between the shoulder blades, or place both hands (lightly!) on the top of the shoulders or the shoulder blades. Ask yourself: How does my back feel now? How is my breathing?

I can ask myself:

☐ Would I like a holistic body treatment? What is available locally?

☐ If I don't know what is available, where could I get information?

☐ Would I like to receive or exchange a massage with my mate? Or can I think of a friend who would be glad to help me with a massage?

Pay Attention to Emotions

Emotions still come and go in waves. Grief usually peaks on special dates, such as an expected due date, holidays, family gatherings or anniversaries. Overall, emotions may not be quite as overwhelming now as they were in the beginning. I like to think of this process as moving upward in a slowly spiraling fashion. Emotions, thoughts and themes preoccupy us for a while, and we work with them the best we can. Gradually, they recede to the back of the spiral—out of our awareness—but we continue to work on them unconsciously. Issues we haven't resolved come to the foreground of our spiral again, but on a different plane. Refer to chapter 3 for help in working with recurring emotions.

I can ask myself:

☐ What emotions have I experienced since the loss?

☐ Have unresolved issues of the past reappeared? If so, what are they? How do I want to deal with them?

☐ Are there any special dates that trigger my grief?

☐ Which emotions, themes and thoughts are at the "foreground of my spiral" right now?

☐ In what order do I want to deal with them?

☐ What resources do I have now to work through what is happening inside of me?

☐ If I seek therapy, what are my goals?

Telling Your Story

It's still important in this phase to talk about what happened, to tell people your story. Dr. Glen Davidson writes in his excellent book, *Understanding Mourning* (1984):

> . . . *Telling your story will be the most important thing for you to do as a mourner, because in the very act of telling it you are putting your life back together. By telling your story you will discover that your facts change, not because the facts themselves are changed but because your choice of what is important changes. You may discover that your initial impressions of what happened were incomplete or even inaccurate. The more unexpected the death, the more likely it is that initial impressions were wrong.*
>
> . . . *As you first tell your story, you will probably not be able to provide an ending. Some people try. They say things like, "This is God's will" or "It was meant to be." More unfortunate are those mourners who, in trying to tell their story, are given endings by other people. . . .*
>
> . . . *You will need to tell your story of loss and change again and again in order to get your facts straight, clarify how you are part of the facts, discover how your life has been changed by those facts, and finally determine how you fit into the arrangement of the universe. . . . Without telling our story again and again to others, we find it nearly impossible to recover a sense of order.* (pages 13-15)

It's true that you also need time for yourself, but grief is harder to process in isolation. Handling it on your own can make you lonely. Now, more than ever, you need others who will listen to your story.

I can ask myself:

☐ How has my story changed since I started telling it?

☐ Who is still willing to listen to my story?

The Power of Internal Images

Earlier, I mentioned the power visualizations can have on our feelings and on our body. Just as we create our world to an extent by how we think of it, we do the same when we visualize it. (You can find several books on this topic, such as *Creative Visualizations*, by Shakti Gawain). To get in touch with your inner images, relax through one of the ways described earlier and focus on your breathing. You may want to prepare by stroking your forehead (moving your fingers from the center of your forehead to the temples).

❧ Visualize yourself as *a person possessing qualities that would be useful to you* in this situation (as suggested by Judy Tatelbaum in *The Courage to Grieve*, 1980). First try to remember which qualities you have found helpful to you or others in difficult situations in the past:

- ☞ acceptance (being able to say *yes* to the death and integrate it in your life)
- ☞ patience (with yourself, allowing yourself the time you need)
- ☞ resilience (the capacity to renew yourself)
- ☞ an inner light (having a higher dimension shine through you)
- ☞ confidence (that you will be OK in the end)
- ☞ humor (to help restore yourself)
- ☞ trust (feeling that you are safe even in the storms of life)
- ☞ serenity
- ☞ surrender
- ☞ or: _____

❧ Visualize yourself having these strengths and qualities:

- ☞ Each day, preferably at the same time, spend time at your special place if you have created one (see page 237), or sit in a quiet spot.
- ☞ Relax, allow your breath to flow naturally and be receptive to new images that may appear.

☞ Recall scenes from your life where you or someone else had these qualities.

☞ Visualize yourself or that person in such a situation. Observe as closely as possible. What is the facial expression? The posture? The look in the eyes? The way of walking? Revive or reinforce these qualities in yourself. If you only know these qualities in someone else, visualize yourself in every detail embodying this person's qualities, as if you possessed them. Those who have practiced this exercise regularly have grown in strength and developed great survival and coping skills.

❧ *See yourself as healed and full of new energy.* "Look" intimately at yourself. Be aware of the look in your eyes, the expression of your mouth, the gloss of your hair, the color of your skin, your posture. What does your breath tell you about yourself? How do you move when you walk? What feeling do you radiate? How do you interact with others?

❧ *View nature as a model.* Visualize and follow the changes in a tree over the seasons of the year. Observe how spring follows winter—how buds appear, bit by bit, and the tree, which once appeared barren, eventually stands again in full bloom.

❧ *View nature as a healer.* Let calming, healing images appear before your mind's eye. These places may be familiar or imaginary. Perceive with all your senses:

☞ a sandy beach (look at the tiny grains of sand; let the fine, white sand trickle between your fingers; feel its warmth)

☞ the ocean (look at the horizon; smell the salty air; listen to the roar of the surf; watch the waves coming and going)

☞ a forest (look at the individual trees, see details of the bark, examine a leaf, see the branches swaying in the wind, look at the mossy or grassy ground; what else do you see? what does it smell like?)

☞ a meadow filled with wildflowers

☞ a mountain lake

☞ the desert

☞ the star-lit sky, the universe

☞ or: _____

❧ *Climb a mountain.* Imagine yourself hiking up a mountain. Follow the winding path step by step, feeling the ground under your feet, being aware of your surrounding in great detail, smelling the air, feeling the wind, the sun. Become aware of how your steps take on a certain rhythm with time, and become aware of your breathing. When you reach the top, look at the scenery, the panorama, your closeness to the sky. Be aware of how you feel. Savor the feeling before you start down from the mountain again, refreshed and rejuvenated.

I can ask myself:

☐ Which of these visualizations do I want to try? Or does something else come to mind?

☐ What previously described centering exercise could I use to improve my visualization ability?

Creativity Enhances Healing

☙ *Getting absorbed in some creative act or leisure activity* can order your thoughts, and, for a short time, help you forget your anguish.

In the previous two chapters I have indicated that drawing or painting is a way to process what has happened. You need absolutely no talent or previous experience with art to get a lot of good from this exercise. All you need is (preferably) a large pad of paper and a supply of colors (such as pastels, crayons or a large set of chalks). Having a special place to go is helpful. Place a hand over your heart and allow a theme to come to you; for instance: "My journey through grief— where am I now?" "healing," "letting go," "finding meaning," "being stuck," or "new life" and decide to draw a series of 7 to 10 pictures over time.

☙ Other creative expressions include *playing a musical instrument, composing songs, singing, drawing, silk-painting, photography, sewing, weaving, knitting, crocheting, embroidering, macramé* and *jewelry-making.*

☙ Many bereaved express their feelings in *poetry, prose* or *fairy tales,* which they write to or about their child who has died.

☙ *Making a memorial quilt* for your baby can be meaningful and healing.

I can ask myself.

☐ What creative activities have I liked to do in the past?

☐ What do I feel drawn to now?

☐ What topics and questions would I like to approach through drawing?

The Power of Spirituality

A deep faith can brace and console us in difficult times. But after the death of a child, some people despair of a God who has afflicted them with so much sorrow.

> *God can get lost! I've always tried to be a good person. I've never harmed anyone. If God exists, then why has He taken away something so beautiful and destroyed all my happiness?*

Some people become alienated and bitter. But for many, it is precisely by allowing themselves to express and feel this harsh "no" that they eventually come to a deeply felt, unambivalent "yes"—much clearer and stronger than ever before. Still others, through the caring love and deep dedication of people around them, profoundly experience God's love and a feeling of being supported and carried in the storms of life.

> *The sentence, "All is His—nature and grace" rings in my ears. Yes, I have experienced both—the cruelty of nature and then again so much grace through the love of so many dear people.*

Others may develop a yearning for a higher spiritual dimension and for finding a way "home," with the deep peace this can bring. They set out on a spiritual journey. In their search, they find new insights and inspirations. Doors open that had been closed.

> *Every evening I would lie down on my bed and think about my child. I felt her presence. A joy beyond description would fill my heart. I realized I had just found what I had been searching for, for ages . . .*

So often it takes nothing less than a terribly tragic event to connect us to a Power greater than ourselves. *In the end, genuine healing always means growing spiritually.* We can enhance ourselves on this path.

- One way is through *meditation*, which can bring deep inner peace and serenity. Through meditation we can also listen for answers and spiritual guidance. See Appendix 3 for ideas.

- In their despair, many people discover the *power of prayer* to heal and transform, even those for whom this door may have been closed for years. If this appeals to you, let the prayers rise from the depth of your heart. Some prayers are listed in Appendix 3. Strength and inspiration can also be derived from the prayers in the monthly published booklet, *Daily Word* (see page 254).

❧ You can be consoled by the Psalms; for example, 6, 23; 25:6-7, 17-18, 20-21; 30:11-12; 34:4, 7-18;   37; 61: 1-4; 116; 121; 126; 130; 132:16; 139: 1-18, 23-24. The readings in Appendix 3 can bring peace and comfort.

❧ If you are a member of a church congregation or a religious or spiritual community, your pastor, priest, rabbi or spiritual leader can give help and support.

❧ Accepting forgiveness and forgiving others are keystones of spiritual growth (see bibliography).

❧ If you are not religiously oriented, but are interested in developing spiritually, try some of the following suggestions:

☞ The exercise "Let yourself be carried" (see page 32) can help prepare you to surrender yourself to a higher power.

☞ Holistic and transpersonal therapies and practices essentially contain the potential for spiritual healing.

❧ If you are familiar with the basic 12-step program, you could use a modification of the steps (which have been applied to living in all kinds of ways) for dealing with your loss. Just replace the first step with "I am powerless over the loss/disability/illness of my child." Some of the mottoes, such as "Let go and let God," "One day at a time," and the serenity prayer (below) can be helpful. The 12-step program is a program for growing spiritually.

> God grant me the serenity to accept the things I cannot change,
> The power to change the things I can,
> And the wisdom to know the difference.

❧ You may want to record the following exercise, called "Encounter with the Wise One," on a cassette, to play when you are ready to try it.

Go to your "special place" or get settled comfortably at some tranquil spot. Close your eyes.

Follow the flow of your breath—in, out, pause . . . in, out, pause . . . With every breath go deeper to a "quiet place" within yourself.

In your mind's eye, visualize a candle. At first the flame flickers a bit, then it becomes more intense. Watch the flame as it grows brighter and brighter. Inside the large bright flame, a tiny flame emerges. Look deeper and deeper into the flame until you see only blue light. In the heart of the flame, a figure emerges. Look into his or her face. You just know it is a very wise person. Perhaps it is someone who really exists who you are familiar with, or perhaps you have never seen this person before. Look into her or his eyes. In them are total love, compassion, kindness and wisdom—and that person is now here *just for you!*

Now, ask the Wise One for help with your life and pose all the questions you are burning to ask. Then listen. Be totally open for receiving answers in whatever form they may appear. Perhaps the Wise One has a message for you. Tell her or him that you are ready to hear that special message. Listen . . .

Now look at issues in your life that still cause you concern—perhaps feelings of guilt, not knowing what to do with anger, relationship problems, questions pertaining to life and death . . . the Wise One understands.

Maybe there are decisions that you must make. Ask the Wise One for guidance, and again, listen. . . .Thank the Wise One for being there just for you with all that wisdom, love and kindness. Say good-bye and know that you can call on him or her at any time . . . because he or she is part of you!

ই You may want to write down or make a drawing of what you have just experienced.

I can ask myself:

☐ What are my feelings about God?

☐ Do I also allow negative feelings if they exist?

☐ In what ways may I have worked through my feelings since the loss of our child?

☐ How do I feel about spirituality?

☐ What religious or spiritual leader do I want to turn to? Who could be a guide and companion for me on my spiritual path?

☐ What prayer, psalm, meditation, ritual, song, quotation or exercise might be helpful?

☐ What spiritual qualities do I wish to develop in myself?

Healing Yourself the Natural Way

Holistic therapies aren't just for curing symptoms—they take into consideration the interactions of body, mind, emotions and spirit. To give an example of how a therapy can heal holistically, I will review in more detail the holistic-therapy form I know best: Middendorf Breathwork® (named after its founder, Ilse Middendorf, who, at 87, is still capable of a greater-than-average work load!). Many of the exercises I have described are based on this work. Middendorf Breathwork is not about breathing techniques. Breath is freed *indirectly* and gently through movement (such as stretching), pressure points or touch. The goal is to experience one's individual, natural breath movement as it comes and goes on its own (not as a result of "taking a deep breath"). The premise of Middendorf Breathwork is that our natural breathing pattern has a deep, self-healing power. A natural pause between breaths brings regeneration. Many other holistic therapies also affect the breath, whether they say so or not.

Breathing is more than a chemical exchange of oxygen and carbon dioxide in our lungs—it is a life-giving force. Breathing is movement. Muscle chains throughout the body distribute this breath movement to every part of us. Breath affects every organ, heart and lung functions, pH balance and overall metabolism—balancing and harmonizing all our body systems. The breath center in our brain is directly connected to the *hypothalamus*, the part of our brain concerned with maintaining basic functions and regulating muscle tone. It is also connected with the regions that regulate hormones, emotions, thought processes and consciousness. This is why breath affects us in all aspects of our being. In Hebrew, the word for breath, "ruach," also means "spirit."

The movement of breath is usually restricted in the bereaved. Breathing is irregular and shallow. The bereaved can feel cut off from breath's life-giving force. With breathwork therapy, you become sensitive to your grieving body. Breath opens you up. Tensions and the feeling of constriction give way to a feeling of "spaciousness." Posture and circulation improve. Thinking becomes less clouded. You feel lighter in body, mind and spirit. Bit by bit, depression lifts.

I can ask myself:

☐ In which ways have I become aware of the interaction of body, mind and spirit?

☐ What holistic therapies do I know are offered locally?

☐ If I'm not familiar with any, who could give me information? How can I find a trustworthy therapist (see also Appendix 4)?

☐ Would I prefer an individual treatment or working in a group?

Natural Remedies

Interest in natural remedies and natural medicine is increasing. Nature offers many remedies derived from plants in various forms. They can help while having no or relatively few side effects, if used as directed by the manufacturer. Of course, too much of anything isn't a good idea. And if you are already taking medications, you need to be cautious about adding natural remedies to the mix. Consult your healthcare professional first. Remember, herbs are drugs in a diluted form. Use them responsibly. Also, don't use herbal preparations if you are pregnant again or nursing. Don't give them to babies or young children.

Aromatherapy

Aromatherapy is a natural therapy, using *pure essential oils* from flowers, fruits and other parts of plants to enhance physical, emotional and mental well-being. In Europe, aromatherapy is routinely applied with great success in the obstetrical wards of many hospitals. Training courses in the differentiated use of aromatherapy are now in great demand by midwives and doctors alike.

- The most common use is applying essential oils for *scenting a room* or as an *inhalant*. Add 5 to 10 drops of essential oils to water and let it evaporate in a scent lamp, diffuser or ionizer.

- Add essential oils to a *full-, foot- or hand bath*. Mix 10 to 15 drops of essence with 3 to 4 teaspoons of honey or dairy cream as emollients in a bottle and shake well. Or you can add 10 to 15 drops of oil to 4 or 5 tablespoons of unscented liquid soap.

- To prepare a *massage oil*, dilute essential oils first in a carrier oil, such as sweet almond oil, hazelnut oil, aloe oil, jojoba oil, grapeseed oil or other "cold-pressed" oils. Add 15 to 25 essential oil drops to 4 ounces of a carrier oil.

Here is a list of scents that may be most useful to bereaved parents:

For shock and fear	neroli, mimosa, cedar
During labor	verbena, lemon, jasmine
Contact with the baby	mandarin, vanilla
Help for letting go	clary sage, verbena, lavender
Dealing with feelings	rose, geranium, cypress, cedar
Enhancing a feeling of coziness and safety	mimosa, gorse, cacao, benzoin, tonka bean
Affects mood in a positive, uplifting way	sandalwood, jasmine, vanilla, rose geranium, narcissus, clementine, mandarin, may rose, coriander
Aids meditation	frankincense, hyssop, iris, cedar
Enhances mental clarity	frankincense, juniper, hyssop
Stops spinning thoughts	marjoram
Helps restore erotic feelings	jasmine, ylang-ylang, sandalwood
Promotes sleep	rose, geranium, balm, cedar, lavender

Use the oils individually unless you know how to make compatible combinations. You can prepare a relaxing massage oil by adding 16 drops of geranium oil, 8 drops of marjoram oil and 8 drops of lavender oil to 4 ounces of almond oil. More information on massages using essential oils can be found in the book *Scentual Touch* by Judith Jackson.

If you are pregnant, of the oils mentioned above, **avoid** juniper berry, marjoram, verbena, sage and hyssop essential oils. **Also avoid** anise, cist rose, camphor, myrrh, clove, oregano, parsley, rosemary, sade, safrole, sage, thyme, cinnamon-rind oils and a few others. They are **contraindicated** then. Consult your healthcare professional. An excellent resource book is *Complete Aromatherapy Handbook—Essential Oils for Radiant Health,* by Susanne Fischer-Rizzi (1990).

Flower Essences

The Bach Flower Remedies

English bacteriologist Dr. Edward Bach, born in 1886, discovered a connection between certain illnesses and certain personality styles. After working first with vaccine therapy and later with homeopathic principles, he developed flower remedies that could help harmonize the emotional imbalances that he believed led to disease. He divided these into seven major areas: (1) fear, (2) uncertainty, (3) lack of interest in present circumstances, (4) loneliness, (5) oversensitivity to influences and ideas, (6) despondency and despair, and (7) overdeveloped concern for others' welfare (which today we may call "co-dependency"). Dr. Bach saw illness from a more spiritual vantage point than other scientists. He came to believe that illness was a message from our inner being calling us to change how we live and our mental outlook. In 1930, he gave up a lucrative practice in London to dedicate his life to working with the plants now known as the 38 Bach Flower Remedies. They are similar to classic homeopathy, but unlike homeopathy, can easily be applied by lay people, too. The flower essences work subtly to affect our sense of well-being. Detailed, practical information for do-it-yourself application is offered in Mechthild Scheffer's book, *Bach Flower Therapy,* and other books.

The best known of the Bach Flower Essences is Rescue Remedy (No. 39), a combination of five flowers to be used following trauma, shock, accident or severe upset. I believe this very effective remedy belongs in every home medicine cabinet or purse. In an emergency you can apply undiluted Rescue drops—which you can order by mail (see page 255)—directly from the stock bottle onto tongue, lips, temples, wrists or creases of the elbows. In general, the method is to add 4 drops of concentrate from the "stock bottle" to a glass of water. Sip this mixture until the symptoms subside and repeat at 15, 30, and 60 minutes thereafter. You can also add Rescue or selected other essences (about 5 drops each of single flowers, 10 with Rescue) to bath water.

The usual way to use Bach Flower Remedies is to add 3 drops each of up to seven (sometimes more, but fewer is better) chosen flowers from their stock bottles into a 30ml dropper bottle. Fill the dropper bottle with distilled water and a bit of alcohol or vinegar (if you can't tolerate alcohol) as a preservative. Four times a day, put 4 drops of the mixture on your tongue. This therapy can be used in combination with any other therapy or medication. Unlike homeopathic medicine, taken as directed on the bottles, you can't go wrong. If you haven't chosen the appropriate flower, it won't help you, but it won't harm you, either.

Bach Flower Therapy can help reestablish your equilibrium after a loss and support the healing process in the time to follow. It's possible to familiarize yourself with this therapeutic method through books. However, especially when thinking and perception aren't as keen as usual, it might be wise to consult an experienced therapist (such as an osteopathic doctor). To find addresses of therapists, contact Nelson Bach USA (see page 255). The following may be helpful after a loss (these simplistic descriptions aren't meant to replace detailed information on the flowers that is available elsewhere):

Agrimony	when you override your feelings and act as if you feel great
Aspen	when you have vague, unknown fears
Cherry Plum	when you're afraid you're losing your mind; chaos, darkness
Chestnut Bud	when you don't learn from your mistakes
Clematis	to clear your thoughts
Elm	for otherwise strong persons who don't feel up to a given situation
Gentian	when you're depressed following a loss; pessimism
Gorse	when you feel deep despair, hopelessness
Honeysuckle	when you're stuck in the past, not making progress
Impatiens	when one partner has no patience for the other, or you have no patience with yourself
Olive	when you are completely exhausted in body, mind and spirit

Pine | when you feel plagued by guilt and self-reproach
Star of Bethlehem | for trauma and great sorrow
Sweet Chestnut | when you feel deep despair, are having a spiritual crisis
Walnut | for transition periods of life; readjusting to life without a baby
Water Violet | when you are proud and reserved and can "do it alone"
White Chestnut | when your head and thoughts are spinning, sleeplessness
Wild Oat | for finding your direction or path in life
Willow | when you are bitter and resentful

The California Research Essences

Since 1978, further studies have been conducted in California on flower essences, and 72 flowers were identified there, creating an even greater possible number of therapeutic mixtures. The mixture and application of these essences are the same as described for the Bach Flowers.

Aloe Vera | for regeneration
Arnica | after a great shock
Borage | when you feel drained from grieving and decide it's time to turn to life again
Chaparral | helps promote sleep
Garlic | to strengthen your immune system on all levels
Lavender | when you feel edgy and oversensitive
Lotus | helps you grow and open up spiritually
Morning glory | helps in finding a purpose and new meaning in life
Quince | helps develop the power of love
St. John's wort | brings you in contact with your inner light, feeling safe
Shasta daisy | for mental clarity and order

More Natural Remedies

The book *Wise Woman Herbal Childbearing Year* by Susun S. Weed contains a lot more information on natural remedies. Or read *Medicine of the Earth* by Susanne Fischer-Rizzi (1997).

Use scent cushions or herbal sachets filled with specific blossoms to improve your sense of well-being. An herbal sachet made up of balm, passion-fruit flowers, honey clover, lavender and St. John's wort (one ounce of each) placed under your pillow at night promotes sleep. (You can get herbs at your health food store or through the mail—see page 255.)

I can ask myself:

☐ Would I like to try some of these natural remedies? If so, what appeals to me?

☐ What conditions would I like help with? What do I need?

☐ In which areas do I feel that natural remedies could enhance my spiritual growth?

When We Get Stuck

Most people recover from grief in their own time. Sometimes, however, we stagnate, or our grief process takes an unhealthy course. Repressing grief can cause serious illness. Not having mourned previous losses can complicate the current grief process. Grief may become chronic, until it seems we'll never find our way out of it ourselves. Then we must look carefully at possible causes.

Unfinished Tasks

In order to find out the reasons you may be "stagnating" at this level, first orient yourself to the five tasks of mourning (four of which are based on Dr. J. William Worden's description in *Grief Counseling and Grief Therapy*. I added one from the perspective of my own research). In your special place, ask yourself where you are in the fulfillment of these tasks. The tasks parallel the phases described in chapters 2 through 5. You can't skip any. Find out what task or tasks may not have been completed and how you can find help to do that.

ε✷ Grasping and accepting the reality of the loss

For those who don't have keepsakes or mementos of their child or have not even seen their baby, the first task is difficult. Sometimes even years later parents feel as though it was only a bad dream. It's hard to say good-bye if you haven't been able to say hello. The result is often denial of the death or an inability to accept it. In chapter 3, I mention several things to do when you have no memories and mementos. If you haven't named your baby, you may want to think of a name now, perhaps based on the suggestions on page 51.

If you haven't talked about the loss or have grieved in isolation, begin to talk. Find people to whom you can tell your story. Begin the process, even belatedly. Perhaps by getting in touch with your inner picture of your child you will eventually accept the reality of her or his death and be able to say good-bye. Ask yourself what would help make your child and your loss real to you.

❧ Experiencing and accepting the pain of the loss and other strong emotions

Feeling all your emotions is naturally a part of this. When people get stuck, it is often because they have repressed anger or guilt. But pain, too, is hard for many people to let themselves feel. Ask yourself what feelings you have no outlet for, why, and what defense mechanisms you have developed. Refer to the suggestions in chapter 3. How can you help yourself express the pain you feel now?

❧ Gradually adapting yourself to a life without your baby

If your being stuck in grief is related to the accomplishment of this task, it will show itself through persistent helplessness and withdrawal from friends and family. If this description applies to you, ask yourself why you are finding it hard to adapt to the situation and what you need to do so.

❧ Letting go and becoming free for new commitments

If you don't manage this task, you won't be able to risk new relationships. Find out what is hindering you from letting go of your baby so that you can enter into other relationships or embark on new activities. The reason may be past ambivalence, guilty feelings or irrational, unconstructive thinking (see below).

❧ Giving meaning to the experience

People who can't find meaning in the experience get stuck in resentment and bitterness. People who do manage to find some sense in it are often transformed in some way. Meaning will reveal itself if we mourn deeply and intensely. Have you given yourself enough time to grieve? You can support yourself in this through talking, visualizing, drawing and telling your story over and over (see pages 126, 31, and 125), as well as through meditation, prayer, retreats and spiritual exercises.

Formulating Helpful Thoughts

> *And at night you will look up at the stars. My star will just be one of the*
> *stars, for you. And so you will love to watch all the stars in the heavens. In*
> *one of those stars I shall be living. In one of them I shall be laughing. And*
> *when your sorrow is comforted (time soothes all sorrows), you will be content*
> *that you have known me.* (Antoine de St. Exupéry, *The Little Prince*)

Our thoughts are the foundation of our reality and largely influence our emotions and our actions. The attitude we have towards life, death and suffering shapes our experience to some extent. If we believe that suffering is as much a part of our lives as joy, and that we can grow even from difficult experiences, then we will have the courage to live through the emotions and pain that are associated with suffering. If we are convinced that, down the road, we will recover from our pain, perhaps having grown a bit, then it will be easier to accept the difficult stages along the way. Contact with others who have had a similar experience can help us develop the confidence that we, too, can make it.

If you seem stuck in your grief process, you might assess your beliefs concerning mourning by making a list of them in your journal or on a sheet of paper, as Judy Tatelbaum suggests in her book, *The Courage to Grieve* (1980). (That book includes a lot of ideas to help you heal.) Your beliefs might be:

ใจ Not showing emotion is a sign of strength.

ใจ This is only a minor loss. Other people have gone through much worse.

ใจ No one recovers from such a loss.

ใจ The longer I grieve, the more I have loved my child.

ใจ I have to pay for previous wrongdoing with this loss, so the worse I feel now, the more redeemed I am.

ใจ Mourners aren't allowed to feel joy.

ใจ The best way to go is to forget everything.

ใจ If I have another child, I will be unfaithful to my dead child.

ใจ Mourning is a normal human experience.

ใจ The expression of feelings is healthy.

ใจ I can get help if I need it.

ใจ Or: _____

After some time, reread what you have written. Discuss it with your mate or friends.

Reflect on how these beliefs affected you in your life; which beliefs have been and are helpful; which convictions work against your healing.

Formulate new core beliefs that can help you drown out the hampering messages. For example: "It is in the nature of things to turn back to life again and live it to the fullest after a time of mourning;" "Grieving means a lot of hard inner work from which I will emerge healed in the end;" or . . . ?

Formulate personal affirmations that will promote healing:

ॐ It's OK and good to feel my emotions.

ॐ I have the courage to face my feelings.

ॐ I have the strength to live through this experience.

ॐ I have mastered other difficult situations in my life, and I will get through this one, too.

ॐ Even if they seem strange, I know my feelings are normal in people who grieve.

ॐ I will give myself the time I need.

ॐ I will not be ashamed for being envious of mothers with babies.

ॐ I will grow from this experience.

ॐ Or: _____

Read over your personal affirmations several times a day, or record them on a cassette and listen to them regularly to reprogram your mind. Put up notes on a mirror or the refrigerator. Ask others to give you these affirmations as "you" messages. Even if it seems difficult and strange, *act as if* you already believe these messages. When you feel stuck, consciously apply yourself to formulating reasonable goals that can help you let go of futile grief patterns and give you a new, positive direction.

If you don't know how to get by on your own, get professional help. Find someone who specializes in death and bereavement counseling and therapy. Or, find a therapist who has been trained in a type of therapy, such as Jungian or Gestalt, that is compatible with your beliefs. There is quite a variety and it may take some research on your part (for resources, see Appendix 4). A therapist can help you achieve closure, enabling you to say good-bye to your baby and let go. With repressed grief, it's possible even years later to reactivate repressed feelings and to relive and work through the experience. You may also want to turn to a religious or spiritual guide for help, especially with issues concerning guilt.

When Is Professional Help a Good Idea?

The following summary of symptoms may mean therapeutic help is advisable when (also based on Dr. J. William Worden):

& the five tasks of mourners have not been completed (see above)

& there is a feeling of intense grief whenever talking about the loss, even though years have passed

& you overreact to small incidents

& you do not feel able to clear the nursery for a long time

& you have persistent phobias concerning illness and death

& you harbor hostility, anger or repressed anger which leads to a "rigid" behavior

& you show depression symptoms well after 18 to 24 months

& you are unable to function in everyday life after 18 to 24 months

& you neglect social relationships over an extended period of time

& there is no perceptible adaptation to the situation (progress should be evident, even if at first it is in the "wrong direction")

& the subject of loss comes up repeatedly in conversation

& you have extremely low self-esteem over a long period

& you have self-destructive impulses (for example, alcohol and drug abuse, compulsive overeating, suicide threats), developing a dependency on chemical substances (you may want to get in touch with a self-help group such as Alcoholics Anonymous or Overeaters Anonymous)

& you have persistent relationship problems (mutual accusations, resentments)

& in children, when they exhibit a decline in school performance or display aggressive, hostile conduct or self-destructive impulses

5

Reorientation and Renewal

I felt as though I had awakened from a deep sleep.

Eventually every night comes to an end, and a new day begins. Every winter is followed by spring. At some time or other we do reach the bottom of our despair, and that is a turning point—perhaps even a turning point for our life as a whole.

Just like trees in the spring, when the sap runs and fills them with new life, we, too, sense an energy surging within us, an energy we may have believed was lost forever. Gradually vitality and spirit reawaken, along with an interest in activities and relationships. A certain normality returns to life. Concentration, memory and mental powers return to normal. Sleeping and eating, too, are restored to a healthy balance. More and more frequently we experience moments of equilibrium and peace within ourselves. For many people, the first anniversary of the baby's death is a milestone. If we have succeeded in wrenching a positive meaning from this terrible experience, we come away having matured and grown from it. We can honor our baby's short existence by the way we live our lives after loss.

Closures and New Beginnings

Renewal can come gradually. Or we can accelerate it somewhat through deliberate action when we feel the time is right, such as by a ritual or going on a spiritual retreat.

"To every thing there is a season, and a time to every purpose under heaven . . . a time to weep, and a time to laugh; a time to mourn, and a time to dance." (Ecclesiastes 3, 1 and 4). Yes, there is a time to end mourning. Perhaps you will know just when that time has come. The more you have come to rely on your inner voice, the more you will be in tune with your own proper rhythm and timing.

ᘖ You might have a *memorial rite* with a circle of chosen friends and family. Create a ceremonial atmosphere, using symbols, flowers, poems, readings and music of your choice. Reflect on what impact your baby has had on your life. Reflect on the traces her "unlived" life has left behind, who has been touched by her and in what ways. Your friends and family can share in this by making their own statements. You may talk about the meaning you have found, the bittersweet gifts you received, and what was created out of the vacuum left by her death. You may want to look ahead and think about how you want to live your life so it will be a tribute to your baby. Perhaps your pastor, priest, rabbi or spiritual leader could help create a ceremony like this.

ᘖ If you feel you are ready to bring mourning to a close, a *fire ritual* can be effective. Prepare a wide, shallow bowl with a candle, matches and a dish of water and arrange them in your "special place" or other dignified spot. Also prepare two sheets of paper. On one sheet write: *I let go*. On the other write *I retain*. You may want to do this alone, as a couple or with special friends and family who will validate your ritual. If you desire others' presence, let them know the procedure and possibly their part in it.

Play meditative or classical music, close your eyes, and give yourself time to let your life pass before your mind's eye—your life before and after your loss. Then contemplate everything you want to let go of. Open your eyes and write down your baby's name (if you truly are ready) and anything else that comes to mind on the first sheet. Then meditate on anything that has come to you after, and maybe as a result of, the loss of your baby—insights, friends, spiritual qualities, and so on. List those on the second sheet. Read over both sheets again and make sure that you can truly subscribe to everything on them. Cross off anything you aren't sure of, and add anything else that might still come to mind.

When you are ready, light the candle. Then say loudly, "I let go of . . .

[read aloud what you have written on Sheet 1]". Then hold the "letting go" sheet over the flame. Turn it over to the fire for transformation. Allow yourself any emotions that might come up. Your companions, if there are any, or your mate acknowledge your statement by saying loudly, "We/I have heard you." Wash your hands and dry them off. Then say loudly, "This is what I keep," and read what you have written on Sheet 2. Your companions or mate will acknowledge this, too, by saying: "We/I have heard you." Then it is your mate's turn. Allow yourself a moment of quiet and feel if and how the energy in you changes. You may end by saying "Thank you."

ટ Trust yourself to know what it is *you* would like to do. (I felt I had to go to a mountaintop all by myself.)

ટ On a smaller scale, others have experienced a turnaround when they actively counted their blessings on a daily basis, maybe with the help of a journal.

If we have surrendered ourselves to mourning, we *will* be changed—enriched by this profound and tremendously difficult experience.

> *I have been changed by this horrible event. I've become more open, more emotional, more accepting. For the first time in my adult life, I have been "out of control"—very strange. A part of me opened up that I didn't know existed.* (Green 1992)

Our child will live in our hearts forever, but it will become less and less painful to think of our baby. Time really does heal wounds. It's common to feel flooded by ocean-like waves of grief during the first year of mourning. But as months pass, the waves become smaller and the intervals between them longer. With time, new dimensions of growth will probably open, and we will continue to experience closures of a new quality.

> *Seven years had gone by since my daughter's death. I felt I had integrated the experience into my life. I was grateful that my life had been able to unfold in much deeper dimensions than before. I had become a new person. Then, shortly before the seventh anniversary of her death, I was surprised by my preoccupation, vivid memories and so many overwhelming feelings. I had to make time for them. I wrote a lot in my journal, planted a rose bush on the anniversary and once again symbolically said good-bye to her with a fire ritual. After this, I felt a strong surge of energy and felt freer than I had ever felt before. I have always been aware that my life ran in seven-year cycles, but still I was amazed that this would also hold true with the loss of my daughter.*

Probably throughout life, waves of grief will keep splashing at us here and there, especially on birthdays, the anniversary of death and family holidays. Just as waves come and go, so our painful feelings will move on if we accept them and allow them to surface.

Shall We Try Again?

Not only the body must be healed and ready before you consider a new pregnancy. It is even more important to be able to open yourself *emotionally* to a new baby—a child with his own identity and a unique name—who can take his own place in your family and not be a replacement for the baby who has died. Suzy, who became pregnant only six weeks following her stillbirth, experienced great emotional turmoil:

> *I thought I was going crazy many times during the new pregnancy. One day at lunch I burst out crying because suddenly I wasn't sure anymore whether I wanted this child. Well, I wanted the child, but did I want it as much as I wanted the first one? I felt I was being unfaithful to my first baby. I went to the cemetery all the time.*

And Joanna, whose third child had been stillborn, says about her following pregnancy:

> *Looking back, I know that I became pregnant again too soon. I had to lie down a lot during this pregnancy, something I didn't do in my earlier pregnancies. On an emotional level this pregnancy was premature. Psychologically, I couldn't open myself to something new. It takes time to develop this basic trust in the course of nature and enough strength to survive the worst.*

This description confirms Donna Ewy's statement: " . . . the parents must have recovered enough emotionally to have the strength to face another pregnancy, another birth and, as one couple put it, another death if it is to be." (Ewy 1984) The more we can accept death as a natural part of life, the more freely we can live life. Learning to let go is a life-long process for most of us. In each encounter with death lies the opportunity to let go a little more of our fear of it, as Melissa did:

> *I had always been horrified of death. Now I don't dread it anymore. Death has lost its terror.*

I can ask myself:

☐ Am I healed enough to attempt another pregnancy?

☐ Am I ready to give my love to a new baby?

Subsequent Pregnancies after a Loss

In subsequent pregnancies we are challenged to overcome our fears and find new confidence. Some mothers are afraid to bond with their baby because they are afraid they'll be hurt again. The more intensively and completely we have gone through our grief process, the more strength we will have gained from it.

Avoiding bonding doesn't protect you from pain. To risk entering into a relationship, even timidly in the beginning, can make your pregnancy less complicated and your lives richer.

> *I felt much closer to this baby than to my other children. Yes, I was afraid it could happen again, but if it were to happen, then at least I wanted to be sure I knew this baby better than I had known the last one.*

If you have had previous losses—and this includes miscarriages in an early stage of pregnancy—it is especially important in a subsequent pregnancy to surround yourself with people with whom you can share your feelings openly. Perhaps you can talk to good friends, or can share experiences with people from the bereavement support group you have attended or with someone from your childbirth education class or breastfeeding support group, or the leaders of either group. Some hospitals sponsor support groups for pregnant couples after a previous loss. If you can't find resources nearby, you may want to talk on the phone with a member of a bereavement support group, such as SHARE. You can find a forum and information on subsequent pregnancies after loss on the Internet, too.

It is especially important for marriage partners to share what they feel. Otherwise, reactions might be easily misunderstood. You can support each other by being open to the needs of the other but also by honestly letting your needs be known.

Where available, you may decide to use the services of a midwife or a doula (see page 78) during a subsequent pregnancy, someone who will visit you at home and who will take time to listen and who at the same time has sound professional knowledge. Or you need to find a doctor who will not pay exclusive attention to medical facts. Don't be afraid to ask "silly" questions. If something bothers you, talk about it and ask questions until you get the answer you need. If you feel you need more checkups than usual to reduce your fears, then get them.

> *When I became pregnant again, I was afraid at first, but eventually the fear subsided, and I was OK. But during the last weeks of pregnancy the fear returned, intensified. I needed frequent checkups for reassurance. I didn't care whether the doctor thought I was hysterical or not!*

Paying attention to our body's signals tells us what is good for us. Positive thoughts and images can counteract anxieties. Focusing on your natural breath can calm you. Perhaps some of the suggestions in chapters 2, 4 and 5 can be useful now.

I can ask myself:

☐ Do I have people I can share my feelings with openly? Can I share them with my partner?

☐ What would help me overcome fears: people, writing, drawing, meditation, prayer, dance, creativity, holistic therapy, checkups, consulting a midwife, positive images or thoughts, or something else?

Our Baby Is Born

Even if this pregnancy occurred when you were fully open and prepared for a new baby, you may experience the birth with myriad emotions. Certainly there is unbelievable joy. We will treasure this baby's life and health all the more because we have learned that these can't be taken for granted. We have developed a different understanding of happiness. Confidence and self-esteem may have been reestablished. But these positive feelings can be mixed with sadness because we are reminded so much of our baby who has died. It's important not to be overprotective with this newborn child because that hinders his development.

> *The child born after my stillbirth got sick in his first year with severe whooping cough. I was scared to death. After I prepared myself to accept everything as it came, I relaxed and became filled with a deep peace.*

I can ask myself:

☐ What emotions do I feel?

We Aren't Having Another Child

Perhaps you have decided against another pregnancy, for personal reasons or because genetic tests have discouraged you, or you feel that your biological clock has run out. It may be that fate has decided for you. Allow yourself time to grieve over that, too. If you need support, find it. If you are thinking about adopting a child instead, you need to consider the ramifications of that carefully.

I can ask myself:

☐ If we involuntarily remain without children, can I cope with the situation or do I need help? If so, in what way and from whom?

Giving the Experience Meaning

We can't prevent sorrow in our lives. But whether we get stuck in despair and hopelessness because of it or it prompts us to further growth is up to us. The search for meaning is an important aspect of the grief process. It enables us to transform suffering into a positive force. (Miles/Crandall 1983) People who can't find some meaning in the experience often remain caught in confusion and despair.

> *Just as when I was told I had cancer, I asked myself over and over, "How can I make something positive out of this terrible event?" So far I haven't succeeded.*

The Jewish neurologist and psychiatrist, Viktor E. Frankl, who spent several years of his life in a concentration camp, said that our greatest sufferings can lead us to recognize the real meaning of our lives, discover our life tasks, and abolish negative attitudes within ourselves (Frankl 1963, 1981). How we deal with suffering is our choice. Whether we deal better or worse with our fate is also due to grace.

The questions of "why" can lead us to ever-deeper spiritual questions about ourselves, life and death, God, our fellow men and about what is essential to us in life. We can come to acknowledge death as a part of life.

The search for meaning in no way spares us intensive, long-lasting pain at the loss of our child. We can, however, channel the pain in a way that will lead to healing and help us contribute to the common good. (Cassem 1975) Through renewal, we can give our lives a new orientation. Beverly, a single mother, changed her life completely after the death of her daughter Jennifer:

> *Perhaps her little soul was just too good to go through the hell in which I had lived with her father. I worked 10 hours a day. I didn't want to live on welfare. I couldn't expect any support from him. For the last years we had stayed with his parents, living day to day. Although I didn't want to,*

I drank and took drugs along with him. Jennifer's death gave me the strength to free myself from this man and build a new life. I have a good job now, have started to do sports and recently met a man while playing tennis. We've developed a friendship, which is gradually turning into something deeper. To be treated with respect, understanding and caring is so new for me. I owe all this to Jennifer. Without her death I wouldn't have managed it.

Beverly's feeling of being a worthwhile person who deserved more than the existence she had known before was awakened by doing "service" to another. At the cemetery she had met a young woman who had also lost a child and was on the verge of suicide. In talking with her, Beverly realized how much stronger she had grown since the loss of her daughter. This newly gained strength enabled her to keep the other woman from taking her life and to give this woman courage by her own example. Her experience encouraged Beverly to continue on her new path. Helping others can release us from the inherent self-absorbtion of grief and be healing.

When you are alone, think of all those who are also alone. Give your time and love. That will keep you from drowning in an ocean of self-pity. If you need love, give love. It will flow back a hundredfold.

The love that was to be bestowed on our child can flow into many new channels. Some persons feel compelled to support others who have been touched by a similar fate or to help people in general who are needy and suffering in some way.

Our precious babies have not died in vain if our love for those babies continues to direct us to ways of helping others. (Sister Jane Marie Lamb)

Others risk new activities and become better able to follow their true nature and calling. But finding meaning may not show itself in great external deeds at all. The true transformation happens *within.*

Acceptance is the end of a long search for peace.

If we have been able to accept our fate and have lived through our grief—if in a certain sense we have "died" with our child and then come back to life—then we will be blessed with gifts. We may feel more alive and awake than ever, and we may have a greater sensitivity and appreciation for everything around us. Perhaps our relationship with our mate and other loved ones will change. New things become important to us. A door to spirituality may have opened. We are more capable of love. We no longer take things for granted. We have become more grateful.

I can ask myself:

☐ How is my life now different from before?

☐ In which ways does the love for my/our child express itself now?

☐ Have I received gifts during this "long night," and what are they?

Part 2

Caring for the Bereaved

When a person is born, we are happy,
when he gets married, we rejoice,
but when he dies,
we act as if nothing had happened.

(Margaret Mead)

6

Supporting the Bereaved

Part 1 of this book, I hope, can help even those who have not experienced a perinatal loss themselves gain insight into the experience. Part 2 specifically addresses people who, on a personal or professional level, touch the lives of the bereaved. Here is a summary of information and key thoughts for those responding to the bereaved.

Thoughts on Grief and Mourning

- Mourning is a completely normal and necessary process.
- Mourning helps us say good-bye, integrate what we have lost, and eventually brings new balance and helps us find new meaning in life.
- The journey through grief takes much longer than most people think. It can last one to two years and even longer, and follows a wave- or spiral-like pattern. People heal in their own time. Don't have set expectations.
- The extent and duration of grief are determined by the depth of attachment, past unprocessed grief, circumstances of death, inner resources, personality and other factors. These are described on pages 231 to 235 in Appendix 2.

❧ Grief for perinatally bereaved parents can be aggravated by the fact that society belittles this loss, that it is often shrouded by taboo, that the baby is unknown to others and is not perceived as real, that there are no memories to share with others and that parents feel isolated.

❧ *By far the most significant determinant for a healthy grief process is the degree of social support the bereaved have.*

❧ Unresolved grief will "come in through the back door" later, affecting health in one way or another.

❧ The way over grief leads right through the middle of it.

❧ Bereaved people must be able to tell "their story" over and over, until they feel they have processed it (see Phases of Mourning, below). This is essential for reorientation after a loss.

❧ A wall of silence freezes grief.

❧ Mourners must be able to express all their feelings. They may need help finding constructive outlets for their anger and in dealing with guilt. They need permission to laugh again.

❧ For a while, grief makes people very self-absorbed.

❧ Relationships can become strained through the death of a child.

❧ The anniversary of the death, holidays and the expected due date are especially difficult times for bereaved parents.

❧ Physical exercise and movement is beneficial, but grieving people find it hard to overcome their inertia. They often feel paralyzed.

❧ Keeping too busy can bottle up grief. It is important to find a good balance between having time to grieve and getting involved in other activities.

A *reminder:* Perinatally bereaved parents have just gone through birth (or a medical intervention) and been confronted with death *at the same time.*

A Summary of the Phases of Mourning

❧ *Shock and Numbness* (lasting several hours, days or even weeks): The bereaved seem to be in a daze and have great difficulty thinking and making decisions. They function mechanically, may express disbelief, and possibly express uncontrollable emotions, including panic and despair.

❧ *Searching and Yearning* (lasting 4 to 6 months): When shock wears off, strong emotions surface in a chaotic way: pain, anger, feelings of guilt, failure, regret, sadness, loneliness, jealousy, despair, bitterness—but also love, expressed through yearning for what could have been. Searching for answers. Restlessness.

> *Disorientation and Transformation* (lasting on average from about 4 to 6 months until the first anniversary of death, gradually decreasing during the second year): Reality definitely hits home now. State of disorientation. Processing on a deeper level, reassessing previous values, searching for new meaning. No energy, forgetful, depression-like condition, eating and sleeping disorders, possibly unresolved feelings of guilt. Low immunity against disease.

> *Reorientation and Renewal* (mostly during the second year): Gradual integration of the loss into one's life, reorientation towards life. New energy, desire and ability to devote oneself to new tasks or able to give love to a new baby. Self-confidence increases. Assessing changes that have come from loss, perhaps feeling like a different person from before. *(adapted from Glen Davidson)*

Tasks of Mourners

> Accept the reality of the loss.

> Feel the pain of loss and other emotions.

> Gradually adapt to a life without the baby.

> Let go and become free again for new relationships.

> Give the experience meaning.

> *(adapted from J.W. Worden)*

What the Bereaved Need

Practical Suggestions

> You cannot take away someone's pain. It is enough simply to *be there*.

> You will not cause more suffering by addressing their loss. Avoidance and not showing interest (for whatever reason) does more harm.

> Knowing others have also seen the baby reduces parents' aloneness and isolation. Now the baby is real to others as well and they can have more empathy.

> Crying is healing. Encourage parents to cry. Let them know it's OK to cry in your presence.

> A touch, a hug, a sympathetic look, tears in your eyes, or simply sitting next to a person quietly can often have more effect than a thousand words.

> Do consider: In times of crisis, most people can tolerate and need more closeness than normal.

- Your presence is helpful and comforting even if you feel awkward, at a loss for words, and at times uncomfortable. You do not have to talk. Being there to listen is much more important. Feeling speechless and helpless in such a situation is normal.

- Convey to the bereaved that you are open to them. Being a good listener is important. Eye contact and positive body language signals openness. (Sometimes eye contact may *not* be called for. Be aware of individual needs.)

- Gently ask for details and memories. Share your own feelings.

- Sense when silence is needed. Be able to endure a healthy silence!

- Be sensitive about when mourners need time for themselves.

- If the parents have named their baby, refer to him or her by name. This helps parents accept the situation and validates the baby's existence.

- Help parents' sort out the facts of "their story," enabling them to find new answers (see page 125).

- Do not ignore the grieving father.

- If there are siblings, include them.

- If you cannot personally visit the bereaved, phone, or send a letter or a card with a personal message (avoid clichés).

- Take or send flowers.

- Remember the anniversary of death, expected due date or other important dates.

- Support the bereaved in their decision-making but also encourage their self-determination as much as possible.

- When the accomplishment of daily tasks is difficult, offer specific help: Go shopping, help with the household, do laundry, wash the dishes, take care of pets, water the flowers. It is important, though, to find a healthy balance between being helpful and making the other person feel helpless.

- Living children of parents in mourning often do not get the attention they need: Give time, lend them an ear, take them for a walk or invite them to an afternoon of games or other activities.

- After a loss, people often do not pay enough attention to their nutrition. They may aggravate their physical and emotional condition by not nourishing themselves adequately. When visiting, it's nice to bring along a wholesome meal (for example, a casserole with fresh vegetables). Or, offer to cook a meal for them.

❧ Support mourners' becoming physically active. Invite them for a walk, hike or swim or, in later months, jogging.

❧ You may help enhance their physical health by offering a massage (let intuition guide you), tapping on their back (creating the sensation that raindrops are falling on it) or placing your hands gently but firmly on their shoulders or shoulder blades. Ask the other person to focus on the touch. Radiate calmness (see chapter 4 for exercises).

❧ Offer diversion (for example, a visit to a concert or theater, a lunch date or an invitation to a meal at your home); accept it if they "don't quite feel up to it." Be aware that they need a balance between activities and quiet time.

❧ Invite them to an evening of singing. Music is healing.

❧ Lead them in "co-meditation" (see page 169).

❧ Reading aloud to them (for example, inspirational texts or fairy tales) can be comforting.

❧ Guide them in a visualization exercise (see page 119).

❧ Join them in doing relaxation exercises.

❧ Invite them to meditate—just the two of you or in a group. For example, quiet meditation—listening, meditations using visualization (see Appendix 3) or meditations focusing on words, such as "Peace, healing, love, surrender, serenity, letting go" or a comforting thought. Or offer to pray together.

❧ When a co-worker has suffered a loss, put a flower or a card at her work place when she returns to work. Don't avoid her! This goes for bereaved fathers as well.

❧ Allow mourners the right to grieve at their own pace and in their own way. Accept individual needs. Don't conclude that what is good for you is also good for others.

❧ Offer literature that initiates the grief process and leads to healing.

❧ Even if some time has elapsed, express your sympathy and feelings to the bereaved.

❧ During the phase of searching and yearning, suggest attending a support group. Obtain addresses (see Appendix 4).

❧ During the phase of disorientation, it is *you* who must approach the bereaved because they find it hard to ask for help. Go to them. Tell them you will plan to come unless they express wishes to the contrary.

ॐ Be there when others have already turned away and forgotten about the pained parents. The second half of the year following a loss is usually more difficult than the first. Perhaps you can arrange with friends to take turns making contact or making visits. *Remember critical times:* the anniversary of the loss, the previously expected due date, Mother's Day, Father's Day, holidays.

ॐ Giving a donation in memory of the child (for example, to SHARE, The Compassionate Friends, The Sudden Infant Death Alliance or other self-help organizations, such as those in the service of helping people with the disability the child may have had), or planting a tree, may touch parents' hearts and be healing.

ॐ Be aware of the signs of a possibly unhealthy grief process (see page 141) and suggest seeking professional help.

ॐ Read "Interacting with Others," page 106.

Helpful Words

ॐ I'm so sorry.

ॐ That must be very difficult for you.

ॐ I'm here, and I will listen to you.

ॐ I've been thinking about you and wondering how you feel.

ॐ Take your time.

ॐ I don't know what to say.

ॐ I don't understand it either.

ॐ How are you doing with all of this?

ॐ It makes me sad.

ॐ How can I help you?

ॐ Do you feel like talking about it/him/her?

ॐ Please don't feel embarrassed to cry in front of me. It's all right. Tears are very healing.

ॐ Is there someone you would like with you now? Who I could call for you?

Remember: Showing interest and caring are more important than finding the right words.

What Pains or Harms the Bereaved

Unbeneficial Behavior

ে Acting as if nothing has happened. Ignoring.

ে Wanting to pacify parents to alleviate their pain. Playing down facts to "make them feel better."

ে Pressuring them to feel better.

ে Judging and condemning their feelings.

ে Protecting them from the reality of the loss or making uninvited decisions in their place (both hinder the grief process).

ে Wanting to spare them painful confrontations; for example, by putting baby things away, clearing out the nursery and avoiding the subject in conversation.

Avoid the Usual Clichés

ে Thank God you didn't know the child.

ে Better now than later.

ে You're young—you can still have other children.

ে Be thankful that you already have two healthy children.

ে It was for the best.

ে It's God's will.

ে Be glad—your child wouldn't have been normal.

ে You're lucky to be alive.

ে I know how you feel [unless you have had a similar experience].

ে Please don't cry.

ে [To the father:] You have to be strong now for your wife.

7

Caring for Bereaved Parents in the Hospital

Professionals working in hospitals often receive little (if any) training in dealing with death and dying. So it is understandable that, when confrontation with death is inevitable, many resort to models developed in our culture over the last century. They include repressing, ignoring, shrouding in taboo, avoiding contact, avoiding talk about it, acting as if nothing had happened—with the idea that all will be forgotten soon. In the past, we have often withheld stillborn and miscarried babies from their parents, believing we acted in their best interest. We seldom knew how people fared after they left the hospital.

A Letter that Changed Hospital Routine

The following letter to the chief of staff of a hospital gives us insight into how life went on for a mother who had not gotten to know and say good-bye to her baby. Many women with whom I have spoken shared similar stories with me.

Dear Dr. E.,

You are probably surprised to hear from me. Three years ago, my child died shortly after a Cesarean section, following a difficult labor. Everybody, including you, said, "It'll be all right. Medically, everything is fine." But I haven't become pregnant again.

I'm writing to let you know what happens to women—or rather, to mothers—who experience what I did. I feel there are several things that you, as a physician (and as a man, who never can become pregnant himself), should know.

During the last three years, I have tried everything to become pregnant again, without success. I have become more and more frustrated. Two months ago I started therapy. Since then, some things have become clear.

I don't know my own child. I don't have a picture of it; I don't know what it looked like. Isn't this strange—that a mother doesn't know her own child? To this day I haven't been able to stop looking, though I know that I won't ever find it. This makes it so difficult to say good-bye.

The child died in fact but hasn't been able to die in my head because everything was taken care of by others, especially you. I had nothing to do with anything that happened. I did not deliver—I was "delivered." You took the delivery, the pain and the grief away from me.

Because of all the sedatives, the whole experience is foggy. I don't really know what happened. The only thing I know is that I came to you pregnant, and then there was nothing. Where is my child? Because of the way things were handled, I haven't been able to "give birth" to my child in three years. I haven't been able to let her die. How am I supposed to become pregnant again when I still haven't given birth? I don't want to blame you by writing you this letter. I just want to point out what to me was a grave mistake—that you didn't offer to let me see my own child. It was my *child. I had that right!*

Everyone was helpless. No one knew how to handle the situation or me—neither you nor the rest of your staff. The tendency seemed to be: Don't stir things up, hush them up, get everything over with as quickly as possible. Maybe for you it was mainly a medical problem, but for me it was life and death, and had a lot to do with my mental health. You should have given me the chance to see my child. Unfortunately, I couldn't ask because I was too medicated. To be frank, that I can't forgive. I have been very upset and angry at you.

For all I know, you have children. Just imagine how you would feel if you didn't know one of them—never to have seen that child, only to know it is dead—and you wouldn't even have carried it inside of you!

For me, it's too late. My child is gone. I'll never know what it looked like. I don't know whether you handle these situations differently now. I'm telling you this so things will change—they just have *to change! Discuss it with your staff. Give mothers the chance to get to know their baby and say good-bye, if not immediately, then a day or two later. It is not up to* you to make this decision. *The only one who has that right is the mother. The next time you encounter this situation, I hope you will think about me and my experience.*

Please understand—I'm not writing to offend you, but if I have, I can't help it. I had to write this letter for the sake of my life, my dead child, my emotional health and my concern for others.

Sincerely,
M.S.

The doctor took the letter in the spirit in which it was meant, and it prompted many positive changes in his hospital. Five years after the above-mentioned letter, Sarah was stillborn in the same hospital. Myriam, her mother, remembers the time directly following her birth:

Sarah was handled with respect and love by all the attendants. We felt like she and we too were "cradled" in a nurturing atmosphere of caring and empathy. Immediately after birth, Sarah was cleaned a bit and then wrapped in a blanket so that only her little head showed. This way, we could begin to familiarize ourselves with her appearance. Naturally we were apprehensive of how she might look—but she looked so sweet. As we held her in our arms, we gazed at her, absorbing every one of her features. The most important thing was that we had the feeling that we could take as much time as we needed. *No one pressured us to hurry. Through the gentle guidance of our caregivers, we were able to overcome our paralyzing fears of this situation. They were there to help us, but more important, they gave us the heartwarming feeling that a little person had been born who deserved to be treated with dignity and caring.*

After we had Sarah's foot- and hand prints made, we dressed her, and a sister came to baptize her. The staff lovingly and spontaneously prepared a place where we could lay Sarah and keep her with us for a while. They placed a pillow on a little table, covered it with a white cloth and decorated it with a rose, which a nurse brought in from the hospital grounds. A lit candle created a solemn atmosphere. Our daughter looked beautiful and peaceful. We had her with us for several hours. Everybody who had been involved was there to help us say good-bye to Sarah. Despite terrible feelings of loss and grief, strangely enough we also experienced something like happiness, and I was really proud of my child.

Frank, Sarah's father, described his impressions in this way:

> *When our child was born, it was a very intense feeling. The birth attendants gathered around us like a protective wall. We felt their closeness, and their great sympathy supported us. That was so important and comforting. I believe most of them cried along with us. That touched me deeply. We felt such strong support. If it hadn't been for that. . . .*

How Can Professionals Help?

The death of a baby is a terrible experience. For most parents, this experience takes place in a hospital. In shock, totally unprepared, parents depend on their caregivers for sensitive support and guidance. How the situation is handled at the beginning determines how this loss will affect the future lives of the bereaved family—even future generations. Issues such as how much support they receive, whether they can express their emotions, whether they can participate in making decisions and live through the situation according to their own values and needs, whether they have time to say good-bye to their child—all these factors influence the outcome of this loss on the family. The circumstances also can affect their experience of subsequent pregnancies.

Based on many years of listening to and ministering to parents whose babies died, Sister Jane Marie Lamb feels that families need to be given information so they can make informed decisions that are in keeping with their beliefs. If you are able to be there with them and not withdraw emotionally, they will not feel alone.

Caretakers Affect the Course of Mourning

We as caregiving professionals play an enormously important role in helping facilitate the best conditions for a healthy grief process. Most professionals are willing to give their best. But they may need help to overcome their own helplessness, which is so natural in the face of death. Knowledge of the process parents go through and of what has proven helpful to the majority of them can help you overcome your initial insecurity and fears. Over time you will learn from the parents themselves.

In the preceding chapter you found basic information and guidelines regarding grief and mourning. *The Rights of Parents When a Baby Dies* and *The Rights of the Baby* in Appendix 1 can be used as a general basis for responding to bereaved parents. I've provided specific ideas at the end of this chapter (starting on page 176) for the care of the bereaved in the hospital during five stages: hospital admittance, labor, delivery and immediate postpartum care, hospital stay, and outpatient follow-up care. This information can be helpful to caregivers in the areas of obstetrics/gynecology, pediatrics/neonatology and nursing. You may want to copy the list and post it in the appropriate areas.

Caring Steps That Help

We all feel more secure and confident when we have enough background information about a particular situation, along with concrete direction as to how to respond. But in the end, a loving presence, caring and the courage to be touched and to face death along with the parents counts more than knowledge and skills.

A Very Important Photo

Photos are often the only concrete remembrance parents have of their baby who has died. These photos are unique. They are usually the only way parents can "introduce" their baby to others. Therefore, whoever takes these photos should do so in a loving and caring way.

Provide a dignified setting. Take many photos—some without, some with clothing. Ask parents what they want. Having the baby dressed in the clothes parents previously set aside can be very meaningful to them. You can take some photos of the child lying on a pillow or in a little basket or bassinet, maybe surrounded with flowers or perhaps just a single rose. Light a candle. Some photographs can be taken of the baby in the arms of his parents, grandparents, siblings or friends, depending on the situation. (When *you* hold the baby lovingly in your arms, those around you will tend to lose their fear and uneasiness.) Encourage family members to take pictures with their own cameras so they can capture their baby as seen through their own eyes, with an emphasis on what is important to *them*. In addition to the parents' photos, take some instant photos to guarantee that they will have photos in case something happens to the undeveloped film. In any case, encourage overnight development. The little book, *A Very Important Photo*, from the Centering Corporation can give you more ideas.

If parents did not want to see their baby and, for the moment, do not want any photos either, keep these carefully under lock and key. (Perhaps label the envelope with a reminder to handle confidentially.) Parents need to be told how long pictures will be kept (in most hospitals, up to six years). Parents may come back years later to pick up their photos.

In one case a couple had expressly requested after the delivery that no photo be taken of their son—they wanted to remember him the way they had seen him. Nine months later, at a support-group meeting at the hospital, they approached us kind of timidly, saying they hadn't wanted photos . . . but "had their orders maybe not been followed, and were there perhaps some photos after all?" We checked and found out that, indeed, their orders had been heeded—no photos anywhere! They were let down by this. After that, we decided to take pictures routinely, because it occurred to us that around the time of the birth, people are not in a good position to judge what their needs will be later. And this is one thing that is definitely irretrievable at a later point.

Keeping Miscarried Babies in the Hospital

In the hospital in which Sister Jane Marie worked, miscarried babies are buried with dignity in a mass burial site. Until the burial, they are kept at the hospital. Sister Jane Marie says:

As I explain to the parents, we keep the baby in an embalming-like fluid. It lies in this clear fluid in a closed bag, with the name of the mother and her hospital-patient number attached, so that clear identification is possible. Then we place the baby in a tiny coffin. It frequently happens that parents change their minds and come back to see their baby. Then we take the child out of the solution, bathe it so the odor of the embalming fluid is diminished, and, if the baby is large enough, we dress the baby in tiny clothes. [It is also possible to use doll clothes—author's comment.] This does not work if the baby is extremely small. We then wrap it in a small, warm, homemade blanket, about the size of a square washcloth, in green or yellow, because we sometimes are not able to identify the sex of the child, and we do not want to attach a sex-identifying symbol. That should come from the parents.

Nurturing Touch

Grief puts us in a regressive state. We know that touch is a basic biological human need. In times of crisis, most people need more closeness than usual. Many bereaved I interviewed said how they wished someone had just held them. When parents hear the horrible news, it is as if the blood in their veins freezes. Touch and being held can melt the "ice." Touch lessens the feeling of shock on a physical level and also softens emotional shock. Physical touch gently brings the bereaved in touch with their emotions. When that happens, healing tears can start to fall.

ટ Touch parents in a nurturing way; for example, putting your hand on their hands, arms or shoulders in a natural, heartwarming way, warmly stroking their hair or putting your arms around them in a caring way is generally appropriate and helpful. Be sensitive to the parents' needs and be aware of your intuition. With those guides, you will probably know when nurturing touch is welcome and needed. If you are natural about it, it will come across as right. If you are unsure, you may want to ask first if they would like you to hold their hands or if they would like to be held or hugged.

∾ You may want to sensitize yourself to the quality of nurturing touch by doing the exercises described on page 28. You may also want to experiment with a partner or colleague to get their feedback.

Meditation Support of Women Delivering a Stillborn

Richard Boerstler, a psychotherapist and practicing thanatologist, describes a method to support persons in their deep anguish and despair in dealing with death and dying in his book, *Letting Go*. He calls it *co-meditation*. An adaptation of co-meditation can be useful in supporting a woman in labor for a stillbirth, especially during early labor. Co-meditation can help the laboring woman let go and open up to the experience. But it can also be useful during the mourning period. An example of co-meditation follows.

The room is warm; the lights are dimmed, distractions should be minimized. The mate (or doula, or midwife), after centering him- or herself (see chapters 2 and 4), guides the woman in a relaxation exercise. The co-meditator instructs her to let her breath in . . . to let it go . . . and to wait until it comes in on its own again. As her "helper," the co-meditator turns full attention to the laboring woman and becomes attuned to her and her breathing rhythm. Over a period of time, the co-meditator simply breathes along with her and is ready to accept whatever happens.

After a while, especially when her breathing is fast and shallow, the co-meditator begins to accompany her out-breath with an "Aaahhhh." The laboring woman can contemplate the tone in her head or concentrate completely on listening to the tone. Or she can tone along out loud. Slowly the co-meditator's toning and the breathing of the woman in labor will interweave, as though in a dance. If it feels right, the co-meditator can also count the woman's out-breaths, up to 10, then start anew. Each time the co-meditator moves to something new, he or she needs to prepare the laboring woman for the change by telling her what will happen next. A co-meditator can also facilitate the toning of a *mantra*—a word or a sentence that is comforting to the spirit. (The laboring woman will usually come up with something that fits well immediately, if she is asked.) Over time, these activities help women begin to feel a sense of tranquillity and the trusting feeling of being nestled inside a greater whole. Boundaries can fall aside, and a feeling of oneness with the dead child can emerge.

Be Aware of Cultural, Religious and Ethnic Traditions

How any individual deals with death is strongly influenced by culture and religion. Persons from different ethnic backgrounds may be more or less strongly embedded in their traditions and cultural rites than we ourselves may be. In many cultures and traditions, death is dealt with in a more healing way than it is to a great extent in our Western culture. When responding to people from other ethnic backgrounds, we need a special sensitivity. We must respect other people's customs and beliefs, but we must also be able to tell where these beliefs, just like some of ours, may sometimes stand in the way of healing.

For example, according to Islamic beliefs, a dead baby, as soon as it is recognized as a person (from about the eighth or tenth week of pregnancy), must be buried and treated with great respect, as are all the dead. If it has cried even once, ritual prayer must be held; otherwise it is up to the wishes of the parents. In the Middle-Eastern world, the dead are not left alone until after the burial—they remain at home, surrounded by family and relatives. Wailing women pour in from all directions to lament with the mother. The burial is the sole responsibility of the men. In the evening, there is a common ritual for all. The Islamic belief allows an autopsy only when it is truly necessary.

Every region of the country has its own primary mix of ethnic and cultural groups. Try to find out what those groups are in your area if you don't already know. Then seek out cultural and religious information that can help you become sensitive to each group's needs with regard to death, dying and burial. Your local library is a fine place to start. If you have a college or university at hand, you may find information through their international studies, religion, cultural anthropology or other departments.

Whenever possible, ask the parents themselves about their cultural and spiritual customs and beliefs, or make inquiries at their places of worship or cultural centers. Tell them what has proven helpful to other bereaved parents who have lost a child and decide together on how to proceed.

The Caregivers' Role

The editors of *Bereavement: Reactions, Consequence and Care* (Osterweis et al 1984), working as a committee to investigate the health consequences of grief-related stress, concluded that not enough attention has been given in the past to the needs of the bereaved. They identified these causes: inadequate education about the effects of loss and grieving; failure of healthcare systems to feel responsible for the follow-up care of the bereaved; failure to plan sufficient time for appropriate activities; and failure to recognize that the care of the bereaved is stressful for healthcare providers and support staff.

Difficulties in dealing with death and mourning for support staff are not just organizational problems but also emotional challenges. In the area of medicine, where ever-more victories over death have been won and where we like to believe that everything is possible, it is easy to experience death deep down as a personal failure. At best it makes us humble.

In the everyday routine of a hospital we do not have time to stop and digest what happens to loved ones (or ourselves) when a person dies. Often we don't have the time we wish we did to dedicate ourselves to caring for the person in need. We are called to the next room, where another woman is giving birth to her baby with great joy. . . .We become aware of how happiness and suffering live next door to each other.

Being faced with death makes us aware of our own mortality. Many people consider the fear of death to be the greatest fear of all. But at best, if we can allow ourselves to really be in the present, we may also experience the *peace* of death, and our fears can gradually diminish.

Too many of us never had helpful models or instructions for dealing with losses in our own lives. Instead of grieving, we may have repressed our feelings and simply tried to move on. We may not have healed adequately from our own past wounds. And so, when encountering death in the professional context, we may find it hard to separate the current situation from our own history: New losses reopen the old wounds. Our own unprocessed grief can make exposure to another person's pain unbearable.

> *It became clear to me that I wasn't trying to shield the parents from looking at their child, but was protecting myself.*

In the book, *Mental Health Issues in Grief Counseling: Sudden Infant Death Syndrome*, Stanley Weinstein notes that it can be just as important to be aware of our own feelings and to face up to *them* as it is to know and understand the grief process. Dr. Elisabeth Kübler-Ross asks in her book *On Children and Death*,

> *How long is it going to take until members of the healing profession realize that Valium® as great a killer in its own way as cancer? How long is it going to take until we teach the prevention of such tragedies by replacing*

drugs with a sympathetic listening ear, by a human being who has his or her house in order and is not afraid of letting a patient express his or her pain and anguish, to make room so that a healing process can take place?

In many of my workshops with caregivers, I have encouraged participants to share their personal experiences, histories, emotions and attitudes towards death, dying and grieving. Taking time and the courage to look at their feelings has been healing to these professionals, who are periodically confronted with death. Death began to lose some of its terror for them.

The questionnaire in Appendix 2 can help you start the same kind of healing process and facilitate your awareness of your attitudes at present. The questionnaire can also be used for mutual peer support in the context of a bereavement-team meeting (see below). It can help you determine if there are unresolved issues in your personal life that get in the way when you want to give support to the bereaved and that you might need help in sorting out. You may even remember an issue or two from your professional life that remains unresolved, for which you might seek supervision to sort out. You may find Elisabeth Kübler-Ross' books stimulating and enlightening, particularly *Questions and Answers on Death and Dying*. *Grief Counseling and Grief Therapy*, by Dr. J. William Worden, offers an excellent theoretical background for helping the bereaved.

Healthcare providers and caretakers themselves need a supportive social network and a place to vent and process feelings. Institutional support for the staff in the form of supervision and continuing education is urgently needed. Peer support can be organized in the form of a perinatal-bereavement team (see below). Some of us are fortunate enough to have compassionate family members who will listen.

When caregivers can overcome their own fears, they may experience a stillbirth somewhat differently than they expected to. Dr. L. described her feelings four hours after the first time she had been present at such an event:

I hardly dare say it, but it's true—there was beauty to it. Until now I had successfully avoided such experiences because I was afraid of them. If someone had told me beforehand that it would no longer be terrible if I actually allowed myself to become fully involved as a person, I wouldn't have believed it. But it's true! It left a very strong impression with me.

Our philosophy of life, too, affects the extent to which exposure to death poses a personal threat or other difficulty. Those who believe that death is the radical end may find it difficult to be confronted with death as a regular part of their job. Others, who believe that everything they accomplish is only the result of their own efforts, tend to be more easily fatigued or burned-out by their work than those who draw strength from sources beyond themselves; for example, through spiritual beliefs.

And finally, burn-out in this and other work can be slowed down and even prevented if we find ways to nurture and regenerate ourselves. To begin with, we need to allow ourselves enough time to process significant events of our life. Caregivers too can draw on the many suggestions for self-care on a physical, emotional and spiritual level given to the bereaved in chapters 2 through 4.

Setting up a Perinatal Bereavement Team

Being part of a support network helps parents. But it also benefits their caregivers. A burden distributed among many shoulders is a lighter burden for each individual. Work with others to assess and plan necessary changes in your clinical practice that can provide for these important support systems. Changes are always easier to implement when the group works from a shared sense of commitment to the outcome.

In fact, *perinatal-bereavement teams*—multidisciplinary teams looking after the concerns of parents who lose a baby—have proved effective. They have become increasingly common throughout the country. Ann Coon, who helped institute such a program at the North Shore Hospital of Miami, Florida, speaks of that program's beginnings:

> *A bereavement team came to life spontaneously after a workshop at our hospital, at which we ourselves had worked on our feelings concerning the losses in our own lives. This made us all very sensitive. The team consisted of gynecologists, neonatologists, nurses, social workers, childbirth educators, clergy and educational-service staff. To begin with, we looked at how we had handled perinatal losses at our hospital until now. It became clear to us that in the past we had hindered rather than promoted the grief process of perinatally bereaved parents.*

A core group of committed staff members was formed. During the first year, at regular team meetings, this group worked out new procedures for the delivery room, the gynecology unit and the neonatal intensive care unit, and they shared their experiences and difficulties. A pregnancy support group was formed. Follow-up care for bereaved parents was also instituted.

A nurse was assigned to the care of the bereaved exclusively. After about a year, we started a SHARE support group. Our cooperation with pathology was sometimes difficult because, after an autopsy, they did not want to return the baby to us at our request.

Periodic regional meetings with staff members at other local hospitals now serve as a forum for exchanging experiences and getting new ideas. A person or a small group may prepare a talk on a specific subtopic; for example, rituals, cooperation with funeral directors or socially tabooed losses (such as issues relating to adoption). By working cooperatively, professionals frequently find it is much easier to examine the many dimensions of a difficult situation or to locate outside resources, among other advantages.

At the meetings, healthcare providers and other support staff can also enjoy an atmosphere of mutual support. The meetings provide an opportunity for participants to reflect on attitudes, beliefs and early experiences that still influence them. As serious as the subject is, however, the mood at such meetings is not gloomy. A healthy dose of humor keeps the burden of work in this sensitive area bearable. I have heard of many positive experiences coming from such meetings, and I highly recommend instituting this kind of a support network in your own setting, if you don't already have one.

Final Thoughts: Bereaved Mothers Speak

Suzy:

At first I just cried. I felt so alone, and the only thing that would have helped is if somebody had just held me. But it took half an hour before someone even thought of that. . . .

. . . As my daughter was being delivered, I instinctively reached for her, but the doctor pushed my hands away. I heard her drop into a bowl they usually catch the placenta with. I will never in my whole life forget that sound—I could tell she was lifeless. As if she had no worth! If only they had held her a bit. . . . ! Then I said, "I don't want to see 'it'."

. . . It would be good if, an hour or two after the birth, women were asked again whether they want to see their baby. Even if they say "no" again, they must be asked at least once more! Right after birth I didn't want anything to do with it at all. Later, I didn't dare ask. Now I'm plagued with self-reproach. What I would give to have seen my child!

Melissa:

> *At first I didn't touch Allison. But finally I ended up caressing my daughter.*

> *. . . If the doctor had insisted on full anesthesia, I might have consented to it. But I am extremely happy that it wasn't done. It was so important to see Allison, to touch her and to experience everything.*

> *. . . But what makes me sad is that I would have liked so much to have had some time alone with her. You can't believe how disturbing it was to have all these other people around. Even now I'm upset with myself that I didn't manage to say, "Please leave us alone for a while—just go away."*

Marian:

> *Jonathan's birth was such a beautiful experience. I gave birth to him in a birthing room. I realize now the importance of a good birthing experience—it is the only happy memory we have. At least something went the way we had imagined it, and that is something I can be proud of!*

Kristin:

> *I'd have liked to have seen my little boy once again, but I was denied this with the remark that he was no longer "worth seeing."*

Penny:

> *I was afraid to see my baby. I think it's important that the doctor or the nurse tell the mother what the baby looks like. It would have been so much easier for me if someone had said, "He is such a sweet little boy, he has red hair and blue eyes; his little body is perfect." Even he hadn't been perfect, if they had said, "He lacks an arm," or "a part of his face is missing," at least I could have prepared myself for it. I believe that it is very, very important to see your baby and hold it, no matter what problems it may have.*

> *. . . I suggest that the staff take a lot of pictures and keep them at the hospital. Then call the parents after a while and ask whether they want them. It is asking too much to have to make so many decisions all at once.*

Guidelines for Parents' Care after Stillbirth, Miscarriage and Newborn Death

Upon Admittance to the Hospital

In the case of stillbirth:

- If the hospital is advised by a gynecologist's office of the arrival of a woman whose baby is thought to have died in the uterus, inform *all* staff members *before* her arrival.

- If possible, involve a member of the perinatal-bereavement team from the beginning.

- If you diagnose an intrauterine death upon admittance, where possible —with the help of ultrasound—let the woman (and her partner, if present) become aware themselves that the baby's heart is no longer beating and the baby is no longer moving.

- In simple, empathetic words, confirm the fact that their child is no longer alive.

- Following confirmation of the baby's death, do not withdraw, *be there,* show empathy.

- Nurturing touch may be needed and appropriate—assess! (For details, see page 28.)

- "Give permission" to grieve. Parents sense in whose presence they may openly express their emotions and when they have to hold back. Adults may be afraid to express such emotions in the presence of "authorities," especially if they felt threatened with rejection as children whenever they showed sadness or other "unpleasant" feelings.

- Assure parents of the staff's support.

- Attend to the father. He, too, has lost his child.

- Be prepared for, and accept variations in, grief reactions: Emotional outbursts are just as "normal" as withdrawal and numbness.

- Shock is a natural form of anesthesia. Because of a high adrenaline output, the parents' thinking ability will be reduced temporarily, though they may appear from the outside to be functioning. Usually improvement sets in after about half an hour (depending on the situation).

- Do not routinely administer tranquilizers—they hinder the grief process.

ễ♥ Let parents know: what to expect, ways they might proceed, what decisions they can take part in, how much time is available for making these decisions, the advantages, disadvantages and possible risks of their options, what has helped others in the same situation in the long run, and what these parents regretted in the end.

ễ♥ Be aware that the thinking process in early bereavement is disconnected and that the bereaved will best comprehend brief comments and suggestions. Avoid overloading them with information.

ễ♥ Include them in the decision-making process wherever possible. (Important: Let them make as many decisions as possible—this helps reduce their feeling of helplessness and restores their feeling of control and self-worth.) Leave ample time for this.

ễ♥ Ask parents if they wish time alone with each other, and tell them how to get in touch with you when they want you to come back.

ễ♥ If you are sure that parents have a support network of friends, family and professionals and if there are no medical contraindications, it may be helpful *not* to induce labor immediately, if parents want to wait. This gives them time to grasp what has happened and prepare for the birth (see page 28). The woman may need to be told why not rushing into things might be beneficial. Help parents get in touch with other bereaved parents or a support group. Possibly arrange for or suggest home care through a nurse or nurse-midwife, where available, and contact their clergy, if they are part of a religious community. Be at least in telephone contact with the parents.

ễ♥ Assess who might be predisposed for a pathological grief process (also see Appendix 2): Inquire about possible previous losses and how they were handled (for example, possible traumatic situations or negative hospital experiences, unresolved grief, no social support) as well as information about additional current stress factors. Know about possible earlier emotional or mental problems. Gauge the degree of social support available now and after hospital discharge. Determine where the support of a social worker and/or postpartum intervention in the form of grief counseling or therapy may be indicated. Refer or initiate necessary arrangements. Advise the family physician.

ễ♥ Be aware that women without partners may need additional care and attention because they may lack adequate social support.

ễ♥ It would be optimal if one person from the nursing staff or bereavement team could dedicate herself without other interruptions to the care of the parents.

From *Help, Comfort and Hope after Losing Your Baby in Pregnancy or the First Year*
© 1997 Hannah Lothrop. All rights reserved.

When there is a miscarriage:

- ≿ Many of the points above also apply to the treatment of parents who come to the hospital because of a spontaneous miscarriage (especially after the first trimester).

- ≿ Miscarriage is often treated as a surgical intervention. Medical terminology, such as "conceptus" or even "fetus," masks the loss, making it harder for parents to feel they have "permission" to grieve. Be aware that bonding starts early in the pregnancy. Most parents would like to have acknowledged that they are losing their baby.

- ≿ In the case of an emergency, medical aspects take priority. But here, too, the human factor determines the course of mourning. Here, too, emotional care is so important.

Attendance and Support during Labor

- ≿ Enter into the experience. "Be there." Don't withdraw.
- ≿ One thing at a time: Usually women cannot deal with birth *and* death simultaneously.

For the labor process and delivery:

- ≿ Ask parents how they had envisioned labor and birth and what their wishes were.

- ≿ Encourage them to implement as many of these wishes as possible.

- ≿ Inform the woman of pros and cons of certain procedures. Wherever possible, include her in the decision-making process.

- ≿ Don't administer medication routinely. Instead, consult with the birthing woman (see page 37).

- ≿ Give a lot of recognition as to how well she is managing labor under these difficult conditions.

- ≿ Physical contact—for example, holding her hand or placing a hand on her shoulder—may help.

- ≿ Warm water (for example, in a bath or shower) can soothe and aid relaxation.

- ≿ Help parents resume bonding with their baby, which is usually interrupted by news of the death. Completing bonding with their dead child is helpful for the course of mourning and helps them to say good-bye. Not being able to bond with their child leads to feelings of disassociation, tension and tightness.

ॐ Help women reconnect with and accept their baby by massaging the woman's abdomen, as if lovingly addressing the dead child in the womb. Suggest to the mother and the father that they stroke the abdomen and talk to their baby. The goal of these efforts is to help parents accept the child as their own.

ॐ Through gentle and sensitive questions, help parents resume a bond with their child. For example: "What were your first thoughts when you found out you were pregnant? How was your pregnancy? When did you feel the first movements? Was the baby quiet or active? Had you picked a name? Will you want to give that name to your child now? Or has another name come up?"

ॐ Provide a "release valve" for them to express their disappointment about lost dreams and hopes, and help them become conscious of the reality. Be aware that occasionally relief can be part of the rainbow of emotions. Respond sensitively and gently.

ॐ Let the parents know that they may talk and ask about anything they want to. Listen for unspoken questions. Try to grasp emotions intuitively. Depending on the situation, perhaps ask directly: "What is your biggest fear?"

ॐ Encourage the father to assist as much as possible in the care of the birthing woman. Especially if they had prepared together for the birth, let them apply what they have learned. If he is unprepared, guide him in ways to help: holding her hand, massaging (back, head, feet, thighs, abdomen), effleuraging, placing his hands quietly on her shoulders or the shoulder blades, wiping her face, holding her in his arms, supporting her as she sits, kneels, stands, squats (letting her lean against him, supporting her back by sitting behind her).

ॐ If the father is not present (or in the case of women without partners), encourage the presence of someone else close to the woman who can serve as a labor doula, coach or support person.

ॐ Possibly instruct support persons in co-meditation (see page 169) or guide the woman yourself in co-meditation, as the occasion warrants.

ॐ Slowly prepare the couple for the decisions ahead of them—saying hello and good-bye to their child, naming, baptizing, other rituals, autopsy, burial.

ॐ Inform the parents about their options and tell them what has been helpful to others: "I have spoken with many women who later regretted very much that they hadn't seen their child. But I have never met anyone who was sorry to have seen their baby," if this was true to your experience. Be sure not to pressure couples.

From *Help, Comfort and Hope after Losing Your Baby in Pregnancy or the First Year* © 1997 Hannah Lothrop. All rights reserved.

&> Allow plenty of time for all decisions: "You don't need to decide right away. Take your time. I'll come back this afternoon, and we can talk about it again." When there is a time limit, let them know precisely how much time they have; for example: "We will hold your child here for two days. You may change your mind at any time."

&> If parents do not want to see their baby, it could mean: (a) "I'm afraid that it will only cause me more pain" or (b) "I am afraid of what I could see."

&> In the case of (a), acknowledge to parents that it might indeed be more painful at first to see their baby, but that in the long run their memories will aid their healing.

&> In the case of (b), tell them that it is normal to be afraid of the unknown, that they can take it step-by-step and change their minds along the way at any time. Assure them that someone will be there for them, if they wish. Ask them (especially if abnormalities are expected) whether they feel it might be helpful for someone to describe their child to them before they decide whether they want to see their baby.

&> Even if the husband or other support persons present don't feel that the mother should see her child, say: "We are morally and legally obliged to meet the wishes of the mother."

&> In case the nursing staff rotates shifts and if extending the shift isn't possible, introduce the person who will care for the parents next, say good-bye to them and let them know when you will be on shift the next day. Continuity is important. If you had good rapport with the mother and/or father and think they might leave before you come back, let them know how they can contact you if they need to talk.

Delivery and Postpartum Care

Women often perceive the birth as completely detached from the death. Because of this we should strive to make the birthing experience as positive as possible (whatever that means to the couple). Wherever possible, help couples to live through birth as they would have if their child had been alive.

Saying hello, saying good-bye:

&> Handle the delivered child with care and dignity.

&> Recognize the woman's delivery performance.

ठ✿ Where women have come to feel assured of their caretakers' acceptance and support and know that they can feel free to follow their instincts, at birth they may display similar bonding behavior as women giving birth to a living child—first they will look, then touch the baby with their fingertips, then touch with the palms of their hands, then perhaps pick up the baby. Allow this process to run its course! Let the parents take the lead.

ठ✿ If parents ask that their child first be described to them, try to look at the baby as parents would. Then tell them about their baby lovingly and clearly. Leave time for them to grasp the details. Where appropriate, make eye contact and use touch (for example, place a hand on their shoulder or arm), relate positive things you have noticed (for example, a tiny snub nose, little dimples, a cute little face).

ठ✿ If parents seem afraid to see their child, you can gently help arouse their curiosity and bridge the gap. Help make their baby real—go step-by-step and acquaint them gradually with the description. Remember that the mind of a newly bereaved person works slowly— after supplying information or asking questions, allow plenty of time for processing before going to the next step.

ठ✿ Start by asking whether they would like to know if it is a boy or a girl.

ठ✿ You can then ask whether they have considered a name for their baby. (If they have chosen a name, refer to the baby by name.)

ठ✿ Ask whether they would like to have a card or certificate containing _____'s name and the baby's foot- and hand prints. Prepare a card including date and time of birth, information on weight and length, any special features and (if available) a lock of hair.

ठ✿ After a while you may say something like: "So, you're afraid to see your baby, hm? What are you afraid of?" After they have told you, you may be able to dispel their fantasies or ask if they would like to know what their baby *does* look like.

ठ✿ If they would like to know what their baby looks like, describe it lovingly (see above). If the baby looks peaceful, you can certainly say so. Find kind but realistic words to describe what parents can expect to see: "Nita looks like she has raspberry-red lipstick on. . . .There are a few dark spots on her sweet little face, just as if she had bruised herself. They usually go away after a day or so. . . .There is a little bit of skin peeling off her leg, just as it does sometimes when we've skinned a knee." At this point, you have taken away a lot of the unknown in the situation, and parents' curiosity usually overcomes their fears.

From *Help, Comfort and Hope after Losing Your Baby in Pregnancy or the First Year*
© 1997 Hannah Lothrop. All rights reserved.

&❧ If there are physical abnormalities and if the parents want to know about them, explain them in a caring way, being very careful not to use words that can create scary images. Parents can take almost anything if they are sufficiently prepared in advance. Wrap the baby in a blanket or cover her in such a way (for example, with a bonnet) so the abnormalities won't be the first thing they notice. They can then decide for themselves how much they want to look at. Help them see what is special about their baby: facial expression, perfect little fingers, possible resemblance. Parents often overlook the abnormalities anyway as they focus on what is unique in their child.

&❧ If the parents see their baby for the first time dressed or bundled, be sure to let them know that they are free to unwrap or undress their baby if they like. Many parents need to do this, but they are often afraid to if they aren't told specifically they may.

&❧ Provide enough time, privacy and support for parents to say hello and good-bye to their baby.

&❧ Respect the intimacy of the parents. Give them time to be alone with their child. (Fathers often have difficulty showing their emotions in the presence of others.) Let them know how they can reach you when they want you to come back.

&❧ Offer parents the opportunity for any parenting action they wish: "Would you like to wash or bathe your baby? Dress her? Hold him? I'm here to help, if you want me to." Remember that this is *the only opportunity* parents will ever have to parent their child. To the extent that it is feasible in the given situation, let them do everything that they would do with a living baby, if they like.

&❧ Be aware that you are a model for the parents. If you tenderly touch and hold the baby, and if you speak with the baby, it will be natural for parents to do so, too.

&❧ If the parents are afraid to hold their baby, leave it in the room with them for a while. Eventually their curiosity may overcome their fears.

&❧ If the parents have not named the baby, perhaps this question will come up now.

&❧ Create mementos:
  ☞ hand- and footprints (use an ink pad)
  ☞ impressions with alginate impression material (order from ICEA, page 250)
  ☞ a lock of hair (if already available)

- a crib card, indicating the name, date of birth, time of birth, and other data that would be given for any living child

- a Certificate of Life; these are available from SHARE or through Perinatal Loss, for example (see Appendix 4, page 245)

- baby's identification band

- sensitive photos of the baby (see page 167)

- the blanket in which the baby was wrapped

- a little gown or bonnet—anything that touched the baby's skin

- possibly a mask of the baby's face or footprints made of plaster of Paris

> Create a ritual. Many helpful ideas for aiding parents in creating rituals can be found in the manual *Bittersweet . . . hellogoodbye*, available through the SHARE national office (see page 247), which should be in the library of every hospital.

> Ask the parents if they want their baby baptized or blessed (and then call the hospital chaplain or their own clergy on their behalf, if they wish). Anyone who has been baptized him- or herself may also baptize in an emergency (they must baptize in the sense it is intended, using water and saying the words given for baptism). Possibly provide a Certificate of Baptism, also available from Perinatal Loss.

> A naming service could be offered (see *Bittersweet . . . hellogoodbye*).

> Leave the baby with his or her parents for as long as they wish. Remember that it is the only time they will ever have with their child—and *only they know* when enough time is enough.

> Let them hold and cradle their baby, if they wish.

> If and when desired, lay out the child next to them in the room and hold a type of wake. You can improvise to create a dignified setting. For example, place a pillow on an instrument table and cover it with a white sheet, perhaps light a candle and decorate it with flowers. Or place the baby in a bassinet or basket. Your hospital may have or would like to obtain a handpainted silk scarf with symbolic designs in which to wrap the baby (also a meaningful volunteering endeavor for support-group members). "You can take as much time with your baby as you wish. If you want me to, I can bring your baby back tomorrow."

> Include siblings, if parents want that. Be aware of the different issues with and approaches to death at different ages (see page 97). Children generally deal much better with death when they can see it rather than when it remains an abstract concept. Young children are not yet capable of abstract thinking. Help make the sibling real for them.

ટ•＞ At their visit, prepare them for the fact that Mommy will be sad.

ટ•＞ If parents would like, ask children if they'd like to see their little baby brother or sister.

ટ•＞ If they do, tell them in a child-like fashion what they will see.

ટ•＞ Call attention to special features: "Do you see his cute ears? See how tiny they are?"

ટ•＞ Model touching and stroking the baby.

ટ•＞ Let them hold the baby where possible. Suggest taking photographs.

ટ•＞ You may want to have a puppet available through which you can talk, particularly to little children who are shy.

ટ•＞ You might make children's picture books on grief available, such as *Thumpy* (see page 105), that you can look at together.

ટ•＞ Arrange for grandparents and close friends to see and bond with the baby, if the parents so wish. This reduces parents' isolation in their grief, because now there are others who have witnessed that the child is real. Besides, grandparents have a right to say hello and good-bye to their grandchild.

ટ•＞ If the child died during a Cesarean section or while the mother was under full anesthesia, let the mother see and bond with her dead child after she awakens.

In the case of miscarriage:

ટ•＞ If the baby is intact after a miscarriage by curettage (from about the 12th week on, possibly earlier), ask the parents if they want to see it. Describe beforehand what they will see. You may dress the tiny baby in specially made gowns or wrap it in a tiny blanket. Many hospitals have tiny handmade gowns available for miscarried babies, some donated by support groups.

ટ•＞ Suggest giving a name.

ટ•＞ Issue a Certificate of Life (see above).

ટ•＞ It is not easy to clearly determine the gender before the tenth week. However, from about the eighth week on, you can usually detect the baby's sex with the help of a strong source of light (fluoroscope).

ટ•＞ Tell parents the options they have for taking care of their precious baby's body, and help them in their decision-making by sharing the pros and cons of the alternatives.

Saying good-bye to a dying child:

&❧ When a newborn's life is threatened, offer the parents as much opportunity as possible for contact with and care of their child. Let them experience nurturing self-touch (page 28) so they will become aware of how nurturing touch benefits and affects their baby. Help them overcome possible fears of contact.

&❧ Where possible and originally planned, suggest and enable breastfeeding.

&❧ If the baby is in the neonatal intensive care unit (NICU), prepare the parents for what they will see (the baby attached to tubes, and so on).

&❧ Let siblings, grandparents or other people close to the family see the baby and say good-bye, if the parents would like that.

&❧ If death is imminent, encourage parents to be with their dying child and possibly hold him or her in their arms, so they can be assured that their baby will not be left alone to die.

&❧ If the child dies in the children's hospital and the mother is restricted to her bed, have the dead child brought to the mother.

The Hospital Stay

&❧ Offer the mother choices as to how she wants to be accommodated (see page 42).

&❧ When she rooms with others, be sensitive in your choice of room and roommates. Prepare the roommates for her arrival, giving them information on the basics of grieving (see chapter 6) and the needs of a bereaved mother and father.

&❧ Be sensitive to the fact that initially most bereaved parents cannot bear to hear a baby cry.

&❧ It would be ideal to make family-centered accommodations available—where partner, relatives and friends have free access and overnight accommodations, if desired.

&❧ Mark the door to a bereaved woman's room with an inconspicuous but clear symbol that signals to everyone—up to the housekeeper— that someone in this room has suffered a loss (for example, you could choose a picture of a rainbow, a half-open rose, a tear, a heart . . .). Also mark the bed. Instruct the entire staff to be sensitive and gentle and not to avoid the bereaved.

১৯ Be available to the mother to help her clarify any open questions and fill in parts of the "story" that she does not remember or that are distorted in her mind—offer her the opportunity to speak with the staff members who assisted her during labor and delivery. "When you think about . . . *[baby's name, the delivery or the moment you found out your baby is dead]*, what comes to your mind?"

১৯ If a woman has not seen her baby, gently tell her that she still can, if she wants to. (Do not ask more than three times, or it may come across to her as pressure to see the baby.) *How* you ask makes the difference.

১৯ Don't take anger and emotional outbursts personally. View them as a sign of a healthy grieving and not as an attack on the personnel because of lack of competence.

১৯ Encourage the parents to take part in planning the funeral or a memorial service, but do not push them. Think of ideas for rituals available or recommend literature (refer to the bibliography under "rituals").

১৯ If the mother needs to stay in the hospital for an extended period of time, possibly see to it that the burial is delayed or, where possible, grant the woman leave of absence so she can participate at the funeral (in a wheelchair if necessary). Another possibility is to explore the idea of having the farewell service in the hospital chapel.

১৯ Introduce members of the perinatal bereavement team responsible for follow-up care to the parents and inform the parents about procedures and options they can help with.

১৯ Tell the bereaved gently and undogmatically about the process of mourning.

Upon discharge from the hospital:

১৯ Answer any questions that may still be open.

১৯ Ask whether there will be caring support at home.

১৯ If necessary, arrange for home visits from a nurse or nurse-midwife or social worker.

১৯ Where indicated, refer to counseling or other appropriate support.

১৯ Supply addresses of local perinatal bereavement self-help groups, if available, or phone numbers of national organizations.

ༀ Help the couple establish contact with other bereaved parents, if they desire.

ༀ Ask if you can keep their address in a card file and if later on they would be willing to be contacted by newly afflicted parents. If so, let them fill out and sign an appropriate form. (You may need to contact them about that later.)

ༀ Give them handouts with helpful information, addresses and a literature list.

ༀ Send them home with the photos and mementos, if they want to take them, or let them know how long photos will be kept on file in the hospital, should they not wish to take the pictures at this time.

ༀ Make an appointment for a follow-up, postpartum visit at the usual time after hospital discharge, or earlier if indicated.

ༀ Whenever possible, prepare the partner separately for the potential length and intensity of mourning. Advise of the need to express difficult emotions. Point out possible differences in the expression of grief in mothers and fathers (see also page 87).

8

Caring for the Bereaved after They Leave the Hospital

Accompanying the bereaved means following them on their path, for only they know what their path looks like. (Michaela Sieh)

Care Possibilities

To ensure a woman or couple's healthy grief process after a perinatal loss, it is a good idea to offer continuous follow-up care for at least one year. Continuity of care like this isn't available in many healthcare settings yet, unfortunately.

Hospital Follow-up Care

As I've said, it's desirable for hospitals to offer a perinatal bereavement-care program in the areas of labor and delivery, intensive care and follow-up care after a loss. It's desirable for professionals—including doctors, nurses, midwives, social workers, psychologists and clergy—to be involved. Try to assign one person knowledgeable about grief to be the team's coordinator. Where continuous follow-up care is not offered, *arrange at least one postpartum meeting* between the staff present at the delivery and the bereaved parents. Having the opportunity to hear the "real story" from the attendants' perspective, to be able to ask any questions that may still be open, perhaps even to revisit the facilities where such a tragic event in their lives took place, can help parents close some gaps in their perception of those events, process more of what has happened, and so move forward in their grief process.

Follow-up Care in the Doctor's Office

Immediate follow-up care of perinatally bereaved mothers is generally in the hands of their gynecologists. The emotional trauma of a woman who has lost a baby (even if it is "only" through miscarriage) is far more severe than the physical trauma of a delivery or a surgical intervention. Repressed, unprocessed grief from the event can and will resurface during subsequent pregnancies as illness. In general, unprocessed grief is the source of many emotional, and thereby also physical, problems, as Aaron Lazare (1979) describes in detail. Therefore, the attending gynecologist should not only pay attention to medical factors, but also see that grief is processed in a healthy way. This is not an easy task, but it is a very important one.

Perhaps the family physician, who is likely to be most aware of the family's overall situation, is in an even better position to survey the effects of the perinatal loss on the family as a whole. If needed, he or she can either help or refer.

Miscarriages are common. To a surprising degree, so are perinatal deaths. In 1992 in the United States, one in 78 babies born was stillborn or died in the first month of life. In Canada, approximately 7 out of 1000 babies born was stillborn or died soon after birth. Staff working in gynecologists' or family physicians' offices should be made aware of and educated about loss and grief so they can respond in a supportive way to the perinatally bereaved. They could also help provide continuity of care; for example, by keeping a card file, keeping track of crucial dates, making periodic telephone calls, and at the time of subsequent pregnancies, being aware of previous pregnancy losses.

Home Care by a Visiting Nurse, Midwife or Doula

When women come home from the hospital, they slowly begin to experience the full impact of their child's death. Because we live in a mobile society, women are often far away from family and friends who might support them. They may lack thoughtful neighbors they can count on in times of distress. These truths can make a difficult situation even more difficult. In addition, bereaved fathers often aren't able to stay home from work for any length of time because of a perinatal death. That's not good for them, nor is it good for their partners— bereaved mothers may feel especially lonely. Initial home care by someone who can assess and treat the physical state of a woman after birth or a miscarriage, while at the same time tending to her emotional needs, is important.

An excellent support person for home care would be a practicing (nurse-) midwife in those states where such services are available. Midwives have been called "wise women." Through their experiences with birth, they may have also come closer to the mysteries of death. They may be the best people to feel their way into a deeper level with the bereaved. They can gauge the significance and effect the death had on the family and integrate individual members into the care structure with a home visit. In the home setting they can also best discern when grief takes a pathological course and suggest additional help. A visiting nurse, who perhaps has some additional training in the area of grief and mourning, is another good initial support person for a bereaved mother at home. So is a doula.

Spiritual Care

A pastor, priest or rabbi can also be an important support for parents who have experienced the death of their child. When it comes to questions of baptism or burial, they can contribute substantially in helping parents find peace in this painful situation by their attitude and actions. They or other spiritual guides can also help in phases of grief that will come—quests for meaning or moments of spiritual desolation and doubt. Many clergy have been educated in pastoral counseling and have learned to respond with great empathy. It is part of their pastoral responsibilities to be available to the bereaved. They are in a position to make home visits beyond the initial period of mourning.

Support by a Counselor or Therapist

Mourning is a normal life process. But sometimes, when many aggravating factors appear at once (use Questionnaire 1 on page 231 to assess), the bereaved may feel too overwhelmed to tackle that process alone. Then they need professional help. It is a good idea for the professional to have worked with the bereaved before and to be familiar with the pattern of a healthy grief process. Information on assessment of complicated mourning and grief therapy are given in this chapter on page 201. Suggestions for working with and guiding the bereaved through the phases of mourning are found in chapters 2 through 5. ADEC, the Association of Death Education and Counseling (see page 253), provides continuing education in this field and can also supply addresses of grief counselors nationwide.

Facts for Caregivers

Information on grief and mourning and guidelines for responding to the bereaved are beginning to be taught more among medical faculties and during nursing and midwifery training. Clergypersons may not be prepared for this special situation. Continuing education about perinatal bereavement is becoming more available, but those who are most uncomfortable responding to these families don't always take advantage of it. Good will is not enough. Information is also needed.

A summary of information of special interest to professionals confronted with the treatment and aftercare of the perinatally bereaved follows. It is based partly on worksheets of Sister Jane Marie Lamb, who adapted material regarding perinatal loss from the works of Glen Davidson, M.D., and J. William Worden, M.D.

Principles and Procedures in Responding to the Bereaved

ê» Get to know the history of possible earlier losses.

ê» Explain grief to the parents.

ê» Define normal behavior and normal reactions.

ê» Help parents make their own decisions. (Give necessary information. Allow ample time for decision-making.)

ê» Allow for individual differences.

ê» Provide time to grieve.

ê» Support them in fulfilling the five tasks of mourners (see page 195).

ê» Help parents reflect on how they are handling the loss and, if necessary, plan together more constructive ways of coping.

ê» Strive for ongoing support (make phone calls and/or home visits, talk one-to-one, keep track of important dates, point out self-help groups, put parents in touch with other bereaved, share literature).

ê» Know to whom the bereaved can turn, in case they appear unable to move forward on their own.

Follow-up Care

ê» Initial home visits by a visiting nurse or midwife, as needed

ê» Follow-up meeting with the hospital staff two to four weeks after hospital discharge, when shock has subsided and questions arise

ê» Further appointments (perhaps a month later), thorough checkup between the fourth and sixth month postpartum, and at least one more meeting around the first anniversary of death

ŝ» Where necessary, more frequent contact by telephone (for example, on the monthly memorial dates following the loss)

Assessing the Situation

Questions from Questionnaire 1 in Appendix 2 can facilitate initial communication with the bereaved. The questions may help them better understand the context of the loss. The questionnaire may reveal when intervention is needed.

Offering Support through the Four Phases of Grief

1. Shock and Numbness

☐ Be available. Show compassion. Don't hide behind a professional mask.

☐ Touch is the basic form of human communication at this time.

☐ Help parents grasp the reality of this tragic event.

☐ Prepare parents in simple words for what will happen (decisions ahead, options, pros and cons).

☐ Allow time for decision-making—tell the bereaved how much time is available.

☐ Find out who else they would like to call on for support and who should see the baby.

☐ Facilitate parents' bonding with their baby so they can perhaps process their grief better.

☐ Describe the child, perhaps (look at the baby as a parent would).

☐ Get more ideas for support in chapters 2 and 7.

2. Searching and Yearning

☐ Prepare parents for the normal course of mourning.

☐ Help parents accept and express emotions, especially pain, anger and guilt (see chapter 3).

☐ If anger is expressed against the staff, just listen. *Don't become defensive.*

☐ Help the bereaved search for answers to the questions that preoccupy them. (Possible questions: Was I at fault? Did the baby suffer? What did the autopsy show? Can that happen to me again? Do we need genetic counseling?)

☐ Do not mask grief and hamper your emotions by focusing on medical and physical facts alone.

☐ Offer access to medical records, if desired.

☐ Steer parents to literature that could answer their questions.

☐ Inform the bereaved about local self-help groups (they are particularly open to them in this phase) or provide phone numbers.

☐ Help the afflicted find their own answers.

☐ Remember: Pat answers are not expected, nor are they constructive.

3. Disorientation and Transformation

☐ Be available as a sounding board as they look for meaning, new values and a new orientation to life.

☐ Be knowledgeable about and recommend inspirational reading.

☐ Help them view this phase of disorientation as a normal part of the grief process.

☐ Help the bereaved assess their degree of self-nurturing and attention to basic needs and determine in which area help may be needed.

☐ Suggest measures from chapter 4 to promote good health and healing in physical, emotional, mental or spiritual realms.

☐ Advise against making long-term decisions or major changes at this time.

☐ Suggest a thorough physical examination by the family physician between the fourth and sixth month, when the bereaved are at particular risk of serious illness.

☐ If complicated mourning is suspected by the attending physician, make or arrange for home visits (visiting nurse, midwife). The extent of disorientation can better be assessed in their home environment.

☐ In case of pathological grief, refer the bereaved to a counselor or therapist knowledgeable about grief (see Appendix 4).

☐ In case of addictions, provide information about and suggest attendance at 12-step groups (for example, Alcoholics Anonymous, Overeaters Anonymous).

☐ Where childhood grief from life in a dysfunctional family is surfacing in this loss situation, refer to a local chapter of ACOA (Adult Children of Alcoholics).

☐ Help the bereaved reflect on when they might be ready for a new pregnancy.

4. Renewal and Reorientation

☐ Provide care and support throughout a new pregnancy. Be aware that the couple may be more fearful during this pregnancy.

☐ If a subsequent-pregnancy group is available locally, give the address.

☐ Pay special attention to the woman if she is unable to become pregnant again. This is a special type of loss and grief.

☐ As a therapist, help bring closure to the experience and help the bereaved find a new orientation to life, when they are ready (see chapter 5).

Helping with the Five Tasks of Mourners

1. Grasping and Accepting the Reality of Loss

☐ Help make the baby real.

☐ Help create memories.

☐ Do not administer sedatives routinely.

☐ Help create rituals (for example, a funeral).

☐ Support with empathy. "Be there" for the family.

☐ Remember: This task is easier if parents see their child.

2. Experiencing the Pain of Loss and Other Emotions

☐ Facilitate the parents' becoming aware of and getting in touch with all their feelings. Encourage expression of these feelings.

☐ Listen attentively. Be a sounding board.

☐ Help parents realize how they may block feelings.

☐ Be conscious of your own reactions to various emotions.

☐ Do not try to deaden pain through medication.

☐ Possibly help find constructive ways of expressing anger.

☐ Suggest, and possibly assist with, ways to deal with feelings (see chapter 3).

☐ Offer human closeness. Hold the bereaved, where appropriate, to facilitate the expression of feelings and make it more bearable.

☐ Inform parents of support groups, providing information and addresses, that can put them in touch with other bereaved.

☐ Possibly attend a ritual, if asked.

☐ Remember: Trying to spare pain in the beginning leads to greater pain and possibly complications later.

3. Adapting to a Life without the Child

☐ Help bereaved get in touch with their own inner resources. Through active listening, help them find their own answers, eventually leading to a new orientation towards their experience.

☐ Support them in redirecting the love for their baby into other channels.

☐ Help develop rituals for what was missed (see Appendix 2).

4. Gradually Withdrawing Emotional Energy from the Baby. Reinvesting Love in New Relationships and Tasks without Guilt

☐ Reinforce the parents' decision not to attempt a new pregnancy prematurely (allowing ample time to work through this loss. No child can be a replacement for another).

☐ Encourage the eventual healthy emotional withdrawal from the baby. Give "permission" to welcome a new baby into their lives or to reinvest energy in other ways.

☐ Help them see that letting go of their dead baby does not mean forgetting their child.

☐ Help them think of ways to find closure (see chapter 5).

☐ Make the bereaved aware that grief's "shadow" will always remain and is normal, but that intensity, frequency and length of grief will lessen gradually.

5. Finding Meaning in the Experience

☐ Use active listening techniques to help the bereaved find meaning in the experience.

☐ Possibly help them discover "gifts" from their child, being sensitive to timing and your use of words.

☐ Provide inspirational literature (see Bibliography).

☐ Guide them in applying measures suggested in chapter 4.

☐ Encourage writing or other creative forms of expression.

☐ Possibly accompany them in their spiritual quests.

Conditions that Promote Communication

These positive qualities are important: Nurturing attentiveness, responsiveness, eye contact (unless not called for), warmth, acceptance, respect, empathy, clarity, genuineness, self-disclosure (where indicated), openness to paranormal experiences (see page 199), signaling openness and readiness to listen through body posture, willingness to allow ample time for parents to express themselves.

If the parents have named their baby, refer to the baby by name.

Typical Grief Behavior

☐ Frustration

- When expressed directly, the bereaved makes statements such as "could not see the baby" and the like.
- When expressed indirectly, the bereaved suffers from restlessness, insomnia, nervous activity.

☐ Anger

- The bereaved expresses anger at the partner, the baby itself and attending staff.

☐ Bizarre Behavior and Searching

- The bereaved may play with dolls, hear baby cries, carry around objects of a similar size or weight (this stage reaches its high point two to four months after the loss).

☐ Preoccupation with the Experience

- The bereaved continuously replays in her mind the delivery, prenatal period, finding out about the baby's death, how she was treated by attendants, saying good-bye to the baby.
- Or, the bereaved does things mechanically (for example, peeling a carrot until nothing is left).

☐ Disorganization

- The bereaved may display a temporary inability to carry out ordinary tasks.

Signs of Normal Grief

Sighing, tightness of throat, dullness of perception (touch them to keep them aware of reality), volatile emotions (those who do not cry need more attention), guilt feelings, aloofness (they do insignificant things to avoid contact with others and to distract themselves) and/or a marked change in behavior—all three are normal signs of grief.

Assessing the Attention Given to Basic Needs

By assessing the following factors, we can gauge to what degree the bereaved are coping with the loss or if additional help is necessary (Davidson 1984). These points help us spot the mourners "at risk." It's fine to ask open-ended questions in a casual way, as part of a conversation. Avoid creating a feeling in the bereaved that she is being interrogated.

ê Supportive social network (Proved to be the most essential factor—research shows it improves the immune system): Who can you speak with openly? Can you and your husband talk about what happened? How does that go?

ê Well-balanced nutrition (With a weight gain of more than 20 pounds, expect greater disorientation and more illness): How is your appetite? Have you gained or lost weight? What do you enjoy eating?

ê Sufficient fluid intake (Caution with coffee and tea!): What do you drink during the day? Do you remember to drink enough fluids?

ê Adequate exercise (Physical activity releases endorphins, which improve emotional well-being): Are you getting any physical exercise?

ê Sufficient rest (Processing grief uses additional energy): Can you sleep through the night? Do you get enough rest? Are you able to get to sleep? When do you go to bed? How much sleep do you get each night? Are you taking sleeping medication?

Assessing the Effectiveness of Support Networks

To work best, support during bereavement should come from several sources: 25% from oneself, 20% from one's partner, and 55% from environmental support, including

ê people: family, friends, neighbors, colleagues, professionals, funeral director and others

ê activities: art, music, dance, writing, travel, work, volunteer work

ê meditation

ê faith

ê bereavement or other self-help groups

ê courses and workshops

ê counseling

(adapted from O. Carl Simonton and Stephanie Matthews-Simonton: *Getting Well Again*, 1978)

Extraordinary (Paranormal) Experiences of the Bereaved

In their encounter with death, people often report profound occur-
rences that don't seem to fit into the normal realm of experience.
These can come in the form of dreams, intuitions, visions, sensations
and the like. The bereaved need to be able to talk about these phenomena but often don't because they are afraid they will be considered
"strange," even mentally ill. When you hear an allusion to a paranormal experience, facilitate talking about it. For example, by saying:

> *In context with death, people sometimes have experiences that can't be
> explained. Many people report "encounters" with their child in some form
> or other—others have strange dreams that really affect them. That isn't
> abnormal. Have you experienced anything like that?*

Such a statement assures them of your acceptance. If a bereaved
mother relates this kind of occurrence to you, you will help her clarify
the experience and make it more concrete in her consciousness by
asking about it. That can help her eventually discover what meaning
it might have for her. You might encourage her to draw pictures about
it—whatever comes to her mind. Be careful not to interpret what is
reported to you unless you are trained to do so. By asking questions
about the picture or pointing out what you notice, however, you can
help the woman draw her own conclusions. Bereaved fathers can experience such phenomena as well.

Monitoring the Health of the Bereaved

Grief makes people more prone to illnesses, especially when they have
an inadequate social network (Jacobs/Ostfeld 1977). The lymphocyte
count (important for immunity against disease) can drop drastically,
from 2000 to only 400, within seven to eight months after a loss,
according to research findings. But if a person connects to a strong support system, the immune system improves considerably.

Increased Susceptibility to Disease

A study by E. Lindemann (1944) showed that serious (some even life-
threatening) diseases occur more frequently following a loss, including
heart attack, intestinal cancer, hypertension and diabetes. Aggravation
of some of these diseases can be prevented if they are
recognized early enough. Therefore, a general physical examination is
indicated between the fourth and sixth months. Family physicians
should also pay attention to the following common illnesses in

people who have been bereaved:

ཆ chronic depression

ཆ alcohol, medication or drug dependency

ཆ improper diet (20 to 35 pounds weight loss or gain)

ཆ electrolyte disorders

ཆ suicidal tendencies

These psychosomatic complaints are also frequently attributed to a loss:

ཆ headaches

ཆ lower-back pain

ཆ colds and flu

ཆ chronic fatigue

ཆ impotence or other sexual disorders

ཆ sleep disturbance

Go Easy with Medication

An investigation by Richard Dayringer et al. (1981) showed that 87% of physicians routinely prescribe barbiturates and tranquilizers at the time of a loss. Eighty-three per cent continue to prescribe these a week later. Others prescribe antidepressants. J. William Worden, M.D., observes:

> *It is usually inadvisable to give antidepressant medications to people undergoing an acute grief reaction. These antidepressives take a long time to work, they rarely relieve normal grief symptoms, and they could pave the way for an abnormal grief process.* (Worden 1987)

Professor Glen Davidson recommends using medication only on a temporary basis and only if necessary, dispensing it with discretion. For example, mild doses of tranquilizers and antidepressants should be taken for a maximum of 4 out of 7 nights and only over a short period of time, with the goal of retaining normal functioning during the day. Chapter 4 lists natural ways that have been effective in enhancing sleep, relaxation and inner calm. Helping people work through their experiences is certainly more healthful than prescribing psychiatric drugs.

The Unhealthy, Complicated Grief Process

According to Glen Davidson (1984), only 5 to 15% of the population has unhealthy grief reactions. We need to be aware that "part of the work of adaptation requires a period of depression and personal adjustment." The majority of mourners work through their grief in a healthy way within one or two years. But some people need psychotherapeutic intervention. Of these, there are two groups:

ह» The bereaved who have the feeling of being "stuck in grief" and seek therapy on their own.

ह» Individuals who consult their physician because of physical or emotional problems, without associating their problems with unresolved grief.

In the second group, it can be difficult to trace the source of the problems to unresolved grief. The physician's experience usually determines whether he or she can diagnose unresolved grief as the primary problem and, if need be, make an appropriate referral to a psychotherapist (at best, one familiarized with working with the bereaved) in addition to other treatments. J. William Worden's excellent book, *Grief Counseling and Grief Therapy* (1982), helps readers recognize and respond appropriately to instances of pathological grief.

Varieties of Complicated Mourning

Complicated mourning can take one of four forms.

ह» Chronic grief reactions

Prolonged reactions that do not resolve. Bereaved have the feeling of "not being able to move on."

Question: Which of the tasks of mourners (see page 137) are not being resolved? Why not?

Intervention: Focus on the resolution of these tasks.

ह» Delayed grief reactions

Inhibited, suppressed or postponed grief reactions, surfacing with later losses.

Signs: Reaction to a later loss that is out of proportion; excessive emotional reactions when seeing a film showing loss or when someone else suffers a loss.

Intervention: Support by reactivating and reliving the repressed emotions (see "Second Task of Mourners," page 137) ê❧ Exaggerated grief reactions

Disabling reactions, development of despair and phobias (often centered around death) that do not fade with time.

Background: Often previous ambivalence about the initial pregnancy, resulting in guilty feelings

Intervention: Help to acknowledge and work through feelings

ê❧ Masked grief reactions

Symptoms that are not recognized as responses to loss (for example, psychosomatic symptoms, bizarre behaviors or thoughts, possibly psychiatric symptoms or delinquent behavior)

Background: Not wanting to face the pain of grief

Intervention: Guide through the tasks of mourning

(Categories based on J. William Worden, M.D., 1987)

Indications for Therapeutic Intervention

Therapeutic intervention might help bereaved who show some of the signs below.

ê❧ The five tasks of mourning (see page 137) have not been completed, resulting in: denial of the death; not feeling the emotions associated with grief; helplessness, withdrawal; not being able to find meaning in the experience

ê❧ Intense expressions of grief when talking about the loss (as though it had just happened), though years have passed

ê❧ Relatively minor incidents trigger an intense grief reaction

ê❧ Mother does not clear out the nursery for a long time

ê❧ Self-destructive impulses (for example, alcohol and drug abuse, food addiction)

ê❧ Persistent phobia regarding illness and death

ê❧ Persistent hostility, anger or repressed anger, which leads to rigid behavior

ê❧ Persistent low self-esteem and guilt

ê❧ Lack of normal functioning in everyday life after 18 to 24 months

ê❧ Persistent, gross neglect of social relationships

ê❧ No noticeable adaptation to the situation (a process should be evident, even if it seems worse)

ê❧ Subject of loss comes up repeatedly in conversations

ও In children: continual low-level performance in school and continual aggressive or hostile behavior

ও Persistent relationship problems

(based on J. William Worden, M.D., 1987)

Grief Therapy

This treatment description for bereaved who need therapy to recover from their loss is also based on Dr. J. William Worden's book, *Grief Counseling and Grief Therapy* (1987).

Procedure:

ও Rule out physical illness

ও Set up a contract with client

Time: Limit the arrangement to from eight to ten sessions
Goal: Explore the loss and its relationship to the present problem; that is: Recognize and resolve conflicts surrounding the death that hinder completion of the Five Tasks of Mourners; complete the Five Tasks.

Method:

ও Revive memories of the pregnancy, the birth and the baby.

ও Evaluate which of the Five Tasks of Mourners have not been completed.

ও Deal with the emotions that are revived by the memories (or with the apparent lack of emotion).

ও Explore where things stand in the way of grief resolution, and defuse them.

ও Acknowledge the finality of the death.

ও Help say a final good-bye to the baby.

Grief therapy focuses on the completion of the grief tasks to help overcome inner resistance. Naturally, in the course of grief therapy, underlying personality problems (self-esteem, identity, handling anger and so forth), relationship problems and life-history problems can surface. For example, with adult children from alcoholic or other dysfunctional family backgrounds (see literature), the loss of a baby can intensely revive unresolved childhood grief. In this case, after grief therapy concludes, negotiate new goals for further therapy. Or, refer clients to another professional specializing in the area in question (family therapy, couples therapy, chemical abuse, and so on), or to self-help groups, such as ACOA.

Care during Subsequent Pregnancies

In past years it was customary to counsel women after a miscarriage or stillbirth to become pregnant again soon to overcome the loss. In some individual cases this may not have been harmful. However, experience has shown that a new pregnancy runs more smoothly when a woman is physically *and* emotionally healed.

Pregnant women who have been previously bereaved (this includes miscarriage) need special attention during their next pregnancy and delivery, particularly if they have suffered more than one loss. The fear that "something like this could happen again" often holds them back from completely enjoying and bonding with the baby growing inside them. Relief and happiness mix with anguish and worry. If the baby died early in pregnancy, that same point in the new pregnancy may present a particularly difficult hurdle for the parents to overcome. A previous perinatal loss can bring pathology to subsequent pregnancies, particularly when grief from the previous pregnancy hasn't been adequately processed.

Women who have lost a child generally need strong reassurance from others in later pregnancies, especially when they think the death could have been prevented by a timely intervention. They may press for more frequent examinations, especially in the last weeks. This is understandable. As part of preventive health care, these checkups should not only be made possible, but welcomed.

Women who don't succeed in becoming pregnant, and really want to, need additional support. They may also need help to decide whether to consider adoption. Many couples aren't ready to consider adoption until they have tried to become pregnant for a relatively long period of time. Approaching this possibility early needs to be done with great sensitivity.

9

Spiritual Care of the Bereaved

Blessed are those who mourn, for they shall be comforted. (Matthew 5:4)

Questions of Baptism and Funeral

Chaplains, ministers and rabbis can greatly help bereaved parents. They are important to healing. The first contact of the parents with the clergy usually comes around the time of the loss, with a request for a baptism or blessing of the dead or dying child. Some parents I have spoken with were disappointed when the clergy they approached placed dogma above their pastoral role. There is plenty of latitude in interpreting religious laws and traditions, and an individual may act outside of his or her pastoral duty at his or her discretion.

A Mother's Feelings

In the ecumenically oriented handbook, *Bittersweet . . . hellogoodbye* (for ordering, see page 251), Sister Jane Marie Lamb and others have collected a number of rituals for saying good-bye to a dead baby. The following letter, slightly condensed, gives insight into the emotions of a mother, and can be found in this comprehensive book.

> *Timothy John was stillborn on April 6, 1984. I wanted my baby baptized. My wishes were refused by the hospital chaplain.*
>
> *Being raised a Catholic during my formative years in the 1950s and '60s, we were taught that you did not enter the kingdom of heaven unless you had met the two criteria of faith and baptism. It was this basis that led me to request baptism for my baby. I didn't want him in limbo or hell. He was my baby. I carried him. I felt him move. He was life within me. We had established a relationship. I would pat my stomach and tell him that everything would be OK—that Mommy loves you, baby. I wanted to make everything OK in his death, also, by having him baptized.*
>
> *That the request was denied was an additional stress for me. I did not see why my baby couldn't be baptized—even if the baptism was to make me feel better. Isn't that part of what this healing process is about? Isn't that part of the reason we have chaplains in the hospital?*
>
> *My parish priest did baptize the baby at the graveside service. I will be eternally grateful to this dear, understanding priest for doing this one additional service for my baby.*
>
> *Later, I approached the hospital chaplain on this issue of baptism. He explained it just wasn't done, because baptism was a sacrament for the living. I still don't understand. My baby was alive at one time, even though he was stillborn.*
>
> *It is such a short, turmoil-filled time before the baby is taken away. Can't we at least do any small part to reinforce our faith in such troubled times? Please baptize my baby.* (Reprinted with permission from SHARE.)

A Pastor's Experience

In the same book, a pastor called to the delivery room and asked to baptize a stillborn child describes his thoughts and experience:

> *The mother, father and I spoke softly, stood quietly, and shared a moment of horror. I stroked her hair. As minutes stretched into hours, I began to understand what we were doing theologically and pastorally. This was not a fetus, but a full-term child. The parents would need to grieve the loss of their baby just like the death of any child. But before they could say*

good-bye, they had to have a way to say hello. Baptism is the moment in which the community of faith says "Hello". . . .

I began to understand more. One of the most important elements of the Baptism is the naming. That name generates power that says "this is a real person." . . . *I asked the parents if they would like to name the baby. Yes, they already had a boy's and a girl's name picked out.*

Finally, the baby was delivered. The parents, family and I gathered in the labor room. The nurse brought in the baby and laid it in the mother's arms. As this young mother spent the only moment she would ever have with her baby, we stood in silence and shared the moment. It was powerful. It was a worship experience. After some time, I began to speak. I spoke of God's love and the significance of this baby, no matter what happens.

As I have so many times before, I took the baby into my arms. I looked into his face and spoke the words that are thousands of years old. "What name shall be given this child? . . . Nathan Andrew, I baptize you in the name of the Father and of the Son and of the Holy Spirit. Amen."

In the midst of tears, which is an authentic baptism by water and the Spirit, we offered him up to God and asked that Nathan Andrew be held gently and tenderly for us. The father took the baby from my arms. . . . With the full authority of my office, I told them that they must bury the baby and that we would have a graveside service. This baby would not disappear but have a proper place in history so that we could say "Good-bye." We had just said hello to Nathan Andrew, and now we must say good-bye. But we would do it with the sure confidence that the memory of his life would never be forgotten. This life would be held gently at the breast of God for all eternity.

(Adapted from "Saying Hello and Good-bye" by John D. Stoneking. Found in *The Circuit Rider*, March 1984. Copyright Abingdon Press. Used by permission.)

Parents See Things Differently

Some Christian and Jewish regulations and traditions distinguish among children who were born alive and those who were born dead. Moreover, certain traditional Jewish burial rituals, including the recitation of the *Kaddish* and *Tziduk Hadim*, are only in order after 30 days.

Mothers who have felt life inside them have a different understanding.

> *It makes no difference to me in my pain and grief whether my child took a breath or whether he had already died in my womb. I have felt him alive in me, and the grief is the same.*

Denying a ritual can bring despair and alienation. Conducting a ritual can bring peace and solace.

From my conversations with bereaved parents, I have learned that the issue of a funeral is very important for them. Many fear that their baby has not been handled with respect and dignity. Their fantasies about what might have happened to their child keep them from finding peace. After a funeral, particularly if parents were attended to by their clergy with empathy and sympathetic understanding, they often find peace. This is especially true if the parents strongly desired a funeral.

In some cases, parents may want a home service or a bedside service in the privacy of the hospital room instead of a graveside service. The more personalized a service can be and the more the parents can be integrated into its preparation, the more healing it can bring. Healing the parents emotionally must be a primary consideration and goal.

Powerful Rituals

Rabbi Robert H. Loewy, himself a bereaved parent, writes:

> *In the past, when infant mortality was common, burial and mourning customs commenced if the infant was 31 days old or more. In our time, when infant mortality is rare, and certainly unexpected, it is my sense that we should simply utilize our rituals and customs at an earlier stage. To deny ritual acknowledgment communicates the message that the family's loss is not at all significant, and that their baby was not a real person. Rabbis have a responsibility to comfort mourners through rituals.* (from the Journal of Reformed Judaism, Spring 1988.)

Some traditions from the past aren't quite appropriate today. But rituals are still very important. Perhaps churches should consider ways of giving new strength to existing rituals or of finding new rituals that fit our modern times better and bring real comfort and healing to parents.

Sometimes parents come to their clergy still feeling a lot of pain long after a loss. They can still be helped with rituals at this point, especially when they regret not having done all they felt they might have at the time of the loss. If, for example, no funeral rite was held, clergy might offer to conduct a memorial service—even if years have elapsed. *Bittersweet . . . hellogoodbye* contains many suggestions for rituals. Excerpts from some of these rituals can be found in Appendix 3.

Meeting the Bereaved

Parents with whom I have spoken were not comforted by platitudes. References to "God's will" only made them angry. It felt right to them when their pastors, too, could admit helplessness. The Jewish philosopher and theologian Martin Buber said, "All real living is meeting." When we have a genuine encounter with another person, our words flow from our heart, and God will speak through us. "Behold, I have put my words in thy mouth." (Jeremiah 1:9) For Christians, Jesus meeting his disciples on the way to Emmaus can serve as a model for being with the bereaved through the different phases of mourning.

Sister Jane Marie, who has helped so many bereaved parents, says:

> *Accompany them on their way from the beginning and stay with them when they reach the dark valley. Instead of being left alone in their grief and sorrow, through your presence and support on their journey, God's presence will be experienced. It is not a time to preach to them or to make reproaches about their not being in church very often. Instead, have sympathy and let them show you where they are in their grief process. Through understanding and support, they can find a deeper relationship to God.*

> *Give them permission to experience everything that is part of their journey —pain, confusion, helplessness, anger, doubts about God, isolation and other painful emotions. Many of these feelings may be new to them . . ., they may be ashamed and fearful of admitting to their anger and jealousy.*

When the bereaved get stuck in their grief process, gently ask about possible guilt feelings. We must admit our guilt or our assumed guilt to at least one other person before we can become free of it and find forgiveness. To support other people in their journey through grief, we have faced our own grief and processed it in a good way.

The Question of Faith

Whenever a child dies, the question of meaning usually surfaces. Many persons despair of a God in whom they had believed and trusted until now. Many shake their fists at God, are angry at Him and turn away.

When I was pregnant with Eve I often prayed—not directly to God but to someone who is in charge of everything. I couldn't pray to God because I had sworn and cursed at Him so much after Laura's death.

It's by allowing the bereaved to express this "no" that perhaps in grief a true "yes" can emerge. This process is facilitated by people who accept them unconditionally, and act as a sounding board for their thoughts and feelings. When anger and disappointment have been vented, a vacuum is created that may truly make room for God.

Those who may have lived a materially oriented life before may discover a power that carries them along in the midst of the most agonizing experience of their lives. Their grief opens a door to God. Perhaps human love coming from the people who stand by them in their deep anguish becomes a precious stepping stone along their way.

I've become—I don't know if it's religious, but something in that direction . . . now I have a very sure feeling that there is "Something," whereas before I thought, "There is nothing."

Additional Ways the Clergy Can Help

Pastors, priests and rabbis can help bereaved parents by putting them in touch with other parents who have suffered a similar loss. (Keep a file for this.) They can make their congregation sensitive to the special needs of grieving parents mourning a child whom no one else had gotten to know. They can create a handout that educates neighbors, friends and family about how to treat perinatally bereaved parents. The handout can be made available in the church and synagogue.

Clergy can mark in their calendar "memorial" days where grief peaks (for example, the anniversary dates of the death three, six and 12 months later) and get in touch with bereaved parents at these times, when others think they "must have gotten over it by now." Especially during the period of disorientation (see chapter 4)—usually the second half of the bereavement year—parents need more support than before, because they are searching more deeply for meaning and a new spiritual context. The most important thing is to be there with love.

Ministers, priests and rabbis can encourage the establishment of support groups in their congregations by making meeting rooms available and publicizing the addresses of support groups through a newsletter to their congregation. They can offer meditation times for the bereaved or hold special services for perinatally bereaved parents (see *Bittersweet . . . hellogoodbye*), offering the opportunity for talk afterwards.

10

Support Groups for Bereaved Parents

No one understands bereaved parents as well as other bereaved parents. After losing a baby, we need the support of people who understand what we're going through. Those who have already passed through some stages of grief can give hope to the recently bereaved. They are living proof that the sun *will* shine again. But they can also help the bereaved understand that rocks along the road are part of the experience, and what can help. As time goes on, being there for others in need is healing in itself.

Where no support groups exist for parents who have lost a baby through stillbirth, newborn death or miscarriage, bereaved parents may be motivated to form a self-help group themselves at some point.

If you would like to establish a support group, you may want to connect with a national group such as SHARE (see page 251) and form a local chapter. Make contact with other bereaved parents by putting up a note at your doctor's office. Physicians usually are relieved to have handouts to distribute to parents as "first aid" and to know where to direct them for support, or where there is a meeting parents could attend. You might get in touch with bereaved parents by placing a small ad in the local newspaper. Most town papers will publish a small article on the topic and the concerns of the group. Hospitals may sponsor your group by offering meeting space and other resources. I'll describe the SHARE model as *one* possibility for starting a mutual-help group.

The SHARE Group Model

SHARE (Source of Help in Airing and Resolving Experiences) was founded in 1977 by Sister Jane Marie Lamb and is now directed by Cathi Lammert. Both women have answered thousands of letters and phone calls, giving comfort and help to perinatally bereaved parents.

The SHARE office keeps track of all that relates to perinatal loss, issues a bimonthly newsletter and tries to create public awareness for the needs and situation of perinatally bereaved parents. A short book, *Starting Your Own SHARE Group,* contains many suggestions for getting started. Its newsletter, *Caring Notes,* is directed at and covers concerns of SHARE group leaders. SHARE also sponsors national conferences and educates the public. The group's toll-free telephone number is: 1-800-821-6819.

The SHARE model is suitable for parents who want to support others as well as for hospital staff who want to organize a support group within their institution as part of follow-up care. SHARE groups enlist the cooperation of committed professionals (doctors, labor and delivery nurses, community health nurses, midwives, psychologists, social workers and clergy). The group coordinator sends a letter to all parents whose child was stillborn or miscarried or died shortly after birth to invite them to the group meetings. A little card containing information about SHARE (time and date of regular meetings and the telephone number of contacts who can give information or talk with callers) is routinely distributed at the hospital to all bereaved parents.

Group members plan the meeting. Guidelines provides a sense of safety for the group participants. Meetings might consist of open group discussions or talks on specific topics given by a professional (minister, rabbi, psychologist, funeral director, gynecologist, pathologist, geneticist and others), or both. The speaker is asked to give a short presentation. Having someone talk to the group in the beginning can help allay the fears of parents who are new and find it difficult at first to talk about their situation to a group, or cry. Discussions can also revolve around a specific topic.

Guidelines

These orientation guidelines can be handed out or read aloud at the beginning of the meeting:

1. Each of your experiences is unique and valid. No one is here to criticize or analyze.

2. Feel free to share or not share your feelings and experiences. We will not probe. If you have had a similar experience and care to talk about it, feel free to do so.

3. Note pads are available for you to write down any words or phrases that come to mind. It is OK to write while others are talking. Your notes are for yourself, and you will not be asked to share them.

4. It's OK to cry. There are tissues available and we ask that you be sensitive to your neighbor's needs. We ask your permission to cry, too.

5. If you need to leave, feel free to go. One of us will follow you out of the room to be sure that before you leave, you are ready to drive.

6. Share your feelings about the meeting with your spouse or partner. We do not want to create a communication gap, but rather increase communication.

7. The group time is not intended as a time for medical advice. If you have medical questions, we will respond to them after the general meeting.

8. If you wish to share a bad experience you have had with a hospital, nurse or doctor, feel free to relate the experience. Please do not use names in the discussion, however.

9. Tape recorders, if used, will be turned on for the speaker's presentation only.

10. After the short presentation, you may respond to what the speaker has said or open with anything you wish to bring up.

11. We encourage you to respond to each other.

12. To respect the privacy of each parent, we will not discuss, except among SHARE members, the content of these meetings.

A steering committee provides a chairperson or leader. That job rotates for each meeting. The chairperson moderates the discussion, intervening as necessary to redirect unproductive tendencies to more productive discussion. Leaders should be a little further along in the mourning process. It helps if they have a broad perspective on the overall grief process.

Leaders should be well informed about the resources available in the community (for example, bereavement counselors, therapists familiar with grief, marriage counselors, social workers, clergy and others), so they can refer persons who need additional support. They should be knowledgeable about funeral regulations, costs and other information. (Where are children buried? What types of graves are there? How can one get a special permit for burial, if desired? Where can you get burial cradles for tiny babies? and so forth.) Some groups eventually develop task forces to collect information or to educate the community at a state or local level.

Topics for Group Meetings

The following topics can be helpful for setting up a discussion meeting. The list is based on the ideas of Pat Stauber, member of the Perinatal Bereavement Team of North Shore Hospital in Miami, co-organizer of the 1995 ADEC conference there, and a moderator of hospital-based SHARE meetings.

Grief

Understanding grief

Stages of grief

Tasks of mourners

Dealing with shock

Dealing with anger

Dealing with guilt

The need to cry

Siblings and grief

Surviving holidays and anniversaries of death

When there are no keepsakes of your baby

Meaningful rituals

Relationship with Others

The effect of perinatal bereavement on the couple's relationship

The grief of the mother, the grief of the father: understanding each other

Communication

Sexuality and loss

Reactions from friends, neighbors, family

Meeting the needs of surviving children

Relationship with Yourself

Enhancing your healing—assessing your needs

Promoting good physical health

Paying attention to healthy nutrition

Stress reduction

Self-nurturing; being good to yourself

Relaxation and meditation—two pillars on the way to recovery

Healing the emotions

Self-worth

Self-assertion

Writing as therapy

Drawing as therapy

Talking about dreams or "weird" experiences

Developing your creativity

Doing service as an instrument of healing

The power of love

Time Passes

Finishing unfinished business

Finding meaning

Spirituality

Looking ahead, looking back: How can I find a balance?

Turning towards life again

Growing through the experience of grief

Who am I, leaving this tunnel?

Becoming pregnant again

Subsequent pregnancies

Professional Contacts

> Inviting bereavement counselors and therapists
>
> Emotions of doctors and nurses when a baby dies
>
> Exchanging our experiences and needs with hospital staff
>
> Exchanging our experiences and needs with a funeral director
>
> Pastoral perspectives—different religious rituals and proceedings
>
> Genetic counseling

Showing videos or slide series (see Appendix, page 252) can serve as a good start for group meetings. They are also useful as part of an informational event open to the public.

Hospital Auxiliary Work

A good relationship with your local hospital is important. Service can be beneficial to both of you. Some groups have provided hospitals with little handmade gowns and blankets. Other groups have hand-painted silk scarves with symbolic designs in which to wrap the babies, which they have given to the hospital—a meaningful endeavor in itself. The German mutual-help groups "Rainbow" have donated to their local hospitals little handmade "Moses baskets" in which to place stillborn or miscarried babies. Many hospitals appreciate offers from support-group members to visit newly bereaved parents.

11

Dealing with Death in Childbirth Education

It's true. Expectant parents want to look forward to the birth of their child, and prenatal groups are a place where parents can prepare for their child's arrival and share their joyful anticipation with other parents. As a childbirth educator, you want to strengthen parents' feelings of self-confidence and trust in their abilities, help them adjust to becoming parents and teach them ways to make a rewarding birthing experience possible. A positive attitude fosters positive results. However, this *doesn't* mean we should sweep possible fears under the rug. Deep inside, almost every expectant parent, at one point or another, is troubled by fears that their dreams may *not* be fulfilled, that something could go wrong.

Do I Address Loss?

If the fears gradually give way to a deepening feeling of trust—wonderful! But if parents simply repress fears, these may reappear in a distorted form—perhaps as premature contractions or a difficult labor and delivery, which could endanger the child. Very often they feel better if they have can share their fears and preoccupation with people who will listen with undivided attention. Then they feel they aren't alone.

Many fears turn out to be irrational. For others, parents can develop new perspectives or, through talking with others, find new ways of coping and dealing with their concerns. Even the worst fears of all—that a child might not be healthy or may die—can be managed better by most people once they are talked about.

Discussing Death in Childbirth-Education Classes

The most basic requirement is that you, as a professional, have created a warm, nurturing atmosphere of trust and acceptance in the classroom. In this kind of environment, couples may feel free to admit their greatest fears to themselves and others. It's best if the topic comes up naturally.

Perhaps the subject can be introduced through questions such as, *What am I looking forward to the most? What is my greatest fear?* If the issues of fear of death and disabilities don't surface on their own, gently and sensitively address these possibilities without insisting on covering the topic. Allot time for sharing emerging thoughts and, above all, for allowing participants to express their emotions.

Another way of letting the topic develop naturally is to discuss participants' expectations of the birth event. *What if things turn out differently from what we hoped?* You can prepare couples for dealing with several different unexpected outcomes, such as an extremely difficult labor, contrary conditions during delivery, Cesarean section, separation from the baby after the delivery, the "wrong" gender, a child that does not correspond to their image, and so forth (see also Sherokee Ilse, *Presenting Unexpected Outcomes: A Childbirth Educator's Guide*, 1990). Along with these "safer" topics, the issue of the baby's being not healthy, or even dead, can emerge.

This is a good opportunity to approach the subject of loss in general. Every developmental step, such as becoming a father or mother, means saying good-bye to the past. (Elisabeth Kübler-Ross speaks about the "little deaths" that we have to die to prepare ourselves for our final death.) In this context, you can introduce the notion that grieving is a healthy life process that helps us deal with the losses in our life from major to minor (be it "only" our hopes and dreams), and that it is health-enhancing to express our feelings instead of repressing them. When families can accept that grief and birth can go hand in hand, that their emotions are normal and they are able to find new ways to cope with them, then a new feeling of inner strength can grow. (Limbo/Wheeler, 1986)

You can't plan or predict the course that such discussions take. Each group is different. Be prepared to respond to very direct questions.

Having to be flexible, sensitive and able to "go with the flow" of the group requires that you feel comfortable with the subject of grief and loss yourself and that you aren't stuck with a lot of unprocessed grief.

Another way to introduce the topic of loss naturally is to see if there is a group member who has previously suffered a pregnancy loss. (Statistically, there is at least one in every prenatal group.)

Couples Who Have Had a Previous Loss

Childbirth educators should know something about the background of the couples who come to them. One way to gain information is to have them fill out a questionnaire before the course, asking about possible previous losses, among other things. Mothers who have lost a child have more fears in subsequent pregnancies and are at higher risk for another loss—and therefore need additional attention. Not every woman is cared for by a physician who will also tend to her emotional needs. It would be ideal if you could help bridge this gap by offering couples who have had a previous miscarriage or stillbirth the opportunity to talk with you individually before the course begins. You need to know about the healthy course of a grief process so you can assess where in the process the couples are at the time.

This meeting would offer bereaved parents an opportunity to talk about their previous experience and to assess the consequences it's had on their lives. Together you can reflect on their process of mourning, noting the effects on a physical, emotional, mental and spiritual level. Often it is possible to resolve whatever is still unprocessed in one intensive talk. (Questionnaire 1 on page 231 can be a guide.) It is of particular interest to childbirth educators to learn how the previous loss affects the present pregnancy. Bereaved parents should be able to telephone you between group meetings if they need to. If the preparation offered in the classes (relaxation, breathing exercises, discussion, visualizations and the like) is not enough to help resolve fears, know where you can refer these parents for additional help (for example, therapists, bereavement counselors, holistic body therapists and so on. See Appendix 4).

If parents have felt safe talking with you individually, they may feel comfortable talking within the childbirth-education class setting as well. In an atmosphere of trust, given the appropriate opportunity, couples may matter-of-factly discuss their experience with the group. The parents' account can help others, especially if the bereaved have recovered from their loss.

When a Couple in the Childbirth Class Suffers a Loss

The first person we called when we learned that we would have to deliver a dead baby was our childbirth educator. We asked her for advice regarding medication during delivery, and she coached us on how to deliver the dreadful news to people. Without our even knowing, she immediately called the hospital and arranged for us to be able to see our baby, and gave the people there helpful information for our welfare. I believe we would have accepted gratefully if she had asked if she might come and be with us. We needed someone to help carry our sorrow and to lean on. When the time came to fill out our birth questionnaire, I did it in minute detail because someone was interested and I had such a need to tell . . ." (Ilse 1987).
(Copyright 1987 by International Journal of Childbirth Education and Sherokee Ilse. Reprinted by permission.)

How Can the Childbirth Educator Be Supportive?

The relationship between expectant parents and their childbirth educator is often special. It isn't surprising that the person who shared intimately in the joy of anticipation over their baby is usually the first one to learn about their grief in the case of loss.

If you get a call from a couple informing you of their baby's intrauterine death, you can let them know what has helped other parents in this situation and what others wished they had done and regretted. You can encourage them to go through labor and delivery as they had planned. You can offer to serve parents as a *doula*—a labor companion—and be with them during the delivery, just as you may at times do for births that take place under more joyful conditions. Parents may even ask directly if you would attend them at birth. Your presence and support as they say hello and good-bye to their beloved baby can be very meaningful to them. And although it is certainly no easy task to be available to people in this situation, it can be unbelievably enriching to you as well.

When a baby is born sick, you can accompany the parents when they visit their baby in the intensive-care unit. You can encourage them to bond by holding their child in their arms and participating in his or her care as much as possible. You can help them tune in to their own desires and reinforce them in seeing they are met as far as possible.

If you learn through someone else that "something has gone wrong," make sure to call the parents (they may be in too much shock to make contact) and offer a listening ear: "I heard that your baby was stillborn. I'm so sorry. If you would like to talk about it, I would very much like to hear more about your baby, the birth and what happened." Generally parents appreciate it if someone gets in touch with them and doesn't try to avoid them. You can show your interest by asking questions about what happened, about whether they were able to spend time with their child, what their baby looked like. A childbirth educator I know helped parents get a second chance to do what they had missed earlier—to see their child days later. Perhaps you can learn about possible feelings of fear, anger or guilt and help them deal with these emotions. Don't forget the father, who is all too frequently overlooked by others.

For parents, writing a birth report is important for processing what has happened. This is even more the case for parents whose child has died. To be able to "tell their story" helps them, bit by bit, to grasp what has happened. They too should be asked to write a birth report if this is normally done.

These suggestions also apply to leaders of breastfeeding support groups if a woman who has attended meetings during pregnancy suffers a loss.

How Can the Group Be Supportive?

The extent and quality of support people receive after a loss is decisive in determining the outcome. Now that something terrible has happened, it is best for them not to be cut off from a peer group where close relationships have developed. Naturally, other group members will probably feel helpless and perhaps irrationally guilty that *their* children are alive and well. But with their group leader's help, they can come to accept these feelings as normal.

It is good to invite the bereaved parents *in person* to the follow-up meeting of the prenatal group. Many may decline. Others, particularly those who have reconciled to their grief and their loss, will accept. Having no child to "show," it is all the more important for many parents to be able to talk about the birth of their baby. To be recognized for their achievement—giving birth under such agonizingly difficult conditions—helps. In everyday life it is unlikely they would find a forum for sharing details about their birth. Joanne, a childbirth educator, has had positive experiences inviting bereaved couples:

At first, you could sense a general helplessness. Then one of the fathers admitted he felt awkward by saying he didn't know how to react to John

*and Linda and asking them to please tell him what they needed. That broke
the ice. It became clear to the group members that although they could not
take away the couple's pain, it felt good to be there for the couple. Linda
admitted she was jealous and had thoughts about how she would love to
kidnap a baby.*

*Later I heard from the couple how important it had been for them that
someone had listened to them. They had received positive feedback. It was
important for them to have had their birthing experience validated as
equally important to those of others. They were proud of their birth. Even
with the unfortunate outcome of their pregnancy, they felt nurtured and
accepted by the group, and they could maintain the friendships that had
developed earlier. In another case, the bereaved mother began to cry very
hard when she saw all the babies, but she asked if she might hold one. All
the women in the group cried with her. Only after the couple had told about
their birth was it possible for the others to share their experiences.*

In the warm, personal atmosphere of childbirth-education classes,
lasting male friendships may form. Men from the prenatal groups may
therefore be better able to emotionally support a grieving father, who
would probably not have much opportunity to show his feelings otherwise. This support is especially important after a few months, when
others have probably pulled back. (The leader can give some basic
information about the average course of the grief process and the needs
of bereaved parents.)

It is nice for leaders and participants of the childbirth and/or
breastfeeding groups to keep in touch with the bereaved with telephone or personal contacts. Especially on the first anniversary of the
death, it is a nice gesture to telephone, visit, send or bring flowers to
show that someone remembers.

12

Funeral Directors and Grief Support

The Influence of the Funeral Director

Next to hospital personnel and clergy, funeral directors hold a critical position in the grief process of parents who have lost their child. You as funeral director may not be aware of how much you can help ease the grief of parents and facilitate their mourning.

> *The funeral director was really nice. He told my mother that our little daughter looked so beautiful and peaceful and asked if maybe someone would like to look at her again. My mother wanted to spare me the pain and declined without even asking me. I am very sorry about that, although his statement alone has brought me some comfort.*

Some professionals have hampered healthy grief resolution by depriving parents of an irretrievable experience:

> *The one thing I still regret is that the funeral director didn't let us see our daughter again, and we let that happen. We had bought a little baptismal gown for her, and she wore her Mom's ring around her neck. We had held her in the hospital, and we would so much have liked to have seen her one more time in her little dress and with the ring. We will always regret that we didn't see her once more.*

An Ethical Question

A passage from an article by Thomas Attig, author of *How We Grieve: Relearning the World* (1996), helps us reflect more deeply on this procedure:

> *A couple contacts a funeral director and urges him to arrange a quick and simple funeral for a stillborn just delivered by their young adult, single daughter. They are trying to protect their daughter from a difficult experience, which they believe will compound her pain and suffering. They are acting as they believe parents should, inviting the funeral director to do what they hope will be in their daughter's best interests. They make no mention of acting either at her request or with her consent. In short, they are acting paternalistically, and they are asking the funeral director to do the same. Should the funeral director accede to the parents' wishes? Is there a preferable course of action? More than that, are there professional obligations to the contrary? If there are obligations, what is their ethical foundation?*

Thomas Attig speaks out clearly against the paternalistic model, and he justifies his position this way:

> *. . . possible involvement by the bereaved is important, given that helplessness is a frequent component of the grief experience and a major aspect in personal vulnerability. One of the principal dangers for the bereaved is that their experienced helplessness will be reinforced, that their perceived incapacity will become real and chronic, that unrevealed depression will ensue, and consequently emotional accommodation to death, reorientation, and a return to competent human functioning will not be achieved. Failure to acknowledge, or denial of, opportunities for meaningful action feeds, rather than dispels, what temporary incapacity there is in the lives of the bereaved. Thus, paternalism might in fact undermine effective grief work.*
> (Attig 1983)

How Funeral Directors Can Facilitate the Grief Process

Knowledge about This Special Situation

To be of real assistance, funeral directors need to know about the grief process in general, and the special circumstances of perinatal bereavement in particular. Quotes from parents in this book will have helped you learn about their needs. Chapters 6, 7 and 8 show how knowledge about the phases of grief and the tasks of mourning can translate into action. Below are thoughts that might be of particular interest to the funeral director.

What Is Helpful

Do everything that will help parents accept the reality of the loss.

ৎ Offer parents one last opportunity to see their child, particularly if they have not seen their baby yet. Ask both father *and* mother in person. (One may mistakenly want to protect the other, who later regrets having missed the opportunity, causing resentment between partners.)

ৎ Allow the father to carry his child to the car if he wishes, and to accompany you to the mortuary.

ৎ When parents have not seen their child, prepare them for the viewing with kind, empathetic words.

ৎ Don't decide for yourself whether the child is "worth seeing" or not. (Parents see differently—"with the eyes of the heart.") If they so desire, describe the child to them.

ৎ Offer them the possibility of parenting their child (it is their only chance to do so): Ask if they want to wash or dress their baby, or if they have a special set of clothing for their baby—possibly doll clothes for a very tiny baby.

ৎ Ask parents if they have given a name to their baby or if they may still want to do so. If they have named the baby, use that name in referring to her or him.

ৎ Offer parents the opportunity to place their baby in the casket themselves or be present at the closing, as another milestone in their grief process.

ৎ Arrange the funeral date after the mother's discharge from the hospital to enable her participation. If necessary, arrange for postponement of the funeral.

Help integrate the family.

ৎ Children should be allowed to see the baby if they wish, together with an adult of their choice. The adult would be someone with whom they feel comfortable and of whom they can ask any questions. Prepare them for what they will see.

❧ Encourage children to place something in the coffin for "their baby" (some do this secretly): a little note, a little picture, a toy, or dolly, or . . .?

❧ Encourage grandparents, family members and friends to see the baby if they have not done so. Then they will understand the grief of the parents better and be able to support them better. Suggest that they too can bring something for the baby.

Promote ritual expression.

❧ Invite the parents to help create a ritual that is meaningful to *them*: Tie balloons to the coffin or release balloons into the sky, read a poem aloud, select a particular text or sing a meaningful song. Offer them options and let them make as many of the decisions as possible. Decorate the room in a special way, including symbols meaningful to the parents. A variety of rituals can be found in the excellent book, *Bittersweet . . . hellogoodbye* (see page 251).

❧ Because a supportive network is crucial for parents in mourning, suggest they include family and friends in the farewell ritual, but do not pressure them. Taking part in the funeral will make the baby more real to all these people. Suggest that friends could participate and share in the preparations for the funeral service. A friend may want to carry the coffin.

Bury miscarried babies, if that is the parents' wish.

❧ Consider practical, inexpensive ways for the burial of tiny babies. Discuss burial possibilities of very small babies with appropriate authorities.

❧ Respect the parents' attachment to their baby and their wish to bury that baby, even though he or she is not considered a person by law. If you are unsure of procedures, check with the SHARE National Office for direction. If a burial procedure for miscarried babies hasn't been established, you can call SHARE for direction to put this practice into place.

❧ Though parents were not able to register their baby (depending on state and provincial laws), ask if they have chosen a name for the baby. Use the name and encourage parents to place it on the headstone, if there is one.

Bob, a funeral director, reports:

If there is a family grave nearby, we bury the miscarried babies, for example, with the grandmother. I personally build a little white box, which I line inside to create a dignified setting.

You may want to encourage a father or grandfather to build a little coffin for the baby (this might be a creative, meaningful outlet for a man's grief). There are also reasonably priced, sensitively made burial cradles available for tiny babies (see page 249).

Help promote a healthy grief process.

ಈ Inform the parents about the course of a healthy grief process (see chapter 8) and let them know possible long-range effects of certain decisions.

ಈ Give parents information about the options they have, the pros and cons, and let them share in the decision-making.

ಈ Respect the autonomy and the values of the parents, being aware that the best possible healing will take place if parents can act according to *their* values and desires.

Promote networking of bereaved parents and cultivate contacts with groups.

ಈ Funeral directors can promote the establishment of support groups and know the addresses of local groups, or, if not available, of national groups.

ಈ If possible, set up an address file to promote networking of bereaved parents (include parents only with their permission).

ಈ Periodically meet with bereaved parents to find what has helped them and what changes need to be made. Work together to form helpful procedures.

Appendix 1

Rights of Parents When a Baby Dies

To be given the opportunity to see, hold and touch their baby at any time before and/or after death, within reason.

To have photographs of their baby taken and made available to the parents or held in security until the parents wish to see them.

To be given as many mementos as possible; for example, crib card, baby beads, ultrasound and/or other photos, lock of hair, feet and hand prints and record of weight and length.

To name their child and bond with him or her.

To observe cultural and religious practices.

To be cared for by an empathetic staff who will respect their feelings, thoughts, beliefs and individual requests.

To be with each other throughout hospitalization as much as possible.

To be given time alone with their baby, allowing for individual needs.

To request an autopsy. In the case of a miscarriage, to request to have or not have an autopsy or pathology exam as determined by applicable law.

To have information presented in terminology understandable to the parents regarding their baby's status and cause of death, including autopsy and pathology reports and medical records.

To plan a farewell ritual, burial or cremation in compliance with local state regulations and according to their personal beliefs, religious or cultural tradition.

To be provided with information on support resources that assist in the healing process; for example, support groups, counseling, reading material and perinatal loss newsletters.

Rights of the Baby

To be recognized as a person who was born and died.

To be named.

To be seen, touched and held by the family.

To have life-ending acknowledged.

To be put to rest with dignity.

Appendix 2

Questionnaire 1: For the Bereaved
What Is My Particular Grief Situation?

This questionnaire can help you as bereaved parents get a better perspective of the circumstances of your loss and your experience. It can also be useful to doctors, therapists, nurses, midwives and other professionals who wish to help you explore your experience. In addition, it can help assess whether complicating factors warrant additional help for working through grief. It's OK to answer these questions in your head or to use them as part of a discussion with others. You don't have to write down your answers.

1. Intensity of the relationship

How much attachment had already formed? How deep had my love for my baby grown? Had I been holding back my love out of fear of a possible loss? Had I, as the mother, already felt my child inside, or had I, as the father, not yet been able to establish a relationship? Did I have ambivalent feelings towards my child?

2. What else was connected to this pregnancy for me?

Did I feel better than usual? Had my feelings of self-worth and importance increased as a result of being pregnant? Had I received more attention than usual from my partner? Or did my partner seem more distant than before? Did we hope that a baby could help "glue together" an ailing relationship? Did I want to get out of an unpleasant situation (for example, place of work, away from parents)? Was this child the long-desired daughter or son? Did I have the feeling that in becoming a parent I was truly fulfilling a task that was intended for me? How likely is it that we will not be able to have other children?

3. What were the circumstances of death?

Did I have a premonition? Did I have the feeling from the start that something was not right? Or did the news of the baby's death hit me out of blue? Was the pregnancy or death surrounded by a social taboo?

How did I learn about my child's death? How was I told? How was I supported during labor, delivery and after? Did I have the time I needed to say hello and good-bye to my child? Could I handle things according to my wishes and needs? Or what would I have liked to do differently? Could we include the people we wanted to? Could we include older siblings? Do I have any regrets? Do I feel as though I or someone else could have prevented the death?

4. Historical facts

Have I had previous perinatal losses? What were the circumstances? Were any of them surrounded by a taboo? Have we been trying for a long time to have a child? What other losses or traumatic events have I had in my life (do not *only* include losses resulting from death)? How did I handle them? How much or how little support did I have then? What unprocessed grief do I hold? How do I deal with the "little daily deaths" of life? Had there been untimely deaths in my family as a child? If so, how were those dealt with? What messages did I receive about mourning from my family and social circle? Are my parents still alive? Did one of them die early? If so, are there any unresolved issues? What has the general state of my emotional health been so far? Have I gone through periods of depressions in my life? If so, what were the causing factors and circumstances?

5. Personality factors

Can I tell other persons how I really feel or do I tend to settle things inside myself, on my own—in other words, am I more extroverted or more introverted? Do I tend to process things that happen more with my head or more with my feelings? Are my perceptions more of a concrete nature, using all my senses, or more of an intuitive nature? (Am I more of a pragmatic person or more of a person who follows his or her intuition)? Do I live in the moment, or do I tend to be more occupied with the future or the past? Do I like to bring things quickly to a close, or can I allow them to follow their own course? Can I live well with open-ended issues?

   Do I tend to be overly self-reliant or can I accept support from others? Do I tend to be excessively dependent? What coping resources do I have? What are my general tendencies in dealing with stress—do I feel overwhelmed easily or do I function well under pressure? Can I allow myself to express my feelings, or do I tend to repress or deny them? Can I express what goes on in me? Do I easily feel guilty and/or responsible? What is my self-image (for example, "the strong one," "the emotional one," "why always me?")?

Do I tend to react to emotional pain with physical symptoms? Which feelings are hard for me to show or even reach? Which personality factors does my partner exhibit? Where have conflicts arisen with people close to me based on differing personality traits, and how did I deal with them or resolve them?

6. Social variables

How much support do I have from my friends, my family, my environment, my partner, clergy, professionals? How many other resources do I have outside myself—support groups, literature, activities and the like? How many resources do I have within myself: coping skills based on past experiences, social learning and internalized rituals, creativity, faith and spirituality? Are there people in my life to whom I can entrust my innermost feelings? Is this loss likely to be socially unsanctioned or even condemned by some (for example, as a result of an abortion, in connection with AIDS or chemical dependency, the termination of a wanted pregnancy because of medical or genetic problems)?

7. Philosophy of life and value system

What do I believe about life and death? Do I tend toward a material attitude toward life, or do I consider myself a spiritual person? Do I believe that life comes to a complete end with death? Or do I believe in an afterlife? Do I believe in an eternal life of the soul? Do I believe in reincarnation? Do I believe that as souls we select our parents? Do I believe that we are here on earth by chance? Or do I believe that each person has a task to accomplish in life? Can I give a meaning to my life? Can I give a meaning to the events in my life?

Questionnaire 2: For Caregivers

Personal Experiences with and Attitudes toward Death and Dying

This questionnaire is designed to be used by caregivers of bereaved people. Addressing these questions can help you become clearer about and more aware of your feelings and fears, past experiences, attitudes and their sources, and possible unprocessed events. I encourage you to share your answers, thoughts and insights with team colleagues and others. If you discover unresolved or problematic issues that you feel could be hindering you in your encounters with bereaved parents, you may decide to seek supervision or other professional support. Use a separate sheet of paper for answering these questions.

1. My first personal confrontation with death was at the age of _____, when _____ .

2. I remember having the following emotions at that time: _____ .

3. The first funeral I attended was that of _____ at the age of _____ .

4. My most distinct memory of that event is: _____ .

5. The most recent encounter with death was (date, person, circumstances): _____ .

6. The death that affected me most was the death of: _____ .

7. It was difficult for me because: _____ .

8. Of the people in my life, the death of _____ would be the most difficult for me.

9. It would be the most difficult because: _____ .

10. My way of responding to losses is: _____ .

11. I will know that my grief work after a loss is completed when:

   _____ .

12. It is all right to speak about my own grief process and grief work with bereaved patients when: _____ .

13. When I was young and my family talked about death, I thought/felt: _____ .

14. This is how I imagined death when I was a child: _____ .

15. This is how I view death today: _____ .

16. My present attitude towards death came about in this way: _____ .

17. For me, death means: _____ .

18. My greatest fears regarding death and dying are: _____ . I would want to talk to _____ about them.

19. This is my attitude about the use of life-supportive equipment in the case of persons who are dying: _____ .

For those who have had professional exposure to death and dying:

20. I have had the following experiences with death and loss at work or in the course of my studies or training: _____ .

21. The most difficult part for me was: _____ .

22. I find it hardest to deal with the following reactions of parents at a stillbirth: _____ .

23. This may be caused by: _____ .

24. I would like to talk to someone about or get help with the following issues, feelings, questions, experiences and unprocessed events: _____ .

(Inspired by and based on J. William Worden (1987) and Elisabeth Kübler-Ross)

Appendix 3

Suggestions for Meditation

Variation 1

1. Confirm your inner desire.
"I want to spend time now in meditation."

2. Prepare your special space.
Find a place in your home where you feel comfortable and at ease. It should be quiet and peaceful, with few distractions (visual or audible). Transform this into your special space, to which you can return on a regular basis. You may want to place on a silk scarf or other lovely cloth some meaningful objects or symbols—a statue of an angel, a picture of a heart, a crystal or semi-precious stone, a symbol of religious significance for you . . . anything that opens and soothes your heart, mind and spirit. You may want to use a scent lamp and essences that enhance meditation, such as frankincense, cedar, hyssop, iris, juniperberry and marjoram (see page 133). If desired, keep a journal and pen available. Light a candle each time you go to this place. You may want to decorate it with fresh flowers or a plant.

Prepare a place to sit: a meditation cushion or several harder pillows, one on top of the other, or a stool or hard (wooden) chair with a flat surface (check out the height you need so you sit naturally with straight, upright posture—it's best if your lower and upper leg can be at a right angle to each other—if not, correct with blankets).

Pick a time of day at which you can regularly come to your special space for a specific length of time to meditate. Prepare yourself for the transition from activity into quiet meditation and when possible, avoid an abrupt ending of meditation. Enter and leave this space mindfully and with respect. It will develop a special energy with time.

3. Align yourself with a higher goal.

Use a word or phrase to help you become focused on a higher goal—open yourself to a meditative state:

- Finding inner peace
- Healing
- Feeling oneness
- Infinite love
- Know forgiveness
- Let go and let God

4. Foster a meditative state through your body posture.

Paying attention to a good way of sitting, creating "order" in your body, will bring order and tranquillity to your mind all by itself. If you sit on a stool or chair, sit on the very edge, with the upper and lower legs forming a right angle to each other, with your feet about eight inches apart, parallel to each other and in good contact with the floor. That way your back will straighten automatically, without straining. Let the crown of your head "grow" gently upwards, like a flower reaching for the sun, making sure that you do not stiffen inwardly. You can give a little tug on a few hairs on the top of your head to find the right direction. Feel the contact with the chair and let yourself become one with it. Raise your arms quickly and as they fall, let them naturally find their ideal place on your thighs, palms down. Let your joints relax—your ankle, knee, hip joints, all the vertebral joints, your shoulders.

Allow the wave of your breath to flow into your body freely and with ease. Let it breathe into you! You feel calmer and calmer. You may want to close your eyes or look straight ahead. Do not stare—it helps to look "softly" (imagine yourself looking from the back of your head, through your head and toward the front). Then direct your attention to the crown of your head and visualize this spot opening up and being filled with a golden light.

You can also meditate sitting cross-legged on pillows. Quiet your thoughts by laying the left hand on top of the right hand, with the palms of your hands cupped upward, thumbs touching each other.

5. Stay centered and in a meditative state.

- Stay focused on the flow of your breath.
- Begin to contemplate sounding a tone ("oh—ah—oo," and so on; see page 30), then tone audibly, if desired.
- Silently recite a mantra (for example, *om, God, yes!, love, serenity, trust, surrender, clarity, consolation* . . .) and let the sensation it creates spread throughout your body.

☙ Or, say a short prayer.

6. Be gentle with interfering thoughts.
When your mind begins to chatter, do not try to erase your thoughts. Let them pass by lovingly and acceptingly, and gently bring your attention back to your breathing and the "here and now."

7. Be aware and accepting of whatever arises.
Give yourself in stillness to whatever comes up. Be without intentions. Just be! Receive. Say "thank you" as you end your meditation. If desired, write down what has come to you in your journal.

Variation 2

Point 5 of Variation 1 can be replaced by a *meditation on a text*. There are many daily meditation books on the market now; for example, *Remembering with Love* (for the bereaved) or more generally, *Each Day a New Beginning* or *Each Morning Brings New Hope* or *The Daily Word* (see page 254). Meditate over these texts and allow yourself to be moved by them. Here is another possible meditation text:

> *My heart is heavy,*
> *And so many questions are within me.*
> *May I become still so I will eventually hear answers,*
> *In the midst of darkness, may light arise in me,*
> *May I come to recognize order in the chaos,*
> *May I find my way through turmoil to peace,*
> *May I feel carried in the midst of calamity.*
>
> *May my body and my soul become healed and open again,*
> *May I receive consolation in my sadness,*
> *May I experience Love in my pain,*
> *May I feel Your strength in my vulnerability,*
> *May a new life and a new spirit come forth.*

Variation 3

You can also *meditate on a picture* that awakens in you your higher qualities; for example, a picture of a kindly, benevolent personage (Jesus, a spiritual guide, a guardian angel, and so on), nature (a beautiful landscape, an impressive tree, a lovely plant, a beautiful flower), a spiritual painting or a mandala.

Memorial Rituals

Variation 1

A telephone call made to Father Thomas Turner, of Kansas City, Missouri, by a mother after a miscarriage, resulted in an annual memorial Mass for miscarried babies:

> "... 50 more people than normally attend a weekday Mass came to our "Mass for Miscarriages." At the beginning of Mass I told the people that we wanted to recognize the presence of their lost children as members of our community. The Catholic tradition has always emphasized that its community consists of both living and dead members; that is, the community of saints. In my introductory comments I wanted to validate or affirm the painful feeling of loss that those mothers had experienced.
>
> Affirming these two realities—the full church membership of these unborn children and the mothers' pain—is at the heart of the ritual. Affirming or talking about these two realities openly in the context of prayer brought a great deal of healing to those who attended.
>
> In the main aisle of our church near the front, where the casket is usually situated at funerals, we had placed a small rectangular table with a white pall on top. Votive lights were placed around the table's perimeter and fresh flower petals were strewn on the middle of the table. At the beginning of the Mass, I asked the mothers and families to prayerfully invite the spirits of their lost children to be present with us during this celebration. I gestured toward the little table as the symbolic focus for the spirits and then with holy water I blessed them ... "

Variation 2

Reverend Jim Cunningham, Director of Pastoral Care, Fairview Health System, Cleveland, Ohio, lets balloons rise to the sky after a special memorial service, saying:

> "With these balloons,
> We remember our beloved babies who have died.
> Death has forced us to let go of the children we would hold.
> As we let go of our balloons, we send forth a message.

To the community, the message is:
   Our babies were wanted,
   were real,
   are loved,
   and grieved,
   and remembered.

To one another as bereaved families, the message is:
   You are not alone.
   With support we survive and grow.

To our beloved children we have spoken of today,
the message is:
   We remember you!
   We miss you!
   And most of all,
   We love you!"

Variation 3

Here is a suggestion for a reading for a miscarried baby:

Today we come together in sorrow over the death of _____ and
_____'s baby. Their child, created in love and eagerly wished
for, has died—never to be nestled securely in their arms in this lifetime. To
these parents, the pain and the disappointment is great and their loss will be
carried heavily in their hearts for all their days. In the weeks and months
ahead, they will miss their child terribly and will be in need of love,
compassion, time and understanding from all of us.

Each life comes into this world with a mission. Sometimes the mission or
purpose is clear; sometimes it is vague and shrouded in misunderstandings.
In time, we will see what the baby's mission was on earth. Could it have
been just to add a little flicker of love that otherwise may never have been
lit? Was it to soften our hearts so that we may in turn comfort others?
Could it have been to bring us closer to our God and each other?

This child's life was short, yet the death has left a huge void in all of our
hearts and lives. Let us remember today and for always the tiny baby who
will never see childhood or adulthood, but will remain our tiny baby forever.

Lord God, today we can say with your psalmist, "My God, my God, why have you abandoned me? I have cried desperately for help, but still it does not come." May we also remember your promise that you do not willingly harm us. We ask you to be compassionate towards us in this time of grief over the child they expected, who now is not to be. As you knew the suffering and death of your own son, so now join us and hear their sorrow and pain, that they may in the days to come be comforted and receive your peace.

(From "Planning a Precious Goodbye," by Susan Erling; copyright 1997 by Pregnancy & Infant Loss Center, Inc. Available through the Centering Corporation. Reprinted by permission.)

Additional Readings, Prayers and Songs

The following prayer can bring comfort and healing:

We Remember Them

In the rising of the sun and in its going down,
We remember them;
In the blowing of the wind and in the chill of winter,
We remember them;
In the opening of buds and in the rebirth of spring,
We remember them;
In the blueness of the sky and in the warmth of summer,
We remember them;
In the rustling of leaves and in the beauty of autumn,
We remember them;
In the beginning of the year and when it ends,
We remember them;
When we are weary and in need of strength,
We remember them;
When we are lost and sick at heart,
We remember them;
When we have joys we yearn to share,
We remember them;
For long as we live, they too shall live,
For they are now a part of us,
As we remember them.

(From *Gates of Prayer: The New Union Prayerbook* (1975), published by the Central Conference of American Rabbis. Used by permission.)

Another prayer for bereaved parents:

God, I pray to you,

Strengthen these parents in mourning with Your Power.

Give them the courage to stand up to their questions and all
uncertainty.

Give family and friends openness and patience

To be there for them and listen as they express their pain

So they can find the courage to face life and joy anew.

A prayer in time of pain:

Father Mother God, out of your understanding and mercy reach out
to me. Hold, comfort me, let me know that I will laugh again from
happiness that is as profound as my grief at this moment. It feels as
though my heart has been torn from deep inside me. The ache is more
than I can bear, and I am not certain I can live with such pain. Touch
me with your tender caress and give me comfort. Give me peace and
comfort.

(Adapted from "Prayer" in *Comfort Us Lord, Our Baby Died*; Centering
Corporation. Used by permission)

A prayer by Sister Jane Marie Lamb when in agony and doubt:

Dear God,

In the past I have experienced you as a God of love and concern for
your people. Now I feel abandoned by you, and alone in this tragedy
and loss. I feel angry with you. My child has died, and my heart is
breaking. I ask "Why?" and find no easy answer to my questions. I
sometimes feel so empty that I wonder if I will ever feel again—or
ever get past my bitter and broken feelings. Because of my loss I
question my faith in and understanding of you. Show me ways to find
new strength. Bring comfort and peace to my spirit again. Give me
memories and hope to hold on to. Be with me, God, as I cannot make
it alone. I need your comfort and support now, more than ever before
in my life. Amen.

A direction for silent prayer by Sister Jane Marie:

You may wish to thank God for the depth of love you discovered in
the life and death of your baby.

You may wish to give thanks to those who surrounded you in your
sorrow.

You may wish to ask for continued guidance in your journey through grief.

You may wish to thank God for your personal growth upon that journey.

(From *Bittersweet . . . hellogoodbye*, page 438. Used by permission.)

Thoughts on Mother Earth:

I stand beside this tiny grave
And place the fruit of my womb
Into the Arms of Mother Earth.
We are well acquainted, Mother Earth and I.
We've often worked together,
My hands deep in her warm, nurturing soil
To plant the trees which bear fruit.
She has cared for the young seedlings
Anchoring them securely within her womb
Holding their roots deep inside her heart
Providing sustenance as I tended them.
We are a team, She and I,
The very best of friends.
We can look into each other's heart
And know what is lying there.
Now I must entrust her with
The care of my most prized possession.
I have come to place my baby into her depths
For safekeeping
Knowing she will hold my little one
Against her breast
Rocking him gently
As she rocks the trees in a breeze
Until the Father calls us on the Last Day
To be reunited.

(by Deborah S. Guenther. Used by permission.)

More Scripture Texts Concerning Mourning:

Genesis 9:13-17; Job 6:1-3, 7-13; 7:3-4, 11, 13-16, Ecclesiastes 3:1-11, 7:3; Psalm 30:11; Wisdom 4:7-14; Ecclesiastes 38:16-18; Isaiah 25:6-8; Isaiah 49:15-16; Isaiah 61:1-3, Jeremiah 1:4-9; Jeremiah 31:13; Hosea 6:1-3; Matthew 5:1-12; Matthew, Luke 6:21.

Appendix 4

Support, Information and Resources for Bereaved Parents

❖*Groups and Organizations in the USA*

Abiding Hearts, Inc.
c/o Maria LaFond Visscher, PO Box 5245, Bozeman, MT 59717.
Phone: 406-285-4408. Fax: 406-557-7197.
Support for parents continuing pregnancy after diagnosis of fatal or nonfatal birth defects.

The Alliance of Genetic Support Groups
35 Wisconsin Circle, #440, Chevy Chase, MD 20815.
Phone: 800-336-4363. Fax: 301-654-0171.
E-mail: alliance@capaccess.org.
Website: http://medhlp.netusa.net/www/agsg.htm

AMEND (Aiding Mothers and Fathers Experiencing Neonatal Death)
c/o Maureen Connelly, 4324 Berrywick Terrace, St. Louis, MO 63128. Phone: 314-487-7582
Offers one-to-one peer counseling, support and encouragement to bereaved parents.

Bereaved Parents Of The USA (BPUSA) National Headquarters
PO Box 95, Park Forest, IL 60466. Phone: 708-748-7672.
Fax: 708-748-9184.
Nationwide support group for bereaved parents, provides support through local chapters, listing of groups worldwide, program material and educational services.

Bereavement Services/RTS
1910 South Avenue, La Crosse, WI 54601. Phone: 608-791-4747 or
1-800-362-9567, ext. 4747.
International bereavement program, curriculum and training for
setting up bereavement support teams in hospitals.

CLIMB (Center for Loss in Multiple Birth)
c/o Jean Kollantai, PO Box 1064, Palmer, Alaska 99645.
Phone: 907-746-6123.
Network for parents bereaved of one twin or multiple; newsletter.

The Compassionate Friends (TCF) National Office
PO Box 3696, Oak Brook, IL 60522-3696. Phone: 630-990-0010.
Nationwide support group for bereaved parents, provides support
through local chapters, listing of groups worldwide, program material
and educational services.

A Heartbreaking Choice
c/o Pineapple Press—Molly Minnick, ACSW, PO Box 312, St. Johns,
MI 48879. Phone: 517-224-1881.
Resources for families making difficult decisions for unborn babies
with fetal anomalies; quarterly newsletter.

National SIDS Alliance
1314 Bedford Avenue, Suite 210, Baltimore, MD 21208.
Phone: 1-800-221-SIDS. Fax: 410-964-8009
Source of information for parents and caregivers dealing with sudden
infant death syndrome.

Pen-Grandparents
co/ Melissa Swanson, PO Box 8738, Reno, NV 89507-8738.
Phone: 701-826-7332. Fax: 702-323-2489.

Pen-Parents, Inc.
c/o Melissa Swanson, PO Box 8738, Reno, NV 89507-8738.
Phone: 702-826-7332. Fax: 702-323-2489.
E-mail: PenParents@prodigy.com or PenParents@aol.com.
Website: http://pages.prodigy.com/NV/fgck08a/PenParents.html
International support network for grieving parents; quarterly newsletter; personalized angel ornaments, Precious Feet pin.

RESOLVE, Inc.
1310 Broadway, Somerville, MA 02144-1731.
National HelpLine: 617-623-0744. Fax: 617-623-0252.
E-mail: resolveinc@aol.com. Website: http://www.resolve.org/
Information, advocacy and compassionate infertility assistance.

SHARE National Office
St. Joseph's Health Center, 300 First Capitol Drive, St. Charles, MO
63301-2893. Phone: 314-947-6164 or 1-800-821-6819.
Fax: 314-947-7486. Website: http://www.NationalSHAREOffice.com
Support by telephone and mail after bereavement; listing of support
groups worldwide; educational services and training for group
facilitators and caregivers; presentations for community groups
and general public; videos; newsletter.

SIDS Network
9 Gonch Farm Road, Ledyard, CT 06339. Phone: 800-560-1454.
Fax: 203-887-7309. Website: http://sids-network.org/

Teen Age Grief, Inc. (TAG)
PO Box 22034, Newhall, CA 91322. Phone: 805-253-1932.
Support for bereaved teenagers; offers training for grief support groups
for teens.

❖*Additional Websites:*

Anencephaly Support Foundation Homepage –
http://www.asfhelp.com/Asftoc.htm

Bereaved Parents' Resources in USA – http://rivendell.org/usa.html
State-by-state listings.

Grief, Loss & Recovery – http://pages.prodigy.com/gifts/grief.htm
Nationwide support-group listings.

GriefNet – http://rivendell.org/about.html

Hygeia™– http://www.connix.com/~hygeia/hyghome.htm
Interactive online journal for pregnancy and neonatal loss; includes
visitors' contribution area, grieving and sharing registries for bereaved
and caregivers.

Literature Regarding Infertility – http://www.inciid.org/bookl.html

Local Support Groups for Parents after Termination of Pregnancy – http://pages.prodigy.com/gifts/ahc2.htm

Miscarriage: Frequently Asked Questions – http://www.cis.ohio-state.edu/hypertext/faq/usenet/misc-kids/miscarriage/top.html

The Miscarriage Support & Information Resources Page – http://www.pinelandpress.com/support/miscarriage.html

Neonatal Diseases and Abnormalities – http://www.mic.ki.se/Diseases/c16.html

SPALS (Support during Pregnancy after Loss) Mailing List & SANDS Home Page (Stillbirth and Neonatal Death Support)– http://www.vicnet.net.au/%7Esands/sands.htm

❖*Other Addresses of Interest:*

American College of Nurse-Midwives
818 Connecticut Avenue NW, Suite 900, Washington, DC 20006. Phone: 202-728-9860.
Professional nurse-midwives giving support to women before, during and after birth, including stillbirth.

American Foundation for Maternal and Child Health
439 E. 51st Street, New York, NY 10022

The Center for the Study of Separation and Loss
PO Box 2087, Blowing Rock, NC 28605.
Phone: 704-295-9501
Editors of the GEI (Grief Experience Inventory) Newsletter.

Depression After Delivery National Office
c/o Nancy Berchtold, PO Box 1282, Morrisville, PA 19067
Phone: 215-295-3994.
Resource for mothers or families dealing with depression following the birth of a baby.

Doulas of North America (DONA)
1100 23rd Ave. E, Seattle, WA 98112
Phone: 206-324-5440.
E-mail: AskDONA@aol.com. Website: http://www.dona.com

For addresses of midwives nationwide: **1-888-MIDWIFE**

National Down Syndrome Society
666 Broadway, New York, NY 10012.
Phone: 1-800-221-4602.

National Funeral Directors Association
11121 W. Oklahoma Avenue, Milwaukee, WI 53227.
Phone: 414-541-2500. Fax: 414-541-1909.

National Organization for Rare Disorders, Inc. (NORD)
PO Box 8923, New Fairfield, CT 06812-8923
Phone: 203-746-6518 or 800-999-6673. Fax: 203-746-6481.

National Women's Health Network
514 10th Street NW Suite 400, Washington, DC 20004.
Phone: 202-347-1140.

❖*Resources: (See also Bibliography: Journals and Newsletters)*

AMEND, c/o Martha Eise, 1559 Ville Rosa, Hazelwood, MO 63042.
Phone: 314-291-0892.
"Special Babies" memory book, memory book for adoption.

Bay Memorial—Tom and Chris Zerbel, 321 S. 15th Street, Escabana,
MI 49829. Phone/Fax: 906-786-2609.
Burial cradles in three sizes for miscarried babies, tiny urns for the
cremains of a baby.

Birth & Life Bookstore, 7001 Alonza Avenue NW, PO Box 70625,
Seattle, WA 98107-0625.
Mail order of most books covering topics surrounding childbirth,
including perinatal loss.

C.A.R.E. (Comfort and Recovery Effort), The Children's Hospital at St. Francis, 6161 S. Yale Ave., Tulsa, OK 74138-1902. Phone: 918-494-2270 (neonatal intensive care unit).
Cards for immediate and follow-up contact with parents.

Centering Corporation, 1531 N. Saddle Creek Rd., Omaha, NE 68104. Phone: 402-553-1200. Fax: 402-553-0507.
Books and pamphlets on perinatal bereavement, sibling grief, men's grief, grandparents' grief; children's books; cards, memory books. Write for catalog.

Cherokee Casket Company, 1-800-535-8667
Caskets for premature infants; portion of profits go to National SIDS Foundation.

❖*A Guide to Resources in Perinatal Bereavement:*

ICEA – International Childbirth Education Association, PO Box 20048, Minneapolis, MN 55420-0048. Phone: 612-854-8660. Fax: 612-854-8772. E-mail: info@icea.org. Website: http://www.icea.org
An international, interdisciplinary organization promoting family-centered maternity care and freedom of choice based on knowledge of alternatives. Certification Programs for childbirth educators, postnatal educators and doulas. Mail order for books covering childbirth, including perinatal loss, pamphlets on grief from ICEA Book Center. Request BOOKMARKS for reviews of new books and listing of available books. Back issues of ICEA Journal available from Book Center.

Memories Unlimited, 1740 Redwood Way, Upland, CA 91784. Phone: 909-920-3336. Fax: 909- 985-6667.
Memory boxes, cards; gowns, blankets and bonnets.

The National Directory of Bereavement and Support Groups and Services, from ADM Publishing, PO Box 751155, Forest Hills, NY 11375-8755.

Perinatal Loss, 2116 NE 18th Avenue, Portland, OR 97212. Phone: 503-284-7426. Fax: 503-282-8985
Publications, videos, memory albums, certificates of life; urns for baby's ashes, bonnets.

Pineapple Press—Molly Minnick, ACSW, PO Box 312, St. Johns, MI 48879. Phone: 517-224-1881. Fax: 517-224-0863.
Two journals: *Lifeline* and *A Heartbreaking Choice;* and books on pregnancy termination for fetal anomaly: *A Mother's Dilemma: A Spiritual Search for Meaning Following Pregnancy Interruption After Prenatal Diagnosis, Yesterday I Dreamed of Dreams, A Time to Decide, A Time to Heal.*

A Place to Remember, deRuyter-Nelson Publications, Inc., 1885 University Ave., Suite 110, St. Paul, MN 55104. Phone: 612-645-7045. Fax: 612-645-4780
Publications, cards, memory box, certificates of life

Pregnancy & Infant Loss Center, Inc. 1421 E. Wayzata Boulevard, Suite 30, Wayzata, MN 55391. Phone: 612-473-9372. Fax: 612-473-8978.
Publications, newsletter, cards, memory albums, video cassettes and slide shows on perinatal bereavement, certificates of birth/baptism or blessing, burial gowns.

Rainbow Connection—Compassion Books (ADEC's official book service), 477 Hannah Branch Road, Burnsville, NC 28714. Phone: 704-675-9670. Fax: 704-675-9687.
Large mail-order collection of books, audios and videos on death and dying, bereavement, comfort, healing, inspiration and hope.

Raindrops/Hospice of Ponca City, 1904 N. Union, Suite 103, Ponca City, OK 74601. Phone: 405-762-9102.
Birth/death announcements, memory pouches, gowns, blankets, bonnets.

SHARE, St. Joseph's Health Center, 300 First Capitol Drive, St. Charles, MO 63301-2893. Phone: 314-947-6164 or 1-800-821-6819. Fax: 314-947-7486.
Bittersweet...hellogoodbye, children's book *Thumpy's Story* and workbook, handbook *Starting Your Own SHARE Group,* 200-page book on rituals; video rentals; "Recognition of Life" certificate and other resources; listing of artists for paintings of babies who have died.

Willowgreen Press, 509 W. Washington Blvd., Fort Wayne, IN 46802. Phone: 219-424-7916.
Books by Jim Miller, including *How Will I Get Through the Holidays, What Will Help Me?* and *How Can I Help? 12 Things To Do When Someone You Know Suffers a Loss;* also videotape, *Invincible Summer: Returning to Life after Someone You Know Has Died,* and audiotape, *The Transforming Potential of Your Grief.*

Wintergreen Press, 3630 Eileen St., Maple Plain, MN 55359. Phone/Fax: 612-476-1303.
Books on perinatal bereavement, miscarriage, prenatal decision, including *Presenting Unexpected Outcomes: A Childbirth Educator's Guide* and *The Anguish of Loss; slides and cards.*

❖Audiovisual Media:

••*Audio and Video Cassettes, Slides*••

Alive Again (video) from Health Sciences Consortium, 201 Silver Cedar Court, Chapel Hill, NC 27514. Phone: 919-942-8731.

The Anguish of Loss (slides) by Julie Fritsch. Available from author, 607 Harriet Avenue, Aptos, CA 95003. Sixty slides portraying the grief process of a bereaved mother through photographed sculptures, suitable for lectures or seminars. Music included.

Pregnancy After a Loss (video) by Abbott Northwestern Hospital, available from Pregnancy & Infant Loss Center, 1421 E. Wayzata Boulevard, Suite 30, Wayzata, MN 55391. Phone: 612-473-9372. Fax: 612-473-8978.

SHARE video library contains many videos for loan to bereaved parents, siblings and caregivers.

Some Babies Die (video) from University of California Extension Center for Media and Independent Learning, 2000 Center St., 4th Floor, Berkeley, CA 94704. Phone: 510-642-0460. Fax: 510-643-9271.

Who Cares for the Caregiver? and **Empty Arms: A Tribute to Jacob** *by Jack Stack, MD* (videos), available from Family Health Institute, PO Box 904, Alma, MI 48801. Phone: 571-463-2779.

•• *Art Work* ••

(You can also check around in your community or with SHARE.)

Arts from the Heart, Betty Halsell, 1703 Fuller Springs Dr.,
Lufkin, TX 75901. Phone: 409-637-1313
Acrylic portraits.

Shirley's Fine Art Studio, Shirley Nachtrieb, 908 Ruth Drive,
St. Charles, MO 63301. Phone: 314-925-1228.
Portraits from photos of babies who have died.

Michael Wilkins, 14711 Major Ave., Oak Forest, IL 60452.
Phone: 708-687-4332.
Full-color pastels or graphite portraits.

❖ Therapy, Counseling, Self-Help, Holistic Self-Care, Spiritual Care

You may receive information and referral lists of therapists from the
following organizations, check the World Wide Web for regional
chapters and organizations, or go to the Therapy Network of the AA
National Directory of Mental Health Professionals:
http://www.dirs.com/therapy/

"How to choose a therapist" can be found at
http://www.coil.com/~grohol/therapst.htm.

CranioSacral Therapy
The Upledger Institute, 11211 Prosperity Farms Road, Palm Beach
Gardens, FL 33410. Phone: 561-622-4706. Fax: 561-627-9231.
Website: http://upledger.com
A light-touch therapy to correct imbalances throughout the body.

Gestalt Therapy
Association for the Advancement of Gestalt Therapy (AAGT),
11611 N. Meridian St. #250, Carmel IN 46032. Phone: 317-571-
7821. E-mail: btohara@aol.com. Website:
http://www.gestalt.org/index.htm and http://ds.internic.net/cgi-
bin/enthtml/health/gestalt-therapy.
A therapy form concerned with integrating or reintegrating "split-off
parts" into a whole person; individual or group work.

Grief Counseling
ADEC—Association for Death Education and Counseling, 638
Prospect Avenue, Hartford, CT 06105-4250. Phone: 860-586-7503.
Fax: 860-586-7550. E-mail: ADECoffice@aol.com
An international, interdisciplinary organization in the field of death
and bereavement, publication of *The Forum Newsletter,* book service
Rainbow Connection, annual conferences (national, international
and regional), certification as death educator and grief counselor,
supplies addresses of grief counselors and therapists nationwide.

Jungian Analysis
For an up-to-date list of analysts, contact Wilma H. Spice, Ph.D.,
N.C.PsyA., 3233 Arapahoe Rd., Pittsburgh, PA 15241-1136. Phone:
412-882-7010. Fax: 412-854-5963. E-mail: wspice@ccac.edu.
Longer-term, deep-level therapy, working with dreams, symbols and
archetypes.

Middendorf Breathwork®
The Middendorf Breath Institute, 435 Vermont Street, San
Francisco, CA 94107-2325. Phone: 415-255-2174. Fax: 415-255-
2174. Infoline: 415-255-2467
A gentle movement and hands-on approach for bringing balance to
the physical, emotional and spiritual realms.

Neurolinguistic Programming
NLP Comprehensive, 4895 Riverband, Suite A, Boulder, CO 80301.
Phone: 303-442-1102. Fax: 303-442-0609. Website:
http://www.inspiritive.com.au/nlp.htm or
http://www.nlpinfo.com/home.htm
Studying the structure of subjective experience, changing belief
systems, teaching lasting life skills.

12-Step Self-Help Groups
Check phone book for local listings
AA—Alcoholics Anonymous
Al-Anon—for Family and Friends of Alcoholics
EA—Emotions Anonymous
NA—Narcotics Anonymous
OA—Overeaters Anonymous

Unity—Daily Word, 1901 NW Blue Parkway, Unity Village, MO
64065-0001. Phone: 816-251-3580 or 800-669-0282
Monthly issues of meditation booklet *Daily Word* with healing
affirmations.

Prayer help: Silent Unity (same address) or call 24 hours a day: (816) 246-5400 or 1-800-669-7729 or check with local or national offices of your own faith.

❖Health Care and Natural Remedies

General:
Vitality Works, Inc., 134 Quincy NE, Albuquerque, NM 87108. Phone: 505-268-9950 or 800-403-4372.

HERBALIFE International Order Dept., PO Box 92459, Los Angeles, CA 90009-2459. Phone: 310-216-7770.

Flower Remedies, Aromatherapy & Homeopathy:
Aroma Vera, 3384 S. Robertson Place, Los Angeles, CA 90034. Phone: 213-280-0407.
Aromatherapy

Flower Essence Services, PO Box 1769, Nevada City, CA 95959. Phone: 916-265-9163 or 800-548-0075. Fax: 916-265-6467. Preparation and distribution of California Research/FES Quintessentials

Merit Homeopathy, 11862 Balboa Blvd., Granada Hills, CA 91344. Fax: 818-831-2024. E-mail: merithomeopathy@themall.net. Website: http://yesonline.com/merit/
FES, Bach Flowers and others.

National Center for Homeopathy, 801 N. Fairfax Street, #306, Alexandria, VA 22314. Phone: 703-548-7790. Fax: 703-548-7792. E-mail: nchinfo@igc.apc.org. Website:
http://www.healthy.net/pan/pa/homeopathic/natcenhom/index.html
How to select a homeopath; nationwide addresses & homeopathic pharmacies.

Nelson Bach USA, Wilmington Technology Park, 100 Research Drive, Wilmington, MA 01887-4406. Phone: 800-319-9151 or 508-988-3833. Fax: 508-988-0233.
Official Bach Flower distributor, referrals, education.

Original Swiss Aromatics, PO Box 606, San Rafael, CA 94915. Phone: 415-459-3998.
Aromatherapy.

Pegasus Products, Inc., PO Box 228, Boulder, CO 80306. Phone: 303-667-3019 or 800-527-6104.
Manufactures and distributes flower essences.

Scents of Harmony, PO Box 28082, 13111 W. Alameda Parkway, #16, Lakewood, CO 80228. Phone: 303- 716-1037. E-mail: harmony@qadas.com. Website: http://www.qadas.com/harmony/
Essential oils, aromatherapy.

Holistic Health Information:
Robert D. Willix, Jr., M.D., PO Box 17477, Baltimore, MD 21298. Phone: 561-368-2747. Website:
http://www.safari.net/%7Elongvity/main.html
Holistic health information, newsletter *Health & Longevity.*

Bibliography

On death and dying

DeSpelder, Lynne Ann, and Albert Lee Strickland. *The Last Dance: Encountering Death and Dying*. Mountain View, Calif.: Mayfield, 1992.

Doore, Gary, ed. *What Survives? Contemporary Exploration of Life After Death*. Los Angeles, Calif.: Jeremy P. Tarcher, 1990.

Grof, Stanislav, and Christina Grof. *Beyond Death: The Gates of Consciousness*. London, England: Thames and Hudson 1980.

Kübler-Ross, Elisabeth. *On Life after Death*. Berkeley, Calif.: Celestial Arts, 1991.

Moody, Raymond. *Life After Life*. Covington, Ga.: Mockingbird Books, 1975.

Redfield, James. *The Tenth Insight*. New York: Bantam, 1996.

Wambach, Helen. *Life Before Life*. New York: Bantam, 1981.

Weisman, Avery. "Death and Responsibility: A Psychiatric's View," *Psychiatric Opinion* 3 (1966): pp. 22-26

Wilber, Ken. *Grace and Grit*. Boston, Mass.: Shambala, 1993.

Grief and mourning

❖*General:*

Attig, Thomas. *How We Grieve*. New York: Oxford University Press, 1996.

—. "Whose Grief Is it Anyway? Towards an Ethic for Funeral Directors." In *Creativity in Death Education and Counseling*. Lakewood, Ohio: Forum for Death Education & Counseling, 1983.

Bowlby, John, and Colin M. Parkes. "Separation and Loss Within the Family." In *The Child in His Family*, edited by E. James Anthony and Cyrille Koupernik. New York: Wiley, 1970.

Bozarth, Campbell. *Life is Goodbye, Life is Hello: Grieving Well through All Kinds of Loss*. Minneapolis, Minn.: CompCare Publications, 1982.

Cassem, N. H. "Bereavement as Indispensable for Growth." In *Bereavement: Its Psychosocial Aspects*, pp. 9–17, edited by B. Schoeberg et. al. New York: Columbia University Press, 1975.

Davidson, Glen W. *Understanding Mourning*. Minneapolis, Minn.: Augsburg Publishing, 1984.

Dayringer, Richard, Glen Davidson, et. al. "Ethical Issues in the Practice of Medicine: A 1980 Study of the Behavior and Opinions of 800 Illinois Physicians," *Department of Medical Humanities Report*, 81/1 (1981). Springfield, Ill.: Southern Illinois University School of Medicine, 1981.

Deits, Bob. *Life After Loss: A Personal Guide Dealing with Death, Divorce, Job Change and Relocation*. Tucson, Ariz.: Fisher Books, 1992.

Frey, William H. II, and Muriel Langseth. *Crying: The Mystery of Tears*. New York: Harper & Row, 1985.

Kushner, Harold. *When Bad Things Happen to Good People*. New York: Schocken, 1981.

Lazare, Aaron. "Unresolved Grief." In *Outpatient Psychiatry: Diagnosis and Treatment*. Baltimore, Md.: Williams & Wilkins, 1979.

Lindemann, E. "Symptomatology and Management of Acute Grief," *American Journal of Psychiatry* 101 (1944): p. 141.

Mander, Rosemary. *Loss and Bereavement in Childbearing*. Malden, Mass.: Blackwell Science, 1994.

Manning, Doug. *Don't Take My Grief Away from Me*. Springfield, Ill.: Creative Marketing, 1974.

Miller, James E. *How Will I Get through the Holidays: 12 Ideas for Those Whose Loved One Has Died*. Fort Wayne, Ind.: Willowgreen Publishing, 1996.

Neeld, Elizabeth Harper. *Seven Choices: Taking the Steps to New Life After Losing Someone You Love*. New York: Crown, 1990.

Parkes, Colin Murray, and Robert S. Weiss. *Recovery from Bereavement*. New York: Aronson, 1995.

Tatelbaum, Judy. *The Courage to Grieve*. New York: Harper & Row, 1980. (also available as a video)

Wolfert, Alan D. *Understanding Grief: Helping Yourself Heal*. Muncie, Ind.: Accelerated Development, 1992.

❖*Children's Grief:*

Blackburn, Lynn Bennett. *I Know I Made It Happen*. Omaha, Neb.: Centering Corporation, 1991.

Dodge, Nancy C. *Thumpy's Story. A Story of Love and Grief Shared by Thumpy the Bunny* (with accompanying workbook co-written with Sister Jane Marie Lamb). Springfield, Ill.: Prairie Lark Press, 1984. (available through SHARE; also available as video)

Erling, Jake, and Susan Erling. *Our Baby Has Died. Why? For Brothers and Sisters*. Wayzata, Minn.: Pregnancy and Infant Loss Center, 1986.

Gryte, Marilyn. *No New Baby: For Boys and Girls Whose Expected Sibling Dies*. Omaha, Neb.: Centering Corporation, 1988.

Kübler-Ross, Elisabeth. *On Children and Death*. New York: Macmillan, 1983.

Nagy, Maria. "The Child's Theories Concerning Death," *Journal of Genetic Psychology* 73 (1948): pp. 3–27.

Pankow, Valerie. *No Bigger Than My Teddy Bear* (for siblings of a healthy preemie). Omaha, Neb.: Centering Corporation, 1987.

Schaefer, Dan, and Christine Lyons. *How Do We Tell the Children?* New York: Newmarket Press, 1986.

Scrimshaw, Susan, and Daniel March. "I had a Baby Sister, but She Only Lasted One Day," *JAMA* 251/6 (1984): pp. 732–733.

Wass, Hannelore. "Death Fears and Anxieties in Children: Three Theoretical Perspectives and Their Implications for Helping." In *Creativity in Death Education and Counseling*. Lakewood, Ohio: Forum for Death Education and Counseling, 1983.

Wass, Hannelore, and C.A. Corr, eds. *Childhood and Death*. Washington/New York: Hemisphere Publishing Corp. & McGraw Hill International, 1984.

❖*Teenagers' Grief:*

Grollman, Earl A. *Straight Talk About Death For Teenagers: How to Cope With Losing Someone You Love*. Boston, Mass.: Beacon Press, 1993.

❖Men's Grief:

Golden, Tom. *Swallowed by a Snake: The Gift of the Masculine Side of Healing*. N.p.: Golden Healing, 1997.

Leach, Christopher. *Letter to a Younger Son*. New York: Harcourt Brace Jovanovich, 1982.

Men's Fitness Magazine. "Growing Through Grief." In *Complete Guide to Health and Well-Being*. New York: Harper Perennial, 1996.

Nelson, James D., ed. *The Rocking Horse is Lonely—and Other Stories of Fathers' Grief*. Wayzata, Minn.: Pregnancy & Infant Loss Center, 1994.

Sjogren, B. "The Expectant Father and Prenatal Diagnosis," *Journal of Psychosomatic Obstetrics and Gynecology* 13/4 (1992): pp. 197–208.

Staudacher, Carol. *Men & Grief*. Oakland, Calif.: New Harbinger, 1992.

❖Grieving Couples:

Anderson, Linda. *Cameo. Springfield, Ill.:* Joyce Productions and SHARE, 1993. (video) Play portraying the emotional story of a couple's grief following the death of their baby.

Conway, K. "Couples and Fetal Loss," *Journal of Psychosomatic Obstetrics and Gynecology* 13/4 (1992): pp. 187–195.

Doerr, Maribeth Wilder. *For Better Or Worse: For Couples Whose Child Has Died*. Omaha, Neb.: Centering Corporation, 1992.

Gilbert, Kathleen, and Laura Smart. *Coping with Infant Loss: The Couple's Healing Process*. New York: Brunner/Mazel, 1992.

Gray, John. *Men Are from Mars, Women Are from Venus: A Practical Guide for Improving Communication and Getting What You Want in Your Relationship*. New York: HarperCollins, 1992.

Keirsey, David, and Marilyn Bates. *Please Understand Me: Character & Temperament Types*. Del Mar, Calif.: Gnosology Books/Prometheus Nemesis Book, 1984.

Childbearing losses

❖*Miscarriage:*

Allen, Marie, and Shelly Marks. *Miscarriage: Women Sharing from the Heart.* New York: John Wiley, 1993.

Chalmers, B., and D. Meyer. "A Cross-Cultural View of the Emotional Experience of Miscarriage," *Journal of Psychosomatic Obstetrics and Gynecology* 13/4 (1992): pp. 773–186.

—. "A Cross-Cultural View of the Psychosocial Management of Miscarriage," *Journal of Psychosomatics in Obstetrics and Gynecology* 13 (1992): pp. 163–176.

Ilse, Sherokee, and Linda Hammer Burns. *Miscarriage: A Shattered Dream.* Long Lake, Minn.: Wintergreen Press, 1985.

Johnson, Joy, and Dr. Marvin Johnson. *Miscarriage: A Book for Parents Experiencing Fetal Death.* Omaha, Neb.: Centering Corporation, 1983.

Jones, Wendy. *Miscarriage: Overcoming the Physical and Emotional Trauma.* Wellingborough, England: Thorsons Publishing, 1990.

Leaney, Cindy, and Michelle Silver. *Using Lullabies* (video). Boulder City, Colo.: INjoy Videos, 1995.

Leroy, Margaret (in cooperation with the Miscarriage Association). *Miscarriage.* London, England: Macdonald Optima,1988.

Pizer, Hank. *Coping With Miscarriage: Why it Happens and How to Deal with its Impact on Your Family.* New York: Signet, 1986.

Rue, Nancy. *Handling the Heartbreak of Miscarriage.* San Bernardino, Calif.: Here's Life Publishers, 1987.

Scher, Jonathan, M.D., and Carol Dix. *Preventing Miscarriage: the Good News.* New York: Harper & Row, 1990.

Williamson, Walter. *Miscarriage: Sharing the Grief, Facing the Pain, Healing the Wounds.* New York: Walker and Company, 1988.

❖*Stillbirth and Neonatal Death:*

Benfield, D. Gary, et. al. "Grief Response of Parents to Neonatal Death and Parent Participation in Deciding Care," *Pediatrics* 62/2 (1978): pp. 171–175.

Berezin, Nancy. *After a Loss in Pregnancy: Help for Families Affected by a Miscarriage, a Stillbirth or the Loss of a Newborn.* New York: Simon & Schuster, 1982.

Borg, Susan, and Lasker, Judith. *When Pregnancy Fails*. Boston, Mass.: Beacon Press, 1981.

Davis, Deborah L. *Empty Cradle, Broken Heart: Surviving the Death of Your Baby*. Golden, Colo.: Fulcrum, 1991.

DeFrain, John, et al. *Stillborn: The Invisible Death*. Lexington, Mass.: Lexington Books, 1991.

Ewy, Donna, and Roger Ewy. *Death of a Dream*. New York: Dutton, 1984.

Friedman, Rochelle, and Bonnie Gradstein. *Surviving Pregnancy Loss*. Boston, Mass.: Little, Brown, 1982.

Ilse, Sherokee. "The Baby Blues and No Baby," *International Journal of Childbirth Education* 2/4 (1987): pp. 12–14.

—. *Coping With Holidays and Celebrations*. Maple Plain, Minn.: Wintergreen Press, 1982.

—. *Empty Arms*. Maple Plain, Minn.: Wintergreen Press, 1982.

Johnson, Joy, ed. *Dear Parents: Letters to Bereaved Parents*. Omaha, Neb.: Centering Corporation, 1989.

Kohn, Ingrid, Perry-Lyn Moffit, and Isabelle Wilkins, M.D. *A Silent Sorrow*. New York: Bantam, 1992.

Limbo, Rana and Sara Rich Wheeler. "Coping with Unexpected Outcome," *NACOOG Update Series* 5/3 (1986): pp. 2–8.

Loewy, Rabbi Robert H. "Miscarriage, Stillbirth, and Infant Death," *Journal of Reformed Judaism* (Spring 1988).

Morrow, Judy Gordon, and Nancy Gordon DeHamer. *Good Mourning: Help and Understand in Time of Pregnancy Loss*. Dallas, Tex.: Word Publishing, 1989.

Panuthos, Claudia, and Catherine Romeo. *Ended Beginning: Healing Childbearing Losses*. Westport, Conn.: Greenwood, 1984.

Rank, Maureen. *Free to Grieve: Healing and Encouragement for Those Who Have Experienced the Physical, Mental and Emotional Trauma of Miscarriage and Stillbirth*. Minneapolis, Minn.: Bethany House, 1985.

Reid, Joanie. *Lifeline: A Journal for Parents Grieving a Miscarriage, Stillbirth or Early Infant Death*. Mullett Lake, Mich.: Pineapple Press, 1994.

Schweibert, P., and Paul Kirk, M.D. *When Hello Means Goodbye*. Portland, Ore.: Perinatal Loss, 1986.

Wheeler, Sara Rich, and Margaret Pike. *Goodbye My Child*. Omaha, Neb.: Centering Corporation, 1992.

❖ *SIDS and the Death of Older Children:*

Arnold, Joan Hagan, and Penelope Bushman Gemma. *A Child Dies: A Portrait of Family Grief.* Philadelphia, Penn.: Charles Press, 1994.

Compassionate Friends. *We Need Not Walk Alone After the Death of a Child.* Oak Brook, Ill.: The Compassionate Friends National Office, 1992.

Donnelly, Katherine Fair. *Recovering From the Loss of a Child.* New York: Berkley, 1994.

MacLennan, Linda. *SIDS: A Special Report.* Edmonton, Alberta: The Idea Factory, 1995. Phone: (403-439-3985)

Schiff, Harriet Sarnoff. *The Bereaved Parent.* New York: Crown, 1977.

❖ *Infertility and High-Risk Pregnancies:*

Borg, Susan, and Lasker, Judith. *In Search of Parenthood.* Philadelphia, Penn.: Temple University Press, 1995.

Bridwell, Debra. *The Ache for a Child.* Wheaton, Ill.: Victor Books, 1994.

Harkness, Carla. *The Infertility Book: A Comprehensive Medical & Emotional Guide.* Berkeley, Calif.: Celestial Arts Publishing, 1992.

Raab, Diana. *Getting Pregnant and Staying Pregnant: A Guide to Infertility and High-risk Pregnancy.* Montreal, Quebec: Sirdan Publishing, 1988.

Semchyshyn, Stefan, M.D. *How to Prevent Miscarriages and Other Crises of Pregnancy.* Seattle, Wash.: Birth & Life, 1990.

❖ *Painful Choices:*

Blumberg, Bruce D. M.D. "The Psychological Sequelae of Abortion Performed for a Genetic Indication," *American Journal of Obstetrics and Gynecology* 122/7 (1975): pp. 799–808.

Brown, Judy M.D. (pseudonym). "The Choice," *Journal of the American Medical Association* vol. 262, no. 19, p. 2735.

Centering Corporation. *Difficult Decisions.* Omaha, Neb.: Centering Corporation, 1988.

Golbus, Mitchell S. et. al.: "Intrauterine Diagnosis of Genetic Defects: Results, Problems, and Follow-Up of One Hundred Cases in a Prenatal Genetic Detection Center," *American Journal of Obstetrics & Gynecology* 1 (April 1974) pp. 897–905.

von Gontard, A. "Psychische Folgen des Schwangerschaftsabbruchs aus kindlicher Indikation," *Monatsschrift für Kinderheilkunde* 134 (1986): pp. 150–157.

Grady, Jodie, and Joann O'Leary, eds. *Heartbreak Pregnancies: Unfulfilled Promises*. Chicago, Ill.: Abbott Northwestern Hospital, 1994.

Green, Rose (pseudonym). "Letter to a Genetic Counselor," *Journal of Genetic Counseling* (1992): pp. 55–70.

Hodge, Dr. Susan E. *An Abortion for Love, Notes From a Friend: A Journal After a Genetic Termination*. Omaha, Neb.: Centering Corporation, 1995.

Hodge, Dr. Susan E. "Waiting for the Amniocentesis," *The New England Journal of Medicine* 320/1 (1989), pp. 63–64.

Ilse, Sherokee. *Precious Lives, Painful Choices: A Prenatal Decision-making Guide*. Long Lake, Minn.: ICEA,1993.

Korenromp, M. J., et al. "Termination of a pregnancy on genetic grounds; coping with grieving," *Journal of Psychosomatic Obstetrics and Gynaecology* 13 (1992): pp. 93–105.

Lloyd, J., and K. M. Laurence. "Sequelae and support after termination of pregnancy for malformation," *British Medical Journal* 290: pp. 907–909.

Lyon, Wendy, with Molly Minnick. *A Mother's Dilemma: A Spiritual Search for Meaning Following Pregnancy Interruption after Prenatal Diagnosis*. Mullet Lake, Mich.: Pineapple Press, 1993.

Minnick, Molly. *A Time to Decide, A Time to Heal*. Mullet Lake, Mich.: Pineapple Press, 1994.

Rapp, Rayna. "The Ethics of Choice," *Ms. Magazine* (April 1994).

Rothman, Barbara Katz. *The Tentative Pregnancy*. New York: Norton, 1993.

❖*Death of a Twin Baby:*

Riehn, A. "Über das Risiko nach intrauterinem Fruchttod eines Feten bei Zwillingsschwangerschaft," *Zentralblatt der Gynäkologie* 104 (1982): pp. 1530–1536.

Swanson-Kauffman, Kristen. "There should have been two: Nursing care of parents experiencing the perinatal death of a twin," *Journal of Perinatal and Neonatal Nursing* 2/2 (1988): pp. 78–86

❖*Becoming Pregnant Again:*

Abbott Northwestern Hospital. *Pregnancy After a Loss*. Wayzata, Minn.: Pregnancy & Infant Loss Center, 1994. (video also available)

Diamond, Kathleen F. *Motherhood after Miscarriage*. Holbrook, Mass.: Bob Adams, 1991.

Ilse, Sherokee, and Maribeth W. Doerr. *Another Baby? Maybe. Thirty Most Frequently Asked Subsequent Pregnancy Questions.* Maple Plain, Minn.: Wintergreen Press, 1996.

Schweibert, P., and Paul Kirk, M.D. *Still to Be Born.* Portland, Ore.: Perinatal Loss, 1986.

Stukane, Eileen. *The Dream Worlds of Pregnancy: How Understanding Your Dreams Can Help You Bond With Your Baby & Become a Better Parent With Your Mate.* Tarrytown, N.Y.: Station Hill Press, 1994.

❖ *Information and Support for Caregivers:*

Briggs, Lauren. *What You Can Say . . . When You Don't Know What to Say.* N.p.: Harvest House Publishers, n.d.

Johnson, Joy, and Dr. Marvin Johnson. *A Most Important Picture.* Omaha, Neb.: Centering Corporation, 1985.

Kübler-Ross, Elisabeth. *Questions and Answers on Death and Dying.* New York: Macmillan, 1981.

Limbo, Rana K., and Sarah Rich Wheeler. *When a Baby Dies: A Handbook for Healing and Helping.* La Crosse, Wis.: Bereavement Services/RTS, 1986.

Lindstrom, Bonnie. "Exploring Paranormal Experiences of the Bereaved." In *Creativity in Death Education and Counseling.* Lakewood, Ohio: Forum for Death Education and Counseling, 1983.

Osmont, Kelly, and Marilyn McFarlane. *What Can I Say? How to Help Someone Who is Grieving: A Guide.* Portland, Ore.: Nobility Press, 1996.

Osterweis, Marian. *Bereavement: Reactions, Consequences and Care.* Washington, D.C.: National Academy Press, 1984.

Worden, J. William. *Grief Counseling and Grief Therapy.* New York: Springer, 1982.

Helping to heal

❖ *Healing through the Body:*

Bartrop, R.W., et. al. "Depressed Lymphocyte Function after Bereavement," *The Lancet* (1977): pp. 834–839.

Benson, Herbert, et. al. "Historical and Clinical Considerations of the Relaxation Response," *American Scientist* 65 (1977): pp. 441–445.

Beringer, Elizabeth. "An Interview with Ilse Middendorf," *Somatics Magazine* (1991).

Biestman, Margot , and Juerg Roffler. *Middendorf Breathwork: The Experience of Breath*. Tarrytown, N.Y. Station Hill Press, 1996.

Boston Women's Health Collective. *The New Our Bodies Ourselves*. New York: Simon & Schuster, 1984.

Brennan, Barbara. *Hands of Light: A Guide to Healing Through the Human Energy Field*. New York: Bantam, 1988.

Inkeles, Gordon. *The New Sensual Massage Book*. New York: Bantam, 1992.

Jackson, Judith. *Scentual Touch: A Personal Guide to Aromatherapy*. New York: Henry Holt, 1986.

Jacobs, S. and A. Ostfeld. "An Epidemiological Review of the Mortality of Bereavement," *Psychosomatic Medicine*, 39 (1977): pp. 344–357.

Lidell, Lucinda, et al. *The Book of Massage: Complete Step-by-Step Guide to Eastern and Western Techniques*. New York: Simon & Schuster, 1984.

Mathias, Wayne. *Baby Massage and Exercise*. (video) Chicago, Ill.: actiVideo, 1989.

Maxwell-Hudson, Clare. *The Complete Book of Massage*. New York: Random House, 1988.

Walker, Peter. *Baby Massage: A Practical Guide to Massage and Movement for Babies and Infants*. New York: St. Martin's Press, 1996.

Wallace, Robert, and Herbert Benson, M.D. "The Physiology of Meditation," *Scientific American* 226 (1972): pp. 84–90.

Watson, Andrew, and Nevill Drury. *Healing Music*. N.p.: Prism Press, 1988.

❖ *Healing through Natural Remedies:*

Bach, Edward. *Collected Writings of Edward Bach*. Hereford, England: Bach Educational Programme, 1987.

Barnard, Julian, and Martin Barnard. *The Healing Herbs of Edward Bach: An Illustrated Guide to the Flower Remedies*. Hereford, England: Bach Educational Programme, 1988.

Chancellor, Philip M. *Handbook on the Bach Flower Remedies*. New Canaan, Conn.: Keats Publishing, 1980.

Cochrane, Amanda, and Clare G. Harvey. *The Encyclopedia of Flower Remedies*. London, England: Thorsons/HarperCollins, n.d.

Collinge, William. *American Holistic Health Association Complete Guide to Alternative Medicine*. New York: Warner, 1996.

Fischer-Rizzi, Susanne. *The Complete Aromatherapy Handbook*. New York: Sterling, 1991.

—. *Medicine of the Earth*. Portland, Ore.: Ruda Press, 1997.

Gladstar, Rosemary. *Herbal Healing for Women*. New York: Fireside, 1993.

Jackson, Judith. *Scentual Touch: A Personal Guide to Aromatherapy*. New York: Henry Holt, 1986.

Kramer, Dietmar. *New Bach Flower Body Maps: Treatment by Topical Application*. Rochester, Vt.: Inner Traditions, 1995.

— *New Bach Flower Therapies: Healing the Emotional and Spiritual Causes of Illness*. Rochester, Vt.: Inner Traditions, n.d.

Lockie, Andrew. *The Family Guide to Homeopathy*. New York: Guild/Penguin, 1989.

Scheffer, Mechthild. *Mastering Bach Flower Therapies*. Rochester, Vt.: Inner Traditions, 1996.

Weed, Susun. *Wise Woman Herbal for the Childbearing Year*. Woodstock, N.Y.: Ash Tree Publishing, 1986.

Worwood, Susan. *Essential Aromatherapy: Pocket Guide to Essential Oils and Aromatherapy*. San Rafael, Calif.: New World Library, 1995.

❖*Healing through Spirituality and Meditation:*

Bishop, Jacqui, and Mary Grunte. *How to Forgive When You Don't Know How*. Tarrytown, N.Y.: Station Hill Press, 1993.

Boerstler, Richard W. *Letting Go: A Holistic and Meditative Approach to Living and Dying*. South Yarmouth, Mass.: Associates in Thanatology, 1985.

Boerstler, Richard W., and Hulen S. Kornfeld. *Life to Death: Harmonizing the Transition—A Holistic and Meditative Approach for Caregivers and the Dying*. Rochester, Vt.: Healing Arts Press, 1995.

Daniel, Alma, et al. *Ask Your Angels*. New York: Ballantine, 1992.

Dossey, Larry, MD. *Healing Words: The Power of Prayer and the Practice of Medicine*. San Francisco, Calif.: Harper SF, 1995.

Goldsmith, Joel S. *The Art of Meditation*. San Francisco, Calif.: Harper SF, 1990.

Harp, David, with Nina Feldman. *The New Three-Minutes Meditator.* Oakland, Calif.: New Harbinger, 1990.

Holmes, Ernest. *The Science of Mind.* New York: R. M. McBride and Co., 1938.

Jampolsky, Gerald G. "Love is the Only Answer." In *Creativity in Death Education and Counseling.* Lakewood, Ohio: Forum for Death Education & Counseling, 1983.

—. *Out of Darkness Into the Light: A Journey of Inner Healing.* New York: Bantam, 1989.

Lammert, Cathi. *Angelic Presence.* 1997. (Available from SHARE.)

Levang, Elizabeth, Ph.D., and Sherokee Ilse. *Remembering with Love: Messages of Hope for the First Year of Grieving and Beyond.* Minneapolis, Minn.: Deaconess 1992.

Thich Nhat Hanh. *A Guide to Walking Meditation.* Nyack, N.Y.: Fellowship of Reconciliation, 1985.

❖*Healing through Rituals and Visualizations:*

Achterberg, Jeanne, et. al. *Rituals of Healing: Using Imagery for Health and Wellness.* New York: Bantam, 1994.

Childs-Gowell, Elaine. *Good Grief Rituals: Tools for Healing.* Tarrytown, N.Y.: Station Hill Press, 1992.

Gawain, Shakti. *Creative Visualizations.* New York: Bantam, 1986.

Lamb, Sister Jane Marie, ed. *Bittersweet . . . hellogoodbye: A Resource in Planning Farewell Rituals When a Baby Dies.* St. Charles, Mo.: National SHARE Office, 1988.

Simonton, O. Carl, Stephanie Matthews-Simonton, and James Creighton: *Getting Well Again.* Los Angeles, Calif.: J. P. Tarcher, 1978.

❖*Healing through Creativity:*

Fritsch, Julie, with Sherokee Ilse. *The Anguish of Loss.* Long Lake, Minn.: Wintergreen Press, 1988.

Goldberg, Natalie. *Writing Down the Bones.* Boston, Mass.: Shambala, 1986.

❖*Inspirational Reading, Search for Meaning, Conciousness and Spiritual Growth:*

Bach, Richard. *There's No Such Place as Far Away.* New York: Delacorte Press, 1979.

Cohen, Alan. *The Dragon Doesn't Live Here Anymore: Loving Fully, Living Freely.* New York: Fawcett, 1993.

Estés, Clarissa Pinkola. *Women Who Run with the Wolves.* New York: Ballantine Books, 1992.

Evans, Richard Paul. *The Christmas Bo.* New York: Simon & Schuster, 1993.

Ferruci, Piero. *What We May Be.* Los Angeles, Calif.: Jeremy Tarcher, 1982.

Frankl, Viktor E. *Man's Search for Meaning.* New York: Simon & Schuster, 1963.

—. *The Will to Meaning.* New York: New American Library, 1981.

Fromm, Erich. *The Art of Loving.* New York: HarperCollins, 1989.

—. *To Have or To Be.* New York: Harper & Row, 1976.

Garfield, Patricia. *Creative Dreaming.* New York: Simon & Schuster, 1974.

Gibran, Khalil. *The Prophet.* New York: Knopf, 1995.

Lee, Scout Cloud. *The Circle is Sacred: A Medicine Book for Women.* Tulsa, Okla.: Council Oak Books, 1995.

Lindbergh, Anne Morrow. *Gifts from the Sea.* New York: Vintage, 1991.

MacLaine, Shirley. *Out on a Limb.* New York: Bantam, 1983.

May, Rollo. *Love and Will.* New York: Doubleday, 1989.

—. *Man's Search for Himself.* New York: Delta/Dell Publishing, 1973.

Miles, Margaret, Shandor Crandall, and Eva K. Brown. "The Search for Meaning and its Potential for Affecting Growth in Bereaved Parents." In *Creativity in Death Education and Counseling.* Lakewood, Ohio: Forum for Death Education and Counseling, 1983.

St. Exupéry, Antoine de: *The Little Prince.* New York: Harcourt Brace, 1982.

Thich Nhat Hanh. *Be Still and Know.* Berkeley, Calif.: Parallax Press, 1996.

—. *Being Peace.* Berkeley, Calif.: Parallax Press, 1987. (Also available as audio cassette)

—. *Transformation and Healing.* Berkeley, Calif.: Parallax Press 1990.

Williams, Strephon Kaplan. *The Jungian-Senoi Dreamwork Manual.* Berkeley, Calif.: Journey Press, 1985.

—. *The Practice of Personal Transformation: A Jungian Approach.* Berkeley, Calif.: Journey Press, 1985.

❖*Counseling and Therapy:*

Brown, Molly Young. *The Unfolding Self: Psychosynthesis and Counseling*. Los Angeles, Calif.: Psychosynthesis Press.

Cameron-Bandler, Leslie. *They Lived Happily Ever After*. Cupertino, Calif.: Meta, 1978.

Cook, Alicia Skinner, and Daniel S. Dworkin. *Helping the Bereaved: Therapeutic Interventions for Children, Adolescents and Adults*. New York: Basic Books, n.d.

Corr, Charles A., et al. *Creativity in Death Education and Counseling*. Lakewood, Ohio: Forum for Death Education & Counseling, 1983.

Gazda, George, M.D. *Human Relations Development*. Boston, Mass.: Allyn and Bacon, 1977.

Leon, Irving G. *When a Baby Dies: Psychotherapy for Pregnancy and Newborn Loss*. New Haven, Conn: Yale University Press, 1990.

Lerner, Harriet Goldhor. *The Dance of Anger*. New York: Harper & Row, 1985.

Satir, Virginia. *Peoplemaking*. Palo Alto, Calif.: Science and Behavior Books, 1972 (Family therapy)

Woititz, Janet G. *Adult Children of Alcoholics*. Pompano Beach, Fla.: Health Comm., 1990.

❖*Miscellaneous:*

Anand, Margo. *The Art of Sexual Magic*. New York: Jeremy Tarcher, 1995.

Benson, Ralph C. and Martin Pernoll. *Benson and Pernoll's Handbook of Obstetrics and Gynecology*. New York: McGraw-Hill, 1994.

Bowlby, John. *Attachment and Loss*. New York: Basic, 1980.

Davis, Elizabeth. *Heart & Hands: A Midwife's Guide*. Berkeley, Calif.: Celestial Arts, 1987.

Enkin, Murray, Marc Keirse, Mary Renfrew, and James Neilson. *A Guide to Effective Care in Pregnancy & Childbirth*, 2nd ed. New York: Oxford University Press, 1995.

Ilse, Sherokee. *Presenting Unexpected Outcomes: A Childbirth Educator's Guide*. Maple Plain, Minn.: Wintergreen Press, 1990.

Kitzinger, Sheila. *The Complete Book of Pregnancy and Childbirth*. New York: Knopf, 1996.

Klaus, Marshall, John Kennel, and Phyllis Klaus. *Mothering the Mother*. New York: Addison-Wesley, 1993.

Lowen, Alexander. *Love, Sex and Your Heart*. New York: Penguin, 1988.

Journals and newsletters

Birth: Issues in Perinatal Care Blackwell Science, Inc., 350 Main Street, Malden, MA 02148. Phone: 617-388-8250. Fax: 617-388-8255.

The Forum, Journal of ADEC (The Association of Death Education and Counseling), 638 Prospect Avenue, Hartford, CT 06105-4250. Phone: 860-586-7503. Fax: 860-586-7550. E-mail: ADECoffice@aol.com

A Heartbreaking Choice (newsletter), Pineapple Press, PO Box 312, St. Johns, MI 48879. Phone: 517-224-1881. Fax: 517-224-0863

International Journal of Childbirth Education, from ICEA, International Childbirth Education Association, PO Box 20048, Minneapolis, MN 55420-0048. Phone: 612-854-8660. Fax: 612-854-8772. E-mail: info@icea.org. Website: http://www.icea.org

Lifeline: A Journal for Parents Grieving a Miscarriage & Stillbirth, Pineapple Press, PO Box 312, St. Johns, MI 48879. Phone: 517-224-1881. Fax: 517-224-0863

PAILS of Hope (quarterly newsletter for those contemplating pregnancy after infertility and/or loss), Pen Parents, c/o Melissa Swanson, PO Box 8738, Reno, NV 89507-8738. Phone: 702-322-4773. Fax: 702-323-2489. E-mail: PenParents@prodigy.com or PenParents@aol.com.

SHARE Newsletter, St. Joseph's Health Center, 300 First Capitol Drive, St. Charles, MO 63301-2893. Phone: 314-947-6164 or 1-800-821-6819. Fax: 314-947-7486.

Shattered Dreams: Coping with Miscarriage (newsletter published four times a year), Debbie Anderson, 2672 Hickson Crescent, Ottawa, ON K2H 6Y6, Canada.

Index

W-X-Y-Z